THE UGLY WOMAN

Transgressive Aesthetic Models in Italian Poetry from the Middle Ages to the Baroque

Italian poetry of the pre-modern era provided the Western canon with enduring models of feminine beauty, such as Dante's Beatrice and Petrarch's Laura. Yet there exists in Italian poetry from the Middle Ages to the Baroque a large number of works that focus on the figure of the 'ugly woman.' This book examines the prevalence and significance of depictions of unattractive women in these works, and how certain negative stereotypes served as a means of defining woman as 'other.'

Drawing on numerous literary examples, from the invectives of Rustico Filippi, Franco Sacchetti, and Burchiello, to the paradoxical praises of Francesco Berni, Niccolò Campani, and Pietro Aretino, *The Ugly Woman* reveals the underlying misogynist stance of the entire corpus. While portrayals of ugly women in the Middle Ages concentrated on types such as the lustful old hag, the slanderer, the wild woman, the heretic/witch, and the prostitute, those of the early modern period targeted social and racial 'others,' such as peasants, mountain dwellers, black slaves, and other marginal women whose bodies and manners transgress aesthetic norms of classical beauty and propriety. Taking a philological and feminist approach, and employing the Bakhtinian concept of the grotesque body, Patrizia Bettella shows how male poetic depictions of female unattractiveness say less about women than about the moral, social, sexual, racial, and aesthetic values of the patriarchal culture which produced them.

The Ugly Woman examines a topic which has been largely neglected and makes a valuable contribution to Italian studies, literary history, and women's studies.

(Toronto Italian Studies)

PATRIZIA BETTELLA teaches in the Department of Modern Languages and Cultural Studies at the University of Alberta.

The Ugly Woman

Transgressive Aesthetic Models in Italian Poetry from the Middle Ages to the Baroque

Patrizia Bettella

UNIVERSITY OF TORONTO PRESS
Toronto Buffalo London

© University of Toronto Press 2005
Toronto Buffalo London
utorontopress.com

Reprinted in paperback 2021

ISBN 978-0-8020-3926-2 (cloth)   ISBN 978-1-4875-4194-1 (paper)

Toronto Italian Studies

Library and Archives Canada Cataloguing in Publication

Title: The ugly woman : transgressive aesthetic models in Italian poetry from the Middle Ages to the Baroque / Patrizia Bettella.

Names: Bettella, Patrizia, author.

Series: Toronto Italian studies.

Description: Series statement: Toronto Italian studies

Identifiers: Canadiana 20210146184 | ISBN 9781487541941 (softcover)

Subjects: LCSH: Women in literature. | LCSH: Ugliness in literature. | LCSH: Misogyny in literature. | LCSH: Italian poetry – History and criticism.

Classification: LCC PQ4055.W6 B46 2021 | DDC 851.009/3522–dc23

This book has been published with the help of a grant from the Canadian Federation for the Humanities and Social Sciences, through the Aid to Scholarly Publications Program, using funds provided by the Social Sciences and Humanities Research Council of Canada.

University of Toronto Press acknowledges the financial assistance to its publishing program of the Canada Council for the Arts and the Ontario Arts Council, an agency of the Government of Ontario.

 Canada Council for the Arts   Conseil des Arts du Canada    ONTARIO ARTS COUNCIL CONSEIL DES ARTS DE L'ONTARIO an Ontario government agency un organisme du gouvernement de l'Ontario

Funded by the Government of Canada   Financé par le gouvernement du Canada

Contents

Acknowledgments vii

Introduction 3

1 Female Ugliness in the Middle Ages: The Old Hag 10
    Misogyny and Female Old Age in Medieval Culture 10
    Rhetoric and the Ugly 15
    Comic-Realistic Poetry: Rustico Filippi and Guido Guinizzelli 18
    Misogyny and *Antistilnovismo*: Cecco Angiolieri and
    Nicolò de' Rossi 27
    Stilnovistic Parody and Antifeminist Bias in Guido Cavalcanti
    and Niccola Muscia 32

2 Transgression in the Trecento and Quattrocento: Guardian,
  Witch, Prostitute 41
    The Old Guardian in Comic Poetry and Franco Sacchetti 41
    Descriptive Vituperation: Guarding and Slandering in
    Minstrel Poetry 52
    The Witch in Burchiello and Giovan Matteo di Meglio 66
    The Old Prostitute: Angelo Poliziano 75

3 The Portrait of the Ugly Woman in the Renaissance: The Peasant,
  the Anti-Laura 81
    Paradoxical Praise 81
    Parody in Rustic Poetry 83

Praised Ugliness/Otherness: The Peasant in Strascino,
Berni, and Firenzuola 89
Transgression on the Margins: The Disgusting Other 107
Anti-Petrarchism: The Anti-Laura in Berni, Doni,
and Aretino 114
'Stanze in Praise of the Ugly Woman' 123

4 New Perspectives in Baroque Poetry: Unconventional Beauty 128
From Ugliness to Unconventional Beauty 128
The Dark Lady 133
In Praise of Dark Hair 138
In Praise of Dark Skin: The Exotic Other 144
Female Old Age Revisited 152
Lice and Fleas: Beauty and Vermin between Witticism
and Parody 158

Conclusion 165

Appendix 171

Notes 187

Bibliography 233

Index 251

Acknowledgments

This book evolved from my doctoral dissertation at Johns Hopkins University, and therefore my first debt of gratitude goes to my supervisor, Professor Eduardo Saccone, and to Professor Pier Massimo Forni.

This work was a long time in the making, and had to be transformed from a thesis written in Italian to a book written in English. During this process I had the good fortune of finding Ron Schoeffel, editor of the Italian Studies Series at the University of Toronto Press. My warmest thanks go to this great editor, for believing in my idea and for showing unwavering support and patience throughout the process of transformation from thesis to book.

I am also grateful to the two anonymous readers, who provided prompt, insightful, and valuable input to improve this work.

Special debts of gratitude go to various colleagues at American and Canadian institutions: to Christopher Nissen of the University of Northern Illinois for his encouragement and intellectual generosity, and to Laura Benedetti of Georgetown University for urging me to get angry about the way men were depicting women in the texts presented in this book and inciting me to look at the texts more shrewdly. I am grateful to Professor Claudine Potvin of the University of Alberta, who offered advice and valuable suggestions in the later phases of this project, and to Professor Enrico Musacchio of the University of Alberta for being a mentor and a guide over the years.

The Humanities and Social Sciences Federation of Canada Aid for Scholarly Publication Programme deserves my thanks for providing financial support for the publication of this book.

Some material published here has appeared elsewhere in slightly modified form. My thanks to *Modern Language Notes*, where material in chapter 3 appeared as 'Discourse of Resistance: The Parody of Feminine Beauty in Berni, Doni and Firenzuola' (113, no. 1 [1998]: 192–203)]. I would also like to acknowledge *Quaderni d'italianistica*, where material in chapter 2 appeared as 'La vecchiaia femminile nella poesia toscana del XV secolo' (19, no. 2 [1998]: 7–23).

Some of the primary sources discussed in this book were not readily available for general consultation; special thanks go to Richard Landon of the Thomas Fisher Library of the University of Toronto for allowing me to consult material from their collection. I am also grateful to Marina Litrico of the Biblioteca Trivulziana for her generous assistance in making some texts available, and to the staff of the Sala Manoscritti of the Biblioteca Nazionale Centrale in Florence.

To Sylvia Vance, my thanks for helping me with the English language.

Finally, my immense gratitude goes to my husband, Ron Ritter, and to my family for sustaining me in this project over the years.

THE UGLY WOMAN

Introduction

Italian literature of the pre-modern era, which contributed considerably to the formation of the Western canon, provided models of feminine beauty still influential in both modern literature and culture as a whole. Today's paradigms of female beauty include attributes such as youth, blond hair, delicate features, and well-proportioned bodies, all characteristics that were already glorified in medieval and Renaissance Italian literature.[1]

In her introduction to *Ideals of Feminine Beauty* (vii–xv), Karen A. Callaghan has pointed out that beauty norms play an integral role in the construction of gender identity in a patriarchal system. Rules of beauty 'serve as a locus of control over the most fundamental aspects of identity – the self, the body, and intersubjectivity' (ix). Women who do not conform to standards of beauty are considered deviant; moreover, feminine beauty is defined primarily for men's pleasure. Beauty standards are part of a cultural discourse regarding age, class, and race. The ugly woman, by not conforming to the norms of beauty, is depicted as anomalous, rebellious, and transgressive. Such a feminine type escapes control and challenges social order. Since she may cause the wild, unrestrained, and chaotic to emerge, she is excluded and punished.

This work focuses on poetic texts that express male views of women. When the texts are anonymous the authorial voice is assumed to be masculine: it is the male subject, in his hegemonic literary-cultural authority, that represents these female transgressive types. The representations of physically unattractive women in the poems examined are unfailingly negative, particularly in the comic-realistic poetry of the medieval tradition; this study sheds significant light on the misogynistic stance that subtends Italian comic-realistic poetry, an issue that has so far been largely ignored or overlooked.[2] This book takes a first step in bridging the gap in the study of antifeminist bias in Italian comic poetry. As part and parcel of a misogynistic outlook comes the conception of ugly woman as a transgressive type. In what sense are ugly women transgressive? Women in the comic and parodistic texts examined are merely objects of male representation, and as such they can hardly be said to take up an active subject position; they are objectified as much as their beautiful counterparts. However, by infringing upon the canon of feminine beauty, these female figures display transgressive behaviours and attitudes, which reveal their potential role as unruly women-on-top. These women are remarkable because their mere presence in poetic texts contributes to a wider spectrum of female portrayal, beyond the limits of conventional representation. However, physical unattractiveness and radical position do not lead ugly women to subversion. Male poets continue to exert their repressive power over them by using verbal attack, disparagement, and figurative dismemberment.

Critics involved in Italian women's writings have noted that the poetic corpus that constitutes Italian literary tradition is marked by the almost complete absence of female voices, particularly in the early period.[3] In pre-modern Italian literature, then, it is crucial to see how male discourse constructs female subjectivity, particularly when the female type does not follow the usual pattern of glorification of the beautiful beloved.

The objective of this work is to diachronically trace the path of development of a literary female type, to account for the presence of the ugly woman in a tradition moulded by male writers, and to unveil the stereotypes, the clichés, and the antifeminist bias that have shaped the image of woman as either beautiful and good or ugly and bad and transgressive. In *The Mad Woman in the Attic* Sandra Gilbert and Susan Gubar have identified two extreme female types, 'mytic masks' that male authors have generated for women: the angel and the monster (17). The ugly woman in Italian poetry bears some resemblance to what Gilbert and Gubar call the female 'monster,' who has long inhabited male texts. Much is known about the beautiful woman as inspirer in literature; hardly anything has been written about the ugly woman in a transgressive – or any other – role in Italian literature.[4] Yet many authors – even those known for creating prominent models of feminine literary beauty – have written about ugly women. The location and discussion of unconventional female figures can provide insight into the limits of the tradition and unveil the characteristics of the female Other shaped by the male imagination. Within the boundaries of the early Italian literary tradition, marked by the exclusion of female voices and women's writing, it is inevitably the male author who portrays women as ugly, old, dishonest, disgusting, and ridiculous; it is the male writer who performs on the feminine literary bodies his rhetorical, misogynistic, and parodistic experiments.[5] Ugly bodies, unfit to provide male gratification, become loci of fierce attack and denigration or a source of scorn and paradoxical praise.

The four chapters show different strategies male writers have adopted to represent the ugly woman: vituperation, parody, paradox, and witticism. Methodologically, this study is indebted to both traditional rhetoric-stylistic text analysis and to a feminist approach, which is effective in unveiling recurring stereotypes and *topoi* involving unattractive women. Freudian study of sexual attraction/repulsion in relation to the sense of smell, with its link to Eros and Thanathos, is crucial to explain medieval comic poetry's insistence on the ugly woman's bad smell. The theory of voyeurism developed in Freudian psychoanalysis and its connection with 'visual pleasure' inaugurated by Laura Mulvey in feminist film theory helps us to interpret medieval poems on the old guardian: the ugly woman guards and also looks, thereby revealing transgressive attitudes punished by the male authors. The Bakhtinian concept of the Carnivalesque/grotesque body helps illuminate Renaissance poetry about lower-class women, whose physical representation disrupts traditional concepts of female beauty in hegemonic literary production. Peter Stallybrass and Allon White's *Politics and Poetics of Transgression* has served as a useful guide to unveiling the connection between bodily representations of high and low strata, social/class hierarchies, and the construction of the female Other as low and degraded. Some theoretical feminist reflection on verbal description as a technique of bodily fragmentation and domination proved relevant to the representation of both the beautiful and the ugly female body. Finally, Julia Kristeva's *Powers of Horror* and Mary Russo's *The Female Grotesque* provided general reference points for the entire study and enabled a delimitation of its boundaries and an option for a definition of 'female ugliness' rather than for the grotesque or abject espoused by Russo and Kristeva respectively.[6]

Medieval and early modern literature, embedded as they are in the patriarchal system, can give a powerful picture of the cultural discourse about female beauty, its norms, and its transgression. The modes of representation of feminine beauty from the Middle Ages to the sixteenth century reflect the classical concept of beauty: beauty is harmony, perfection, decorum, fruition of divine love, ultimately truth. A study of literary female ugliness must necessarily take into account the classical aesthetic models dominant in the Western canon and then focus on exploring instances of infringement on this canon. The transgression of models of feminine beauty works at different levels, from the subversion of distinctive conventional elements (old age, dark hair or skin) to parodistic remakes of the most common models. In the literature of the Middle Ages, an infraction of the canon is embodied in the shift from youth as a symbol of purity, beauty, and morality to old age as a symbol of decay, evil, and sexual excess.[7] In the Renaissance, the transgression of the canon no longer targets age and morals but social groups and manners. Therefore, ugly women are associated with lower social classes, such as peasants, and are ridiculed for their oversize, disproportionate bodies, and filth. Their ugly bodies contravene the rules of proportion and perfection glorified in the refined environment of Renaissance courts and do not conform to the dictates of decorum, elegance, and cleanliness. In baroque poetry, canonical disruption is often minimal. Women are no longer portrayed as ugly and disgusting, but rather as beautiful in their imperfection: canon infraction here targets in particular the colour of the hair and skin. The dark-haired and dark-skinned lady becomes fashionable, while those who are deformed and attractive become fascinating and intriguing, for the sake of poetic witticism.

Chapter 1 of this work opens with general remarks on misogyny, on feminine old age, and on rhetoric and the ugly. Physical description of the ugly woman was already present in classical antiquity and in the Latin Middle Ages. These sources provided valid models for vernacular texts. In Italian medieval poetry the ugly woman, in opposition to the beautiful, angelic figure of the *Stilnovo* and later of Petrarch, is an old hag whose disgusting body is the object of fierce verbal attack by the male poet. In comic-realistic poetry Rustico Filippi, drawing on Latin poetry and medieval *Artes dictandi*, vituperates the ugly woman for her disgusting body and bad odour, which obliquely reveals immoderate sexuality. Misogyny and the obsession with women's deceitfulness lead authors like Cecco Angiolieri to criticize women's use of make-up and Nicolò de' Rossi to attribute to woman a devilish nature. Although Guido Guinizzelli's and Guido Cavalcanti's comic-realistic sonnets on ugly women are generally read simply as self-parody or parody of *Stilnovismo*, there is an antifeminist bias in such texts, where female unattractiveness and old age signal a transgression of codes of conduct. In Cavalcanti and Muscia, the disfigured woman is cynically presented as therapy for the illness of love.

In the latter part of the fourteenth century there emerges – along with the guardian of the young beloved and various other types of hybrid female figures of power who transgress the codes of looking and speaking – the subversive type par excellence: the witch/prostitute, who is the object of the invective. The verbal attack on this feminine figure includes both contempt for her dishonesty and lascivious behaviour and rage against her body, which can no longer provide male pleasure. Burchiello, Giovan Matteo di Meglio, and Angelo Poliziano all illustrate this attitude towards the ugly woman.

Renaissance poetry about the ugly woman follows the paths laid down by the comic-realistic poetry of the Middle Ages, which had established a true genre of the old hag. However, the most notable trend inaugurated in the Renaissance is the paradoxical encomium of the ugly woman. Interestingly enough, moral contempt and the topic of old age, which were the trademarks of medieval texts dealing with the old hag, dwindle in the sixteenth century with the onset of Renaissance secularism; the ugly woman becomes less the object of invective or attack and more and more the parodistic counterpart of the aesthetic model glorified by Petrarchists such as Pietro Bembo. Authors like Francesco Berni and Anton Francesco Doni present with their sonnets the anti-Laura, a comic variation on the perfect beauty of the Renaissance lady. Between the fourteen and sixteenth centuries the codification of feminine beauty, conceived as physical perfection, leads to an orderly and detailed anatomization of the woman's body in descriptive praise or blazon. The process of fragmentation/domination that feminist theory has detected in the descriptive praise of the female body reappears in its negative counterparts. Paradoxical encomia of feminine beauty in the burlesque *capitoli* of Niccolò Campani (Strascino), Francesco Berni, and Agnolo Firenzuola subvert the canon, producing feminine portraits that reify and dismember the female deformed body.[8] Standards of beauty define the discourse regarding social class: hence in the Renaissance ugly women are primarily members of lower social classes, such as peasants and mountain-dwellers. Bakhtinian discourse on the grotesque body, illuminated by Stallybrass and White's reading of politics and the poetics of transgression, clarifies the reversal of hegemonic rules in the representation of female types from lower social classes in Renaissance poems on ugly women. The parody of traditional feminine beauty, embodied by Laura, involves both criticism of the rigid and abstract models of Petrarchan beauty and a derisive look at the appearance of peasant women. Paradoxical exaltations of peasant beauty in Campani, Berni, and Firenzuola are highly ambiguous, since they manifest the poets' opposing feelings of attraction and repulsion towards the female Other. On the one hand, descriptive praise in burlesque *capitoli* makes fun of the peasant woman, whose physical attributes do not conform to the canonical standards propounded by aristocratic classicism. On the other hand, the disproportion, excess, and abundance of the peasant female body has erotic appeal. Scorn for the peasant and her non-canonical beauty allows the elite to reaffirm their aesthetic and cultural supremacy. When difference reaches the extreme margins of the socio-geographical spectrum, the woman is depicted as the disgusting Other. This is the case in Giovanni Mauro's *capitolo* about mountain women and in the pseudo-Legacci's poem about women suited for 'facchini,' both reviving motifs of medieval invectives against the old hag and describing female ugliness not only as stink and deformity, but also as dirt, bodily infestation, and incivility. This book also presents for the first time to modern readers the anonymous 'Stanze in lode della donna brutta' (1547) in praise of the ugly woman, the only text among the ones studied that openly sets female ugliness as its subject. Despite their lack of paternity (given their misogyny, they must be the product of male imagination) and their erratic style, the 'Stanze' sum up features of previous tradition and foreshadow motifs of Italian baroque poetry, such as witticism and interest in the exotic Other, embodied in the dark woman (Ethiopian or Moor).

My last chapter attempts to sketch new trends emerging in baroque poetry that mark the convergence of two opposite areas: feminine representation in Petrarchan poetry and in comic-realistic bernesque poetry about the ugly woman. With its emphasis on wit and 'meraviglia,' as sanctioned by Giambattista Marino, baroque poetry or 'poesia marinista' finds in lyrical laudatory poetry fertile ground for the promotion of unconventional female beauty. Keeping intact the external pattern of Petrarchan lyric, baroque poets draw thematically on anti-Petrarchan and burlesque poetry to present as beautiful a lady whose physical features subvert specific elements of the canon. In Alessandro Adimari's collection *Tersicore* (1637), tainted, irregular, and unconventional beauties are exalted in fifty poems that reveal how the skilled poet can challenge his poetic abilities by paradoxically asserting female beauty even in the most extreme bodily deformities, such as the beautiful hunchback or the beautiful woman with scabies. Many lyricists focus on the dark lady, and pay homage to dark-haired beauty (Marcello Giovanetti, Ciro di Pers, Pietro Casaburi). Others exalt dark-skinned beauty in women who are social outcasts (Marino's beautiful slave) or belong to racial minorities; Moors and Gypsies are frequent addressees of literary homage.

Baroque poets take a different approach to aging women; rather than inveighing against and verbally abusing old women, they engage them in their love experiences, either as recipients of resented laments about lost time and beauty or as an appealing source of mature beauty. Although most 'poesia marinista' affirms the persistence of attraction despite physical decline, its praise of aging beauty is often ambiguous. Poets show more concern for technical skills and narcissistic self-glorification than genuine consideration for aging women's fate, as Salomoni's *canzone* for the 'Bella vecchia' suggests.

With the seventeenth century this study comes to its conclusion. It does not intend to provide a final and exhaustive investigation of the rich and varied literary trends and aesthetic ideas that originate in the baroque. The apparent rehabilitation of women's imperfections and physical defects, in the name of a new concept of beauty, does not suggest positive roles or liberatory prospects for women. A professed attraction towards female tainted beauty or old age in baroque poetry is a mere expedient aimed at the achievement of maximum witticism and virtuosity for the exaltation of the male poet.

chapter 1

Female Ugliness in the Middle Ages: The Old Hag

Misogyny and Female Old Age in Medieval Culture

The presentation of female ugliness as physical and moral deviancy in early Italian poetry is partly attributable to a sentiment of woman-hating that pervades medieval culture as a whole.[1] The cultural discourse of misogyny legitimized the social, economic, and political subjugation of women. Classical and medieval-Christian antifeminist tradition contributed to a misogynist stance. Works such as Ovid's *On Women's Cosmetics* (15–5 BC), Juvenal's *Sixth Satire* (early second century), and the antifeminist works of the church fathers were familiar to all medieval writers.[2] Misogynist writings identified women as lustful, arrogant, deceitful, physically disgusting, loquacious, petulant, vain, and, in general, inferior to men.[3] Also, Horace, Martial, and Ovid in their poetry attacked women, primarily prostitutes, for their immoderate lust. Latin poets often indulged in graphic descriptions of women's physical ugliness. Moreover, as Joan Cadden has shown, medieval medicine and natural philosophy, by constructing a notion of the feminine as the imperfect male, contributed to a discourse 'capable of misogynistic expression' (178).

The Christian tradition was particularly hostile to women and widely contributed to the dissemination of antifeminist prejudice in the Middle Ages.[4] The Bible itself contains numerous misogynist remarks, from the story of creation, which posits woman as only half human, to the account of the Fall, where Eve is held responsible for original sin and comes to embody material corruption, to the assertion of woman's inferiority in Saint Paul, whose epistles, according to Rogers, are 'the foundation of early Christian misogyny' (*The Troublesome Helpmate*, 11).[5] Invectives against lustful, treacherous, and evil women abound in the writings of the church fathers and early medieval priests' sermons.[6] Misogynist literature of this period focuses on women's behaviours rather than on her body. Reference to the woman's physical appearance centres on the deceptive nature of women's ornamentation and apparel. However, in an ideological perspective based on a direct correspondence between internal and external appearance, physical descriptions are often implicit in moral ones. As Umberto Eco shows in his *Art and Beauty in the Middle Ages*, medieval aesthetics espoused the Christian ideal of 'beauty of an upright soul in an upright body' (10), thereby confirming the importance of the beautiful body as an expression of the good soul and of the ugly body as a marker of the evil soul.[7]

All poetic texts in this book, by presenting woman as marked by various degrees and forms of physical ugliness or evil, are by definition misogynist, even when negative female depictions are interpreted by mainstream critics as parody, *lusus*, a rhetorical game, or witticism. In his studies on medieval misogyny, Howard Bloch conceptualizes women-hating through various headings, some of which are particularly apt for this study. For Bloch, antifeminist discourse conceives of 'woman as riot' and as 'scandalous excess,' thereby connecting misogyny with female transgression, the key concept that lies behind the various examples of feminine ugliness given here.[8] The task of this book, however, is to go beyond the mere assertion of pervasive misogyny in poetry about the ugly woman and to study how negative depiction of women's physical appearance is conceptualized by the male imagination through various instances and degrees of transgression.

Bloch notes the obsession of misogynist Christian writers of the early centuries with women's ornamentation. This connection between woman and decoration is attributed to the Biblical Yahwist account of the Creation, where Eve is conceived as the supplement, the secondary, a by-product of man, and therefore is associated not only with all that is inferior, material, and corrupt, but also with derivation and deflection. Bloch establishes the connection between woman and metaphor: 'As the outgrowth of Adam's flank, ... she retains the status of *translatio*, transfer, metaphor, trope. She is side-issue' (*Medieval Misogyny*, 38). The link between the derivative nature of the female and figural representation accounts for the church fathers' fixation on the relation of women to decoration and cosmetics, in what Bloch defines as the 'estheticization of gender in early Christianity' (37). Among the church fathers, Bloch sees the enormous importance of Tertullian's thinking, since he 'articulated the link between the derivative nature of the female contained in the Yahwist version of creation and that of figural representation in a way that has continued to dominate thought on gender well into our own age' (39). The traditional misogynist *topos* of women and ornament and decoration is crucial in Tertullian's treatise on the apparel of women, *De cultu feminarum* (circa 202).[10] This moral tract tackles two aspect of women's ornamentation, or '*cultu.*' Dress and jewels, make-up and coiffure are associated each with one sin: ambition and prostitution respectively.[11] Changing one's appearance to improve one's looks means tampering with one's God-given appearance. Cosmetics reveal unlimited pride. A woman who paints her face, dyes her hair, or attempts to conceal her age is considered a follower of the devil. Tertullian's *De cultu* states:

> In illum enim delinquunt quae cutem medicaminibus urgent, genas rubore maculant, oculos fuligine porrigunt. Displicet nimirum illis plastica Dei; in ipsis redarguunt et reprehendunt artificem omnium. Reprehendunt enim cum emendant, cum adiciunt, utique ab aduersario artifice sumentes additamenta ista, id est a diabolo.[12]

> (For, surely, those women sin against God who anoint their faces with creams, stain their cheeks with rouge, or lengthen their eyebrows with antimony. Obviously, they are not satisfied with the creative skill of God; in their own person, without doubt, they censure and criticize the Maker of all things! Surely they are finding fault when they try to perfect and add to His work, taking these their additions, of course, from a rival artist. This rival is the Devil.)

Such statements had a profound impact on medieval culture. Tertullian invoked Christian modesty to encourage women to limit ornamentation, on grounds that women should never be objects of desire for men because this can excite men's lust, making them vulnerable. Here the issues of beauty and desire intersect. Tertullian's attempt to control – actually, suppress – desire is in line with his religious spirit and misogynistic stance. From other sources, precepts and advice concerning women's clothing, jewellery, and cosmetics were countless. As Carla Casagrande (92) observes, the controversy about overdressed and artificially made-up women filled pedagogical pastoral literature. The special attention given to this theme is due to the fact that clothes and make-up were a way for women to externalize their bodies in society, in violation of the rules of custody. Patriarchal society attempted to impose on women prescriptive codes of behaviour that controlled and limited their public appearance and defined their space as the private realm of the house under the family's or husband's protection.[13] Love of clothes and ornaments revealed a desire to put one's body on display for others, since women dressed up and applied make-up to go out, to appear in public, and to be looked at and desired. Women used the language of their bodies to express themselves in society. This language challenged established social regulations, threatening chaos and corruption.

The antifeminist theme in medieval and early modern Italian literature, and poetry specifically, has been long ignored and largely eschewed. Scholars have noted the relative scarcity of misogynist texts in Italian vernacular in comparison with the French abundance of antifeminist works and have focused on Boccaccio's prose narrative *Corbaccio*.[14] Paolo Orvieto and Lucia Brestolini, in their recent study on comic-realistic poetry, devote some space to misogyny in the Italian vernacular lyric and finally shed some light on traditional antifeminist themes such as the attack on old women, antimatrimonial tirades, and women's excessive use of make-up and ornament, but a systematic and exhaustive treatment of misogyny in medieval and early modern Italian literature is yet to come.[15]

The most ancient example of misogynist literature in Italian vernacular is the anonymous northeastern poem *Proverbia quae dicuntur super natura feminarum*.[16] The text enumerates in monorhyme quatrains women's defects and forms a detailed intrinsic portrait of a woman. This is the longest vernacular text against women before Boccaccio's *Corbaccio*.[17] According to Corrado Bologna the poem includes 'the ethical-educational, epideictic, edifying intent, typical of sacred oratory, intermingled with the tones and forms of the "jongleur mentality" adopted by the Ordini Mendicanti' (460). The piece's author, perhaps a monk, claims to have composed this book for evil women who are disloyal to men. On account of his extensive knowledge of women – he has known both beautiful and ugly ones – the author, who is said to be an old man, claims that they cannot be trusted (lines 633–6). He mentions the three classic groups in which women were categorized: virgins, married women, and nuns, all of which deserve contempt, particularly nuns for their immoderate lust (lines 653–6). The list of women's vices includes fraud, dishonesty, evil, deceit, malice, and greed, the usual misogynist accusations. Women are also compared to different animals: the fox, leopard, basilisk (for her dangerous lustful gaze), cat, and panther. When generalizing about women, the author uses 'femena' instead of 'donna,' a term used for women of lower social class and to emphasize their base nature. The *Proverbia* also tackle the problem of women's ornamentation. Women's external beauty is never authentic but always the result of colour and tincture (lines 357–64); it is deceitful and corresponds to internal evil. Since women know many arts to deceive men, among them make-up and ornamentation, men cannot trust a woman who paints her face: 'Como pò omo credere asdito ni conseio/de femena qe 'ntençese de blanc e de vermeio?' ('How can a man believe and trust a woman who paints herself with white and rouge') (lines 79–80).[18] This theme, inaugurated by Tertullian, will become ubiquitous in antifeminist attacks and will be examined further below in relation to the comic poetry of Cecco Angiolieri.

Misogynistic themes are also found in vernacular poets like Bindo Bonichi and Pieraccio Tedaldi, whose satirical moralistic writings attack women for their vices, defects, and infidelity in marriage, inaugurating the genre of misogamous literature, specifically expressing hate of marriage and, hence, hate of wives.[19] Antifeminist discourse tightly connects with the issue of feminine old age, since the old woman in medieval discourse and in a patriarchal system tends to occupy problematic and often dangerous spaces of power and transgression.[20]

Despite Cicero's positive models of old age as conducive to wisdom and spiritual growth, already in classical antiquity old age was traditionally viewed negatively as a time of decay and senescence. Medieval culture has highlighted the negative aspects of old age and the old body, particularly with respect to women: the male old body was often represented as neutral, but the female old body was perceived as harmful.[21] Medical and scientific texts, as well as religious and popular belief, claimed that the old female body was poisonous because of its retention of menstrual blood. With the onset of menopause, the menstrual blood's impurity remained in the body and caused evil humours. The thirteenth-century treatise *De secretis mulierum*, believed in medieval times to be a work of philosopher, theologian, and scientist Albert the Great, was a very influential source of supposed facts about women's sexuality and reproductive life. In it menstruation, conception, and formation of the embryo are delineated. In chapter 10 the poisonous effects of older women are discussed. Old, and particularly poor, women are said to have fatal effects on children because of abundant evil humours caused by retention of menstrual blood.[22]

Since in medieval culture the physical and the spiritual were closely connected, individuals who were considered sinful were perceived as physically repulsive. Hence old women, who were considered evil, were represented as ugly and disgusting. Lois Banner, borrowing from Simone de Beauvoir's *The Second Sex*, points out the double standard of aging: 'to be a woman other than young in Western culture is to be twice over "the other" ... Aging women suffer the double discrimination of being both women and aging at the same time' (6). In medieval times women in post-reproductive age were considered perverse and dangerous because of their experience and power. Banner also draws an important distinction between aging women and old women: aging women are perceived as sexually experienced and as having possible access to the category of beauty, whereas women in their late years are doomed to decline, ugliness, and complete exclusion from a society focused on youth.

The negativity that accompanies old women in medieval literature, especially in poetry, is closely linked with the preoccupation with ideals of youth and youthfulness in courtly literature. As Erich Köhler has noted, in French troubadour poetry the term *joven* does not simply designate the category of youth but has social and moral implications: *joven* sums up the virtues that define the courtly ideal of refined love, *fin'amor*, based on liberality and pure love. In contrast, old, *vielh*, stands for all the qualities opposite to the courtly ideal.[23] This moral and aesthetic model glorifying youth influenced Italian lyric poets and, on the other extreme, comic-realistic poetry, the main literary area in which women appear as old and ugly. In fact, in comic-realistic poetry ugly old women are depicted as vicious and uncourtly, morally reprehensible, and ultimately dangerous to men.

As Banner has shown, in pre-modern European literature aging women were often presented as sexual beings; they were viewed as more experienced and sexually aggressive and often associated with dangerous and uncontrollable bodily appetite. Aging women were also considered potential witches, intent on dominating men through their bodies. In medieval comic-realistic poetry misogyny is expressed not only through female moral deviancy, but also and more specifically through depictions of physical ugliness and old age with attendant expressions of disgust.

Rhetoric and the Ugly

The physical ugliness of the individual in medieval literature is not as uncommon a topic as one might expect. In fact, during the early Middle Ages, with the refocusing of classical rhetoric as the art of good writing and poetry making, emphasis falls on epideictic oratory, and particulary on personal description of the individual's physical beauty and ugliness.

According to Faral, epideictic or demonstrative rhetoric, which strongly influenced medieval poetry, was distinctive in separating utterances into categories of praise and blame, thereby splitting the concept of *descriptio* into polarized techniques of *laus* and *vituperatio*. Brian Vickers (502) notes that the connection of epideictic rhetoric with the categories of praise and blame results in a clearer link between the epideictic and ethics, so that epideictic rhetoric becomes moralized; praise is the appropriate and only response to virtue and blame to vice. Therefore rhetorics becomes a propagator of accepted moral systems; poetry teaches us how to live appropriately and to recognize and reject vice.

Most medieval *Poetriae*, or adaptations of ancient rhetoric, provided samples of *descriptio personarum* as a form of *amplificatio* that allowed one to expand on the physical and moral description of the individual. Medieval poetry frequently used this technique both for characterization and for praise of or insult to the individual. Examples of detailed description of the individual, both beautiful and ugly, were an integral part of medieval rhetoric handbooks. In his *Ars versificatoria* (early twelfth century), Matthew of Vendôme distinguishes between instrinsic and extrinsic formal portraits and identifies their use for praise or vituperation of the individual:

> Et notandum quod cujuslibet personae duplex potest esse descriptio: una superficialis, alia intrinseca; superficialis, quando membrorum elegantia describitur vel homo exterior, intrinseca, quando interioris hominis proprietates, scilicet ratio, fides, patientia, honestas, injuria, superbia, luxuria et cetera epitheta interioris hominis, scilicet animae, ad laudem vel ad vituperium exprimuntur. (Faral 135)

> (It should be noted that the description of any character can be twofold: one extrinsic, the other intrinsic; extrinsic when the exterior man or the beauty of his members is described; intrinsic when the characteristics of the interior man, namely, reason, fidelity, endurance, notability, injuriousness, pride, excess and other epithets of the interior man, that is, of the soul, are expressed for praise or blame.) [24]

Both descriptive techniques were already employed in twelfth- and thirteenth-century works. Geoffrey of Vinsauf in his *Poetria nova* (early thirteenth century) adds the precision of a descending order to the rules of a person's physical *descriptio*: 'A summo capitis descendat splendor ad ipsam/Radicem, totumque simul poliatur ad unguem' ('From the top of the head beauty descends to the inferior part, and the whole is at the same time made brilliant to prefection') (Faral 215).

Wolfgang Brandt (257) thinks that medieval rhetoricians considered Sidonius Apollinaris's portraits of Emperor Theodoric and of the parasite Gnatho as the exemplary descriptions of beautiful and ugly character. Others view the bride and groom in the Bible's *Song of Songs* as feminine and masculine descriptive models.[25] Descriptive portraits, especially physical ones, were to become fashionable in chivalric poems and in lyric poetry. In the tradition of the conventional portrait, the description of a physical aspect is followed by assignment of moral attributes. External beauty therefore is a sign of spiritual beauty, whereas physical ugliness signals moral deviance.

The depiction of physical ugliness clearly was not uncommon in medieval literature. It was exploited rhetorically to elicit disgust and contempt for the individual. Since rhetorical arts advised one to practise both high and low style, models of descriptive praise are often accompanied by portrayals of invective. As Liborio notes, '*effictio ad vituperium* is an *effictio ad praeconium* in the negative form' (40). To the medieval reader the repulsive physical *descriptio* served as an indication of the evil, morally corrupted individual. Physical ugliness is typical of demonic creatures, devils, witches and, more generally, of individuals linked with deviancy, transgression, and marginality. Moreover, ugliness is associated with persons of lower social class. In medieval Latin comedy, for example, the ugly woman is a servant or a go-between.[26]

Rhetorical manuals propose literary models based on the correspondence of style and genre. The tragic genre, in high style, with its formal decorum, is opposed to the comic, where realistic details and crude language are not only acceptable but endorsed. In Vendôme's *Ars versificatoria* the physical and moral description of Helen provides the exemplary praise of beauty, whereas the deprecation of physical and moral ugliness is conveyed through the invective against old and ugly Beroe. Helen and Beroe become universal models of female representation in literature. Beroe's portrait is not simply a description of feminine ugliness, but also a *vituperatio vetulae*, an invective against the old hag and a deprecation of the moral depravity of the old ugly woman. This dual function of the descriptive portrait is particularly important, since it is reflected in most Italian poems about the ugly woman. By pairing ugliness with old age, Vendôme also introduces one fundamental element in the depiction of feminine ugliness in medieval poetry. As is shown below, throughout the Middle Ages in Italian poetry the ugly woman is the old hag and old age is a recurring feature. Beroe is described with the appropriate low style and crude language. This repulsive portrait includes an orderly enumeration of disgusting physical features, in an obsessive crescendo of revolting details aimed at figuring moral corruption, epitomized in the hag's lust: bold head 'pilis caput erat nudum,' horrible face 'vult horrida,' wrinkled rusty skin 'pelle ... ferrugo rigescit,' ears full of filth 'auris sorde fluit,' livid eyes exuding rheum 'oculi, sanies decurrit, ... fece replet,' flat dripping nose 'naris sima jacet, ... flamen exitiale vomit,' decayed teeth, foul breath.[27] Beroe's portrait is a seminal text for the literary tradition of ugly women; the authority entrusted in rhetorical discourse is responsible for the codification and legitimization of countless aberrant descriptions of feminine ugliness and old age.

Comic-Realistic Poetry: Rustico Filippi and Guido Guinizzelli

Comic-realistic poetry is the principal area where ugly women appear in medieval Italian literature. By this well-established label in medieval Italian literature I refer to a genre of lyric poetry that makes its appearance around the twelfth century and continues well into the early modern period.[28] It traditionally refers to a genre where comic style and realistic, low subject matter is thematized, in contrast to the aulic, tragic style of courtly and love poetry of the *Dolce Stil Novo*. For many years critics have dismissed this genre as the production of popular, trivial, inferior culture, which does not partake in the learned tradition. Mario Marti's essential work on comic-realistic poetry, *Cultura e stile*, has contributed to a new evaluation of the genre as an integral part of the learned cultural tradition on medieval Italian poetry. Marti has shown how this poetry is directly connected to the *Artes dictandi*, to classical, mid-Latin literature, and to aulic lyric poetry. In his view aulic and comic poetry coexist and are two expressions of reality, one low and one high. Marti sees as typical to the medieval mind the tendency to present reality in its opposite forms: the positive and the negative, the tragic and the comic. The comic-realistic exists in constant dialogue with/opposition to high poetry, with the classical motifs of the *Dolce Stil Novo*, particularly in its representation of the woman.

In recent times there has been an attempt to re-evaluate comic-realistic poetry by placing it within a cultural continuum. Paolo Orvieto suggests 'la necessità di ripensare alla poesia comico-realistica ... come repertorio che si alimenta secondo un processo oppositivo, negativo e differenziale degli stessi stimoli del modello positivo della cultura "alta," solo enfatizzandone il loro rovescio' (*La poesia comico-realistica*, 9) (the need to rethink comic-realistic poetry ... as a repertory that, in a process of opposition, negativity, and differentiation, feeds on the same stimuli of the positive model of 'high' culture, just emphasizing their reverse).

A postmodern conceptualization of culture, by exposing cultural hierarchies of high and low, tragic and comic, can yield a richer view of comic literature. Fabian Alfie suggests such an interpretation in his analysis of the comic genre in Cecco Angiolieri's poetry. Angiolieri's and medieval comic authors' literary program of identifying and subverting cultural hierarchies appears comparable to that of postmodern deconstructionists. Comedy favours the culturally disfavoured, the opposite of tragic: 'Comedy prefers the subject-matter and lexicon related to the body, the earth, the lower classes, ignorance and sin, thereby presenting the so-called world turned upside-down' (Alfie 26). Although medieval comic-realistic authors, by embracing negative valences associated with the downtrodden and by highlighting the culturally disfavoured, appear to overturn hierarchical structures, they fail to fully challenge hegemonic discourse or subvert hierarchies. Their poetry ultimately reaffirms orthodoxy. Their position does not valourize the world turned upside-down, but rather leads to a negative perception of the subject, which in the depiction of women is exemplified by a pervasive misogynist stance and by a bleak representation of unconventional female types.[29]

Comic-realistic authors do challenge the established models of female beauty of courtly Stilnovistic tradition. Praise of the beautiful, young lady, a key point of love lyric poetry, is transformed into its opposite in comic-realistic poetry. For the motif of *lauda* (praise) of the young beloved we need only remember Guido Guinizzelli's sonnet 'Io voglio del ver la mia donna laudare' (472), or Guido Cavalcanti's 'Fresca rosa novella, / piacente Primavera, / per prata e per rivera / gaiamente cantando, / vostro fin pregio mando – a la verdura' (491) ('Fresh new rose, / Pleasant spring, / By meadows and by field / Gaily singing, / I commend your fine excellence to the greenery').[30] The tradition of celebratory poems on the physical and moral qualities of the lady love is particulary rich in the *Stilnovisti*.[31] Comic-realistic poetry transforms this praise into invective and the beautiful young lady into an ugly old hag. The connection by opposition of the comic-realistic and the lyrical style is further demonstrated by the fact that often the same author can master both genres. Rustico Filippi, considered by critics the initiator of the comic style in vernacular, is known for his 'bifrontismo stilistico,' since his *canzoniere* contains an equal number of comic and lyric poems. Likewise Guido Guinizzelli and Guido Cavalcanti, who are best known for their love lyrics, occasionally composed comic poems against the old hag.[32]

Rodolfo Renier (124–5) has noted that the aesthetic type of the woman in medieval Italian lyric poetry was completely abstract and conventional, with little connection to real women. With *Stilnovismo* the woman becomes spiritualized and stylized. In Renier's view, *Stilnovisti*, with their 'intimately psychological poetry, focus more on the effects of feminine beauty rather than on the undescribable beauty of the ideal woman' (96). Moral qualities prevail over physical attributes; hence *Stilnovisti* show less interest in detailed description of the woman's physical beauty. However abstract, beauty remains the origin of celebratory poetry, and the seductive sight of the attractive young woman is at the origin of medieval love poetry. The most significant creation of *Stilnovismo* is the figure of the woman-angel. As noted in the discussion of rhetoric, with the link between epideictic and ethics praise of the individual becomes a vehicle for incitement to virtue; in the encomium of the woman moral qualities supersede external beauty, or rather physical beauty is a symbol of moral virtue and good. Cavalcanti's beautiful lady, compared to the 'fresca rosa novella,' is also an angelic creature of high quality, whose beauty and youth is inherent in the simile of the rosebud.

> Tutto lo mondo canti,
> po' che lo tempo vène,
> sì com'e' si convene,
> vostr'altezza presiata:
> ché siete angelicata crïatura.
>
> Angelica sembranza
> in voi, donna, riposa. (42)

(Let the whole world sing, / Since the season approaches, / Just as is proper, / Your excellent highness, / For you are an angel-like creature. // An angelic semblance / Dwells, lady, in you.)[33]

In the medieval mentality beauty and ugliness are opposite categories, and ugliness, as absolute negativity, is represented as antithetical to beauty and confined to the realm of vituperation. In the depiction of the literary woman this ideology creates a clear distinction between opposites: beauty signals virtue, youth, angelic nature, grace, chastity; ugliness, on the contrary, signals vice, evil, old age, disgust, devilish nature, lust. Comic-realistic poets, who attack the conventionality and excessive idealization of women in *Stilnovista* poetry, depict the woman as opposite to the idealized model and inevitably assume a misogynistic attitude. The beautiful, angelic, immaterial creature of Guinizzelli, Cavalcanti, and Dante becomes the ugly, disgusting, all-physical old woman of the realistic poets.

Vituperation and praise, two opposed literary genres, two poles of epideictic rhetoric, were both very familiar techniques to medieval poets. In epideictic rhetoric praise (*laus*) has the moral task of promoting virtue, while *vituperatio* serves the opposite purpose. Comic poets used vituperative verses to attack personal enemies, political adversaries, and women. *Vituperatio* as a rhetorical device is embedded in the low, comic genre and makes ample use of crude language and violent invective.[34] Rustico Filippi, along with Cecco Angiolieri and other comic authors, were very familiar with vituperation and used it in their comic poetry against old women. Rustico Filippi was considered the initiator of such a genre and is famous for his realistic, disgusting, and obscene language. His artfully crafted poetry in comic style draws on rhetoric and Latin models. Rustico was known already in the early fourteenth century as a vituperator of women, as confirmed in Francesco da Barberino's *Documenti d'amore*.[35]

Rustico's corpus includes 'Dovunque vai con teco porti il cesso,' a sonnet against the ugly old hag, a text that needs to be read within the context of medieval rhetoric and the imitation of classical models; and yet one should not dismiss as void rhetorical exercise the tone of fierce misogyny that permeates this comic poem.[36] The old hag depicted in this sonnets fits Howard Bloch's definition of 'woman as riot and excess' (*Medieval Misogyny*), features that mark her as transgressive. This *vituperatio vetulae* is particularly momentous because it inaugurates the genre against old women in medieval comic poetry. In opposition to the idealized lyrical lady of the *Stilnovisti*, this sonnet presents the old, lustful, disgusting woman, the other feminine type of medieval poetry. Rustico's old hag derives both from Vendôme's Beroe and from the Latin tradition, which stand as authoritative examples for full legitimization of this genre. In this violent and outrageous invective the old woman is attacked through both her moral and her physical attributes:

Dovunque vai, con teco porti il cesso,
oi bug[g]eressa vecchia puzzolente,
ché quale-unque persona ti sta presso
si tura il naso e fug[g]e inmantenente.

Li denti.le gengìe tue ménar gresso,
ché li taseva l'alito putente;
le selle paion legna d'alcipresso
inver' lo tuo fragor, tant'è repente.

Ch'e' par che s'apran mille monimenta
quand'apri il ceffo: perché non ti spolpe
o ti rinchiude, sì ch'om non ti senta?

Però che tut[t]o 'l mondo ti paventa:
in corpo credo figlinti le volpe,
ta.lezzo n'esce fuor, sozza giomenta. (Contini, Vol. 1, 364)

(Wherever you go, you bring the stench of the toilet, stinky old whore, anyone who comes near you closes their nose and flees immediately. Your teeth and gums are full of tartar and your breath is foul; toilets smell like balsamic wood in comparison to your stench. When you open your mouth out comes the reek of a thousand tombs; why don't you skin yourself or lock yourself up so nobody can smell you? The whole world fears you; I think your body breeds the fox such foul smell comes out of you, dirty cow!)

This realistic description, with specific details of the woman's body, although not a whole descriptive portrait, evokes Beroe's *descriptio*. Visual repulsion here is closely linked to an olfactory one, which is highlighted by the opening epithet 'vecchia puzzolente.' Beroe too was described by her disgusting smell.

A negative attitude towards old women and a detailing of their bad odours were already present in the literature of classical Rome. In Horace's epode 12 an old prostitute is compared to a goat and other malodorous animals. This old woman's lust and sexual exuberance disgust the Latin poet, who finds her smell repulsive.[37] In Martial's epigram 93 the old prostitute Vetustilla, semi-bald and toothless, is described via animal similes for each part of her body; this old woman also sends out a bad smell similar to that of the goat, the animal which seems most offensive to the Roman nose.[38]

The adjective 'buggeressa,' which received different readings involving the woman's dishonesty, has been more clearly associated by recent critics Mengaldo and Marrani with her lust.[39] The old stinky woman is in fact a whore, whose behaviour is indecent. This interpretation unveils the old woman's rampant sexuality and links this feminine type to the Latin tradition, where the old woman is always a prostitute and practises excessive sex. In the second stanza Rustico explains the origin of such a bad odour. It comes from the woman's mouth; her teeth and gums, full of tartar, produce bad breath. But the repeated references to excrement ('cesso,' 'selle') also evoke the woman's other mouth, alluding to the malodorous body parts in the old woman's genital area. A connection between the woman's mouth and her genitals was common in both ancient tradition and medieval times.[40] Moreover, the foul smell is associated with the animal-like nature of the old woman, who begets the fox, which commentators (Marrani 175) have linked with a proverbial bad smell. In the last verse the old hag is called 'sozza giomènta,' which again refers to an animal, but also refers metaphorically to the woman of immoderate sexual appetite and the prostitute. The disorderly sexuality of the old woman connects the first verse to the last, bringing the sonnet full circle. Rustico's old woman remains forever in our memory not so much for her moral depravity as for the disgust evoked by her foul smell.

Unlike in classical tradition and rhetorical models, where bad smell is one of a multitude of disgusting elements, in this text olfaction is the key point, since the sense of smell clearly defines this woman's transgressive nature. Filth and foul smell were classic ingredients of Rustico's vituperative poetry, but the connection here of bad smell with lust stresses the transgressive nature of the old woman.[41] Patristic writings with their deeply misogynist stance mention the stench of the woman, particularly the prostitute, in connection with lust. The prostitute, transgressive by definition, is depicted as male temptress, and the bad smell is symbolic of sin.[42] Although there's no open mention of the tempting danger of the 'buggeressa,' such a revolting depiction of the feminine is more than a vacant, rhetorical exercise. Rather, as we saw above, since rhetoric includes ethical concerns, vituperation implies moral judgment. That woman can be conceived by male imagination in such a degraded form has to be explained in terms of the inherent threat associated with a female type that exceeds boundaries of decency, gender, and even human nature.

Recent socio-cultural and literary studies on odours have associated smell with perception of the body and sexual attraction/repulsion. Hans

Randisbacher, borrowing from Freud, reveals the close connection between olfaction and sexuality.[43] In *Civilization and Its Discontents* Freud considers olfaction as an integral step in the development of the species and of human beings in primitive societies. Smell has a strong sexual connotation in the animal world, in those species whose reproductive behaviour is based on olfactory stimuli. The rise to upright posture marks a decline of olfaction in favour of vision, which becomes the leading sense of sexual attraction. Although Freud does not further develop his insight on smell and sexuality, focusing instead on that sublimating sense which is sight, Randisbacher reclaims the importance of smell. In his view olfaction remains, even if repressed, strongly connected with sexuality and has liminal and transgressive qualities. In good smell the erotic charge is positive and represents attraction, whereas in bad smell the negative force of *Thanathos* is at play.

In Freudian terms, the bad smell of Rustico's 'buggeressa' brings us back to the primitive, pre-human form of sexual attraction and reveals the transgressive potential of this female type. The old woman's sexuality and her infractious behaviour are implicit in the opening adjective 'buggeressa' and in the final remark concerning her power to beget animals, one indication of her liminal status as half human and half beast. Moreover, 'buggeressa' in its vernacular form evokes the act of sodomy, a grave sin in medieval times, which makes the old woman more transgressive, since sodomy is not only sex against nature but is also a sexual practice primarily attributed to the male; as a sodomite the old woman's deviancy borders on masculinity and threatens gender distinctions.[44] All these elements point to the poet's subconscious rejection of a pseudo-human hybrid feminine, whose danger is conjured up when gender combines with old age, sexuality, and olfaction. The old woman's foul smell triggers the repulsive force of *Thanathos*, since her bad odour is associated with the stench of death that comes from the open tombs. The bad odour of the old woman in combination with lust signifies decay, repulsion, death. Rustico's 'buggeressa,' contrary to the angelic *Stilnovista* lady with superhuman, heavenly qualities, is endowed with dehumanizing attributes. Her body breeds an animal like the fox. The reference to the fox not only reinforces the emphasis on foul smell but also suggests the possible devilish nature of the old woman, as the fox was one of the animals that witches used as a disguise. Although the open accusation of witchcraft in comic poetry will appear only in the fifteenth-century poetry of Burchiello and his imitators, the connection of the 'buggeresssa' to the witch and the prostitute ties this *vituperatio vetulae* very closely together with pre-Renaissance poetry. For her transgression the old woman is violently attacked not only in the offensive language used to describe her, but also in the curse aimed at her body; the poet asks her 'Perché non ti spolpe,' an open invitation to dismemberment of a body whose flesh, far from being a source of male sexual attraction and desire, is marked by disgust and death and therefore is destined to annihilation.[45]

The connection between a woman's foul smell and lust appears also in Dante's *Divina commedia*. In a dream appears to Dante 'una femmina balba, / nelli occhi guercia, e sovra i pié distorta, / con le man monche, e di colore scialba' ('a woman, stammering, with eyes asquint and crooked on her feet, with maimed hands, and sallow hue,' *Purg.* 19, 7–9).[46] Later she turns into an alluring siren with a sweet voice, but her deceptive arts are ultimately disclosed by a holy lady ('una donna apparve santa e presta') interpreted by critics in a variety of ways, who exposes the woman's belly and her foul smell. The deception is unveiled when the women's clothes are laid bare, revealing her belly with its stench: 'fendendo i drappi, e mostravami 'l ventre: / quel mi svegliò col puzzo che n'uscia' ('rending her garments and showing me her belly; this waked me with the stench that issued therefrom,' *Purg.* 19, 32–3). Cervigni notes that in both Dante and patristic writings, stench is a mark of lust and is used to describe tempting women.[47] While Dante's 'femmina balba' fits in the traditional category of the siren-turned-hag, the temptress, Rustico's foul-smelling woman, is a more complex female type in whom the combination of disgusting body, foul smell, sexual deviancy, and gender ambiguity stirs the male subconscious so deeply as to result in bodily dismemberment.

The closest chronological spinoff of Rustico's invective is in Guido Guinizzelli's (1230?–76) sonnet 'Volvol te levi vecchia rabbïosa.' Some critics consider Guinizzelli's adaptation of the low comic style in this sonnet a direct response to Rustico's attack against the old hag (Buzzetti Gallarati, 209 and footnote).

> Volvol te levi, vecchia rabbïosa,
> e sturbignon te fera in su la testa:
> perché dimor' ha' in te tanto nascosa,
> che non te vèn ancider la tempesta?
>
> Arco da cielo te mandi angosciosa
> saetta che te fenda, e sïa presta:
> che se fenisse tua vita noiosa,
> avrei, senz' altr' aver, gran gio' e festa.

26   The Ugly Woman

Ché non fanno lamento li avoltori,
nibbi e corbi a l'alto Dio sovrano,
che lor te renda? Già se' lor ragione.

Ma tant' ha' tu sugose carni e dure,
che non se curano averti tra mano:
però romane, e quest'è la cagione. (74)

(May a thunder take you, angry old hag, and a lightning bolt may hit you on the head: why are you so hidden that a storm cannot come and kill you? May a deadly arrow come from the sky and hit you fast: if your pernicious life ended, it would be for me, without a doubt, great joy and happiness. Why don't vultures, kites, and crows request to almighty God that He surrenders you to them? They deserve you. But your flesh is so hard and rotten that they do not care to have you: and this is the reason why you remain here.)

Guinizzelli's sonnet, like Filippi's, is a *vituperatio vetulae*, a violent execration of an old angry woman. This poem is generally read by critics as an experiment in self-parody. Guinizzelli, the inventor of the lyric genre in praise (*lauda*) of the angelic lady, amusingly deconstructs his personal style and themes and composes an anti-praise or *vituperatio vetulae*. However, this exercise in self-parody is carried out at the expense of an old woman, the female type most targeted by male poets' discrimination and hostility. This old woman is portrayed as physically unattractive with her tough and rotten flesh; she is described as so disgusting that birds of prey would refuse to feast on her body. The sonnet focuses on the old woman's anger, whose cause remains unexplained. The invective reiterates the poet's wish to see this old woman dead, while instead she seems to resist every attack. The verbal abuse against the old hag, who survives every possible calamity, recalls Martial's epigram 93, where the hundred-year-old woman is not killed even by malarial fever. Critics like Cian have seen in the rage of the 'vecchia rabbïosa' the attitude of an old woman who probably prevented the poet in love from reaching the young beloved (312). Anger and rage would be the most common feelings of the old guardian (mother, stepmother, or mother-in-law) towards the young woman and the poet in love. If we accept Orvieto and Brestolini's reading of 'sugose carni' as 'piene di pessimi umori' (*Poesia comico-realistica*, 19), this old woman's body may contain some foul fluids, which reflect the scientific tradition of the *De secretis mulierum*, in which old women are said to retain evil fluids. The poet's desire to see this old woman dead is so strong that the attack falls again on the aged body, for which, just like in Rustico, dismemberment is invoked. Dismemberment through the action of birds of prey implies a particularly slow and cruel destruction of the human body, as if no trace of her physicality should be left intact. The old woman's transgressive behaviour is to be connected with her position of power and her role as the guardian of the poets' beloved, a motif examined in chapter 2.

Misogyny and *Antistilnovismo*: Cecco Angiolieri and Nicolò de' Rossi

Comic poetry, with its program of subversion of the ideology of ennobling love, is constructed, both in style and themes, in opposition to *Stilnovismo*. The old disgusting woman, transgressor of all moral and physical qualities, is the antithesis of the woman-angel of the *Stilnovo*, with her idealized beauty, virtue, and youth, with her power to elevate and bless (as exemplified in Beatrice). It is unfortunate that, despite their program of subverting *Stilnovista* poetry, comic-realistic authors cannot avoid the pitfall of misogyny. Their antidote to the woman-angel therefore is a devilish creature, site of all corruption and evil. Poets such as Pietro de' Faitinelli of Lucca declare that woman is not created in God's image but rather is a diabolic creation.

> En bona verità, non m'è avviso,
> avvegna ch'ello piaccia a la Scrittura,
> che femmena pur veggia il paradiso,
> non che v'appressi a far dentro calura;
>
> né che Deo padre li formasse 'l viso
> a simiglianza de la sua figura:
> anzi fu, per sacramento preciso,
> femmena dïabolica fattura:
>
> La femmen' è radice de l'enganno;
> femmen'è quella che ogni fraude affetta;
> femmene pensan ogni mal e fanno.
>
> Ma ben i' ho credenza ferma e netta
> che alquante, ma ben poche, ve ne vanno,
> per non lassar santa Maria soletta. (Marti, *Poeti giocosi* 423)

(In truth, I do not believe, although it is in the Scriptures, that the female can see paradise, nor that she can enjoy its warmth; nor that God the Father shaped her face in resemblance to his image: rather for a precise sacrament, female was a diabolic creation; the female is the root of deceit; the female affects every fraud; females think and act in all evil. However, I have a firm and clear belief that some, though very few, shall go there [paradise], in order not to leave holy Mary alone.)

For Faitinelli, then, woman is neither a symbol of divine presence on earth nor a medium towards God, but an evil creation of the devil ('diabolica fattura').

Thanks to Tertullian's *De cultu feminarum*, and as documented in the *Proverbia*, misogynistic attacks become physical when the focus is on women's attempts to improve their appearance through ornamentation and make-up. Without make-up women are said to look disgusting and ugly, but they can become attractive and seductive through cosmetics, as Cecco Angiolieri writes in one of his sonnets.

Cecco Angiolieri (1260?–1312) was the best-known comic-realistic poet in Italian vernacular, who challenged in burlesque parodistic poetry the *Stilnovista* concept of love and the image of the lady. He depicts in his verse Becchina, an earthly lover, who is truly the opposite of Dante's blissful Beatrice. By deconstructing the image of the woman-angel of the *Stilnovisti*, Cecco inevitably falls into misogynist stances, which include criticism of women's ornamentation and an anti-matrimonial polemic. Cecco's negative feelings about wives and more generally about marriage appear repeatedly (sonnets 47, 53) in what Lanza considers the beginning of this *topos* in Italian jocose poetry ('Introduzione' xliv).[48]

Cecco tackles the motif of an excessive use of make-up in one sonnet:

> Quando mie donn'esce la man del letto,
> che non s'ha post'ancor del fattibello,
> non ha nel mondo sì laido vasello
> che lungo lei non paresse un diletto,
>
> così ha 'l viso di bellezze netto;
> infin ch'ella non cerne al burattello
> biacca, allume scagliuol e bambagello,
> par a veder un segno maladetto!
>
> Ma rifassi d'un liscio smisurato,
> che non è om che la veggia 'n chell'ora
> ch'ella nol faccia di sé 'nnamorato.

E me ha ella così corredato
che di null'altra cosa metto cura
se non di lei: o ecc'om ben amendato! (245)⁴⁹

(When my lady gets out of bed in the morning, and she has not yet put on her make-up, there isn't in the world an uglier sight, everyone, compared to her, looks delightful, so bare of beauty is her face; until she concocts powder, paint and rouge, she looks like a cursed figure! But when she applies abundant make-up, she makes every man who sees her fall in love with her. She has reduced me to such a state that I care only about her and, here, she has me well punished!)

It is precisely when the woman gets up in the morning to begin her day, when she is ready to interact outside the confines of the house, that she proceeds to apply make-up. Francesco da Barberino's *Reggimento e costumi di donna*, a fourteenth-century handbook of good manners and conduct for women, addresses this same issue and scorns the woman who gets up to 'lisciarsi a matutino' (to put on make-up early in the morning).⁵⁰ In Cecco's sonnet the woman's disguise attracts several men, who immediately fall in love with her. This court of lovers bothers Cecco, who is obliged to devote all his attention to his woman. This for Cecco amounts to a true punishment, perhaps in light of his desire to have an extramarital affair himself. Therefore the sonnet, while originating from the issue of excessive make-up, exposes Cecco's problematic relation with his wife/Becchina.

In this text misogynistic tones are mitigated by the muted moral judgment, in comparison with what appears in religious tracts. Nor is there found the virulent invective that was distinctive in Rustico or Guinizzelli. It is not clear whether the woman, perhaps the malicious and sexual Becchina, is actually old. Most likely Cecco's 'donna' belongs to what Lois Banner classifies as the more mature but not old woman, a type who is sexually more experienced and uses make-up to enhance her appearance. The transformation of the ugly woman into a charming vamp makes it clear that this woman is an object of men's desire, and her allure can threaten Cecco's relationship with her. Instead of being attacked or dismembered, the ugly-turned-beautiful woman is simply ridiculed. Cecco perceives the transgressive potential of his woman's manipulation of her physical aspect to appear different from what she really is. If Tertullian linked cosmetics with prostitution, Angiolieri is not far off in describing the seductive power of the made-up woman to entice men and cause infidelity. Ultimately, the sonnet is ambiguous; the misogynistic tirade against make-up turns into an admission of the poet's weakness and apprehension about his woman/wife's ability to exert power over him. The sonnet's treatment of the poet's relationship with his wife is revealing; the threat of extramarital affairs, made more likely by the woman's use of make-up, reflects Cecco's unwillingness to accept his subordination to his woman's power. Cecco's wife, adorned with cosmetics, can control not only other men but the poet himself. This advantageous position of the woman over the poet is remarked on in Alfie's work on Angiolieri: Becchina is shown to be wicked and, despite her socially inferior position, she dominates the situation and keeps the man under control (35).

The same *topos* of the woman's ugly body and manipulative use of make-up appears in Giovanni Boccaccio's misogynistic narrative, the *Corbaccio*. Given Boccaccio's reputation as a defender of women in most of his works, the *Corbaccio* has left critics baffled and unable to explain the harsh anti-female tone that pervades this book.[51] The female object of criticism is the widow, who left the protagonist so troubled and anguished as to contemplate suicide. Boccaccio's violent tone in describing the widow is well suited to the use of low, comic style, as exemplified in medieval rhetorical handbooks. The parallel with Angiolieri's sonnet are remarkable. Boccaccio's narrator proceeds to deconstruct the claim of the widow's beauty by unveiling its falsehood.

> La quale se a te e agli altri stolti, come a me, possibile fosse stato d'avere quando la mattina del letto usciva, veduta, prima che posto s'avesse il fattibello, leggermente il vostro errore avreste riconosciuto. Era costei, ... , quando la mattina usciva del letto, col viso verde, giallo, mal tinto, d'un color di fumo di pantano, e broccuta quali sono gli uccelli che mudano, grinza e crostuta e tutta cascante, in tanto contraria a quel che parea poi che avuto avea spazio di lecchisarsi, che appena niuno il potesse credere che veduta non l'avesse, come vid'io già mille volte. (109)[52]

> (But if it had been possible for you and for other fools to have seen it, as it was possible for me, when she got out of bed in the morning before she put on her make-up, you would easily have realized your error. When she arose from her bed of a morning, she had ... a face green and yellow, discolored with the hue of swamp-fumes, knotted like moulting birds, wrinkled and encrusted and all sagging, so different from the way it looked when she had time to preen herself that one could scarcely believe it had he not seen it as I did a thousand times in the past.) (53–4)

Thanks to the extended space allowed by prose and to the vivid imagination that informs his writing, Boccaccio has taken up Cecco's point and expanded on the description of the woman's ugly face ('laido vasello' in Cecco's sonnet). The woman's ugliness is described by Boccaccio with more disgusting details. The morning ritual of masquerade produces powerful effects on the male subject. In both Cecco's and Boccaccio's texts the result of the disguise strengthens the woman's seductive powers and makes the man more vulnerable.

Misogyny is intermingled with more open moralistic concerns in Nicolò de' Rossi of Treviso (born in the late twelfth century). His *Canzoniere* exemplifies the main trends of the Tuscan models, from the love lyric in Cavalcantian tones to the comic of Angiolieri. Although comic-realistic themes such as misogyny, goliardic pleasurable life, caricature, and parody are sparse in de' Rossi's verse, one of his most quoted sonnets sums up numerous misogynistic themes:

> La femena ch'è del tempo pupilla
> le plu parte si trova glotta e ladra;
> e quando viene en etate nubilla,
> sendo ben puita, allor se tien liçadra.
>
> Possa ch'è vegla, çamai non vacilla
> ch'ella non sïa rufiana e triçadra;
> et en decrepità, che gl' ogli stilla,
> sortìlega doventa e grand busadra.
>
> Dunque, primo che l'omo a lei se pogna,
> pensi di non tenerla capitale,
> s' el vede ch'essa non tema vergogna,
>
> (per la qual sola talor scifa il male):
> ché femena sfaçata è per natura,
> un dïavole en humana figura. (141)

(Female is the pupil of time, she is mainly a glutton and a thief; and when she reaches the age of marriage, because she is pretty, she believes herself graceful; later when she grows older she ineluctably turns into a treacherous procurer; in her decrepitude her eyes ooze and she becomes a witch and a liar. Therefore, before a man decides to marry her, he should think carefully, if he sees that she has no shame, and does not avoid evil: because female is by nature insolent, she is a devil in human figure.)

This attack against women, including advice against marriage, is couched in moralistic concerns.[53] The poem conflates Faitinelli's claim of women's diabolic nature with an acute and ruthless observation on the time-bound fragility of female beauty. De' Rossi describes the woman through the different stages of life and connects her physical aspect to the passing of time. Several misogynistic *topoi* are at play: woman's deceitful nature, the decay of woman's beauty in time, and the risks man incurs in marriage. The woman's unattractiveness is mentioned in relation to old age, that time of decrepitude when good looks are lost forever and the eyes are oozing. This last detail links the poem to Beroe's disgusting, trickling eyes, and hints at the authoritative voice against old women promoted in rhetorical discourse. The old woman is characterized in de' Rossi not only as treacherous, a procuress, and a liar but also as a witch ('sortilega'), an element that hints at the transgressive potential of any woman, particularly an older one, and links this text with Rustico's. The polemic with the *Stilnovismo* is also evident in the use of the word 'femena,' selected already in the *Proverbia* for its negative connotation, instead of 'donna,' the natural choice in high-style lyrical poetry.[54] The diabolic creation of de' Rossi and Faitinelli stands as a negative counterpart to the *Stilnovista* idealized woman-angel.

Stilnovistic Parody and Antifeminist Bias in Guido Cavalcanti and Niccola Muscia

As Genette has argued, parody always presupposes a palimpsest, because at its origin there is another text that is counterfeited.[55] Despite the limited corpus of parodistic texts in the medieval period, there are some remarkable parodies of the lyric on the beautiful young woman. The motif of the old ugly woman as opposite of the young and beautiful must have been well established. Cenne da la Chitarra uses the *topos* in one of his sonnets on the twelve months, composed in opposition to Folgore da San Gimignano's cycle of sonnets praising the pleasures of the months. Among Cenne's parodistic *enuegs* is one about the 'vecchia nera, vizza e ranca' ('a dark, wrinkled, and limping old lady'), so the old woman appears again as the opposite feminine figure. In medieval literature parody is often self-parody, as seen in Guinizzelli. Likewise Guido Cavalcanti, the leading figure of the *Dolce Stil Novo*, composed a sonnet on the old woman in which parody and self-parody are foregrounded.

Guido Cavalcanti (1259?–1300) is best known for his lofty love poetry.

Cavalcanti celebrates the beautiful lady's love and examines the joys and torments of love. The lady's cruel indifference causes anguish and pain, which are considered to amount to a true love illness. The predominance of grief, anguish and death in Cavalcanti's verse has led critics to call his account of love 'a poetry of pathology.'[56] In this context of love viewed as illness comes the following sonnet, which is read by critics primarily as *lusus*, parody, and self-parody.[57] However, reading this poem only as a comical escape and stylistic exercise on low genre overshadows the misogynistic stance of a text that not only depicts woman as deformed, unattractive, and ridiculous, but also frowns upon her by portraying her in a transgressive attitude towards medieval codes of conduct for courtly women.

> Guata, Manetto, quella scrignutuzza,
> e pon' ben mente com'è sfigurata
> e com'è drittamente divisata,
> e quel che pare quand'un poco s'agruzza!
>
> Or, s'ella fosse vestita d'un'uzza
> con cappellin' e di vel soggolata,
> e apparisse di die acompagnata
> d'alcuna bella donna gentiluzza,
>
> tu non avresti niquità sì forte,
> né saresti angoscioso sì d'amore,
> né ssì involto di malinconia,
>
> che tu non fossi a rrischio de la morte
> di tanto rider che farebbe 'l core:
> o tu morresti, o fuggires'tu via. (234)

(Take a look, Manetto, at that little hunchbacked woman / And note well how she is garbed / And how she is downright deformed / And what she is like when she shrugs! // And if she were dressed in a cape / With hood and wimpled with a veil / And should appear in daytime in company / With some beautiful high-toned lady, // You would feel no rage so strong / Nor would you be so anguished by love / Nor so wrapped in gloom // That you would not be in danger of death / From the great laughter your heart would provoke: / Either you would die or you would run away.)[58]

In full respect for the rhetorical precepts of practising opposite styles and genres, Cavalcanti engages in a comic-realistic sonnet of self-parody, and by choosing the rhyme in '-zz' he shows his intention to distance himself from his natural high style and to practise parody.[59] However, such a reading alone reveals neither the prejudice against the older/deformed woman nor the transgressive attitude in which the woman is imagined, and that makes her the true other, the opposite to the *Stilnovista*, immaterial angel embodied in Dante's Beatrice.

To be sure, this sonnet lends itself to multiple readings and has been the object of intense examination in recent years.[60] Three interpretive poles have been identified: one – espoused by critics like Marti (*Cultura e stile*), Cassata, and De Robertis – that sees 'Guata, Manetto' as a variation on the *vituperatio vetulae*, one – put forward by Giorgio Agamben – where the ugly old woman serves as cure for the love illness; and, finally, one – suggested by Ciccuto ('Una figura') and Gorni – that views the Cavalcanti comic sonnet as a true *Antistilnovista* manifesto. To these interpretations one should add the most recent by Claudio Giunta, who rejects all the previous approaches and focuses on the sonnet's finale. Giunta evokes cultural memory, rather than precise intertextuality, and sees Manetto's risk of dying of laughter at the end of the sonnet as germane to the death of Greek artist Zeuxis, as reported in Latin author Phestus; Zeuxis really did die of laughter after staring at the painting of an old woman he had created (315–17). Putting aside the specific weaknesses of Giunta's interpretation, his focus on this sonnet demonstrates the importance of such a text, not only in Cavalcanti's corpus, but also in the context of the debate about parody and misogyny.[61]

This sonnet is to be connected with the tradition of *vituperatio vetulae* and should be read as parody of Dante's Beatrice. Moreover, the 'scrignutuzza' is to be considered as old and transgressive since the attitude in which she is imagined, an old woman posing as young and indulging in coquetry, contravenes codes of courtly behaviour.

The focal point in this sonnet is the old unattractive woman, who is mocked for her appearance and her behaviour. The attitude of the poet towards the 'scrignutuzza' is not one of hostility and aggression, as seen in Filippi or Guinizzelli, but rather of derision. The poet's scorn highlights the prejudice against a female type who transgresses the rules of modesty accepted for courtly ladies. Perhaps it is the frustrating experience of love towards the *Stilnovista amata* which generates the antifeminine bias we find in this sonnet. If the beautiful courtly lady of *Stilnovista* poetry is distant, cruel, and unsuited to satisfying the poet's erotic desire and his need for knowledge, then constructing an ugly and laughable feminine figure can lead to the male reaction of reprisal that pervades the sonnet. The poet, sustained by complicity with a male friend, Manetto, established in the opening line, can indulge in the scornful depiction of ridiculous and grotesque femininity. Male authority and judgment over the 'scrignutuzza' serves as a temporary reprieve for the poet, who normally appears enthralled and anguished by the domineering beloved ('domina') of Stilnovistic lyrics. Moreover, the 'scrignutuzza' cynically serves as a curative therapy for the illness of love.

The deformed and ugly woman takes centre stage through the same act of male looking that medieval literary and scientific discourse place at the origin of erotic experience.[62] Cavalcanti himself describes this situation in the sonnet 'Chi è questa che vèn, ch'ogn'om la mira,' where the sight of the beautiful angelic woman causes admiration not only in the poetic self but in everyone who looks at her.

In 'Guata, Manetto' the poet calls a male friend to join in the act of looking at the woman. Contrary to 'Chi è questa che vèn,' where looking collectively at the woman generates in men an appreciation of her beauty, in 'Guata, Manetto' the men looking at the 'scrignutuzza' can gain, not visual pleasure, but gratification through an affirmation of their authority over the woman's ridiculous, paradoxical situation. Manetto and the poetic voice can also gain validation by passing moral judgment on the woman's inappropriate behaviour. Disapproval adds to ridicule of a woman imagined in transgressive attitude, all dressed up and coquettishly garbed, yet disfigured and old. The paradox of the scene (second stanza) lies in the opposition between the 'scrignutuzza' and 'Alcuna bella donna gentiluzza,' the young, beautiful, graceful lady who evokes Stilnovistic love. The ugly woman, far from inspiring feelings of love, is depicted as a laughingstock for being deformed and hunchbacked and for her inappropriate behaviour and attire. As Ciccuto noted, the crooked back of the 'scrignutuzza' symbolically highlights a lack of moral rectitude and human dignity, qualities that always endow the *Stilnovista* lady typified in Dante's Beatrice ('Una figura,' 24). In the sonnet's finale the hunchbacked woman is made the instrument of curative therapy against the 'niquità' and 'malinconia' that burden Manetto, Cavalcanti's alter ego. The 'scrignutuzza' as a *remedium amoris* is the ultimate insult to a woman who becomes a victim of male cynicism.

Does the 'scrignutuzza' belong to the long list of medieval old hags? At first sight one could, as some critics suggest, exclude her from the aging and malevolent women who populate the medieval male unconscious.[63]

And yet, as mentioned above, many critics see this poem as a variation on the *topos* of the old hag.[64] This sonnet is not just a parody of Cavalcanti himself, but is also indebted to Dante's *Vita nuova*, of which it parodies some crucial points. Gorni and Ciccuto ('Una figura') even suggest that the 'scrignutuzza' is a precise and pointed parody of Beatrice, a true non-Beatrice, disguised here as a completely non-idealized feminine figure. For Gorni, this parody indicates Cavalcanti's deprecating tone towards Dante and marks the permanent break of the *Stilnovista* with Dante's new poetics and its privileged role entrusted to the woman.[65] Cavalcanti is poking fun at the *topos* employed by the Sicilian School, exploited by himself (II, 9) and amplified in Dante's *Vita nuova*: the motif of the beloved moving within a group of other ladies of which she is the youngest and the most beautiful. In chapter 3 of *Vita nuova* Dante describes his sighting of Beatrice among a group of older ladies: 'Avvenne che questa mirabile donna apparve a me vestita di colore bianchissimo, in mezzo a due gentili donne, le quali erano di più lunga etade;' ('It happened that ... this marvelous lady appeared to me dressed in purest white, between two gentle ladies who were of greater years').[66] In Cavalcanti's sonnet the situation presented in this episode of the *Vita nuova* is reversed. Where in the *Vita nuova* Beatrice, the young lady at the centre of male attention, appears together with two older courtly ladies – probably her chaperons – and is marvelled at by the poet, in Cavalcanti it is the hunchbacked woman who is accompanied by beautiful courtly ladies ('alcuna bella donna gentiluzza'). The 'scrignutuzza' is the negation of the *topos*; she becomes the subject of male attention and of poetry for being the ugliest and the most ridiculous and, additionally, the oldest of the group of women.[67] Moreover, as a reversal of the courtly lady the 'scrignutuzza' should be old by definition, since in the logic of medieval binary oppositions the beautiful/young stands as contrary to the ugly/old. All the beautiful ladies with whom Stilnovistic poets fall in love are young: Beatrice lures Dante when she is only nine years old, and Cavalcanti's lady Primavera, a manifestation of spring, is compared to the blossom of the rose bud ('Fresca rosa novella/piacente primavera'). As opposite to the *Stilnovista* lady, the ugly woman of Cavalcanti's sonnet then should be included in the list of the old. Even the deformity of the hunchback, in the rhetorical tradition of *descriptio mulieris*, is an attribute of Beroe, the ugly and old woman par excellence.

Cavalcanti's unrelenting humour at the expense of the 'scrignutuzza' targets not only her disfigurement but also her attitude. The exceptional figure in the sonnet is a woman who makes a spectacle of herself when appearing in public, in broad daylight and inappropriately garbed, infringing codes of proper behaviour. The iconographic sketch of her gown, veil, and hat denotes an indulgence of female vanity. As Tertullian explains in his *De cultu*, woman's interest in dress is linked to sinful ambition and can excite men's lustful desire, and courtly ladies of the *Stilnovo* are rarely described in terms of their attire.[68] The attention to the woman's clothing paid here highlights her coquetry and her attempt to appear as an object of desire. The emphasis on the hunchback's apparel stresses the contrast between the seductive nature of her clothing and the impossibility of physical seduction by this deformed woman. She becomes an object of ridicule, under male scrutiny, for masquerading, for making a spectacle of herself, in a way inappropriate to a *Stilnovista* courtly lady, and for attempting to appear young and beautiful when she is not. De Robertis's commentary on this sonnet reinforces the idea of the vanity of this woman who seems so interested in ornamentation. He defines the 'scrignutuzza' as a 'bertuccia azzimata,' ('dressed-up ape'), a designation denoting an ugly and graceless person caught in the act of imitating or copying someone's behaviour; the trappings of masquerade negate the possibility of the 'scrignutuzza' being like the 'fanciulla gentile.'[69] 'Gentile' is indeed the attribute of all the ladies of the *Stilnovo*, but the 'scrignuttuzza' is merely a caricature of the 'bella donna gentiluzza' who accompany her. If in *Stilnovista* poetry the sight of the courtly lady can be so powerful that it becomes unsustainable, the sight of the 'scrignutuzza' is likewise unbearable to the poet, who is left with two possible reactions: death by laughter, or flight.

Although this sonnet is linked by critics to the tradition of the *vituperatio vetulae*, it is not in itself an invective against the old woman. Its tone is comic and parodistic, but neither as vicious nor as destructive as was Guinizzelli's or Rustico's. The 'scrignutuzza' is identifiable as old, or perhaps simply of an older age, when Cavalcanti's sonnet is read in connection with the episode in the *Vita nuova*. The 'scrignutuzza' can be seen as an older woman in the group of younger ladies, in reversal of the situation in chapter 3 of the *Vita nuova*.

The woman's old age is substantiated also through a close reading of Cavalcanti's comic text with sonnet 'Deh, guata, Ciampol, ben questa vecchiuzza,' of uncertain attribution but most likely by Niccola Muscia da Siena, a poet friend of Cavalcanti.[70] This sonnet is modelled on Cavalcanti's 'Guata Manetto,' since it repeats the rhymes in '-uzza' and uses the rhyming words 'amore' and 'core,' but it displays a more openly misogynistic tone and more offensively lingers on disgusting details of the woman's body. By reading the two sonnets in tandem we can confirm the old age of the 'scrignuttuzza.' For Muscia the 'scrignutuzza' is 'vecchiuzza,' and she also displays all those other features of old age:

> Deh, guata, Ciampol, ben questa vecchiuzza
> com'ell'è ben diversamente vizza,
> e quel che par quand'un poco si rizza,
> e come coralmente viene 'n puzza,
>
> e com'a punto sembra una bertuzza
> del viso e delle spalle e di fattezza,
> e, quando la miriam, come s'adizza
> e travolge e digrigna la boccuzza.
>
> Che non dovresti sì forte sentire
> d'ira, d'angoscia, d'affanno o d'amore,
> che non dovessi molto rallegrarti,
>
> veggendo lei, che fa maravigliarti
> sì che per poco non ti fa perire
> gli spiriti amorosi ne lo core. (Angiolieri, *Le rime*, 398)

(Ugh, do observe that ancient hag, Ciampol. / No other half so foul you're like to meet. / Yet see her strut and swell. Upon my soul / She cannot know her odor is not sweet. // I' faith, she seems a very Barbary ape, / And is one too, in gestures, form, and face. / Just look at her. She'll twist as at some jape/ Her ugly mug into a lewd grimace. // Therefore, you should not tear your heart out so / With anger, or, with anguish, or with love / That for rejoicing you do not have room. // Why? Just this marvel which will end your gloom! / Seeing her does, and has, and will remove / All amorous thoughts, and this you ought to know.)[71]

Although this poem is considered less perfect and more repetitive than Cavalcanti's, structurally the two sonnets are remarkably similar. They both use the allocutory formula to attract the male friend's attention to the exceptional sight of the unattractive lady, whose disfigured body is described.[72] The harsh rhymes in '-zz-' are amplified here, since they appear in almost every rhyming word of the sonnet. It is by reading these two sonnets together, as a medieval *tenzone*, that we can also connect Cavalcanti's 'scrignutuzza' with the tradition of old hags, whose vituperation is inaugurated by Rustico. In Muscia's sonnet there reappears Rustico's emphasis on the bad smell of the old woman. Here both olfaction and sight are negatively affected by the presence of this type of woman, whose liminality is confirmed by the ape-like nature of the 'vecchiuzza.'

Muscia reinterprets the inappropriate behaviour of the 'scrignutuzza' by calling the old woman 'bertuzza,' an epithet that recalls both the unattractive features of a monkey and the feminine attitude of imitating and aping younger women. De Robertis referred to the 'scrignutuzza' as a 'bertuccia azzimata,' de facto reinforcing the negative judgment of the woman's behaviour. Effectively, then, male poets and the male critic join in a nasty solidarity of male voices willing to intensify their authoritative judgment on standards of gender, beauty, age, and female behaviour. The 'vecchiuzza' of Muscia displays the anger, evident in her facial frown, that is a reaction to the male act of looking at her. Anger in the old woman further connects this sonnet to the tradition of *vituperatio vetuale*, as it is elaborated in Guinizzelli's 'vecchia rabiosa,' who again could be reacting to such an intrusive male attitude.

In the third stanza both sonnets propose this feminine type as a remedy for love sickness, defined by the symptoms of anguish, pain, and anger. The concept of love as illness was already present in Greek Aristotelian philosophy and in Arab medical and scientific texts, and it reappears in both medieval medical and literary discourse.[73] Denigration of the woman as the cause of love sickness and the need to discuss some therapy or remedy for the negative effect of love appear in literary texts such as Ovid's *Remedia amoris* and Andreas Cappellanus's third book of *De amore*. This literary tradition is sure to have influenced Cavalcanti as well as realistic poets. The idea of proposing the old woman in her disgust and deformity as an effective antidote to love sickness is exploited in both literary and medical discourse.[74] What in Cavalcanti and Muscia is a cynical comic expedient reappears in medical discourse as a pseudo-scientific remedy for *hereos* or love illness. The bad smell of the deformed woman in Muscia connects this sonnet not only to Rustico's 'buggeressa,' but also to Dante's 'femmina balba.' This negativity towards old women in poetic as well as medical texts clearly reveals that medieval culture and literary and medical discourse pursue the same misogynist agenda. Bernard de Gordon (d. ?1318), professor of medicine at Montpelier, discusses *hereos* in chapter 20 of his *Lilium medicinae*. The detail of the bad smell, together with other disgusting elements of feminine old age, appears prominently in this text, which became very popular after its publication in 1305.[75] The smelly old woman is mentioned here as the cure for extreme cases of *hereos*, love illness with excessive melancholy. As Cherchi noted, in Gordon's medical text as well as in Dante's 'Purgatorio,' and additionally in Muscia's sonnet, the disgusting and malodorous woman is presented as having the therapeutic effect of curing love sickness. Although it is not possible to demonstrate whether any of these poets were familiar with Gordon's medical text, or vice versa, the use of the same rhetorical strategies and offensive tones towards old women is remarkable. Be it in the comic vein of Cavalcanti and Muscia or in the serious tone of scientific literature, we witness an attitude of pervasive negativity towards old women. Medical and literary discourse rely on the same misogynistic clichés to condemn women's deformity and age.

chapter 2

Transgression in the Trecento and Quattrocento: Guardian, Witch, Prostitute

The Old Guardian in Comic Poetry and Franco Sacchetti

The recurring characteristic of the ugly woman in medieval comic poetry is her advanced age. This element continues to be dominant during the fourteenth century, but the focus moves to a special category of old woman: the guardian. The guardian is a recurrent character in medieval romance. In the *Roman de la Rose* (circa 1275), and its Italian rewriting in Dante's *Il fiore* (circa 1285–90), she typifies the duenna, the shrewd old woman who, rather than chaperoning and protecting the young woman's chastity, indoctrinates her in all the tricks to gain the lover's favour.[1] The Vielle of the *Roman* (and its Italian variation La Vecchia in the *Fiore*) is the archetypical medieval literary Old Woman who survived a life in the sex war and now acts as a guide to younger women. In this sense the guardian, as half bawd/half go-between, finds an antecedent in Ovid's Dipsas and reappears again in pseudo-Ovidian *De vetula* (mid-thirteenth century), a Latin comedy, where she personifies the lascivious old woman. In this comedy, which was quite influential in Italy, the old woman, who promised the lover Ovid to help in arranging a rendezvous with his beloved in her bedroom at night, takes the opportunity to replace the young girl in the amorous encounter. Ovid is so taken aback by the deceptive plan that he runs away in disgust.[2] Although Latin comedy seems to have more influence on narrative and novellas, it is important to identify the guardian as an established female figure who will appear prominently in poetry on the ugly woman.[3]

In Italian comic poetry of the trecento the guardian appears within the *topos* of *vituperatio vetulae* and as a particular variation of the Latin comedy and Romance examples. Instead of being a go-between and indoctrinating the inexperienced woman into the arts of seduction, the guardian of comic poetry acts as an obstacle to the love affair, and she is often accused of and cursed for not understanding young people's need for love. In the comic poems on the old guardian the poet inveighs against the custodian of the young beloved. Hostility towards the old woman reflects the poet's feelings towards a female figure who is an impediment to union with the beloved, and who appears to control the situation. These poetic texts are particularly significant since they reveal how male fear of a woman in a position of power is expressed through virulent misogynist attack. What is particularly disturbing to the male poet is the fact that a woman appropriates the gaze.

Feminist philosopher Rosi Braidotti notes the primacy of looking in Western culture, where the gaze and sight are the main locus of legitimation of knowledge and where the woman serves as passive object, as a flat surface to reflect the male subject (71–2). The insistence and polysemy of the act of looking by the guardian disclose mechanisms of visual power that subvert the line of gaze allowed to a woman in medieval culture. Rules of conduct for medieval women prescribed that both young girls and more mature women refrain from looking at others, particularly in public and in the presence of men. In Francesco da Barberino's *Reggimento e costumi di donna* (circa 1314–16), we find repeated mention of the importance of women keeping their eyes lowered, particularly in public, not returning the male gaze, and in older age even not spending time at the window or at the door, to avoid possible visual contact with the outside.[4]

The old guardian who looks thus transgresses the rules of appropriate behaviour is attacked in invectives not only because she guards the poet's beloved but also because she insists on looking. Let's examine more closely the mechanisms that rule the lines of the gaze in courtly poetry, the essential reference point for comic-realistic poetry.

The sense of sight plays a particularly important role in medieval love poetry. According to the love phenomenology presented in Andreas's *De amore*, falling in love happens primarily through the eyes and vision: 'Amor est passio quaedam innata ex visione et immoderata cogitatione formae alterus sexus' (4) ('Love is a passion that originates innately from the sight of and immoderate thinking about a person of the opposite sex'). Sight and looking are so important that Andreas almost excludes the possibility of falling in love without seeing the object of desire: 'caecitas impedit amorem, quia caecus videre non potest, unde sus possit animus immoderatum suscipere cogitationem, ergo in eo amor non potest oriri' (16) (Blindness impedes love, because the blind cannot see, hence in no way can his soul generate the thinking, therefore in him love cannot be born). Andreas's discourse is addressed to the inexperienced young man ('novum amoris militem'), who should be taught the art of love, and in general it is addressed to a male audience. As Lobanov-Rostovsky observes (198–9), the Platonic theory of vision accepted in the Middle Ages conceived of the eye as active and penetrating, thereby gendering it as male.

In courtly and lyrical poetry, sight is a focal point of the love relation and the male gaze is the privileged locus of amorous passion; the young woman appears mainly as passive object. Poets of the Sicilian School explain how falling in love originates with the sight of the beloved.[5] In the thematic repertoire of the *Siciliani* we find numerous examples that confirm this point: feelings of love begin with the sight of what one likes. Giacomo da Lentini well illustrates this phenomenon:

> Amor è un desio che ven da core
> per abundanza de gran plazimento,
> e gli ogli en prima generan l'amore,
> e lo core li dà nutrigamento. (16)[6]

(Love is a desire that comes from the heart for abundance of pleasure, love is generated first in the eyes and it is nourished by the heart.)

The lines of the gaze, from the eyes of the lover to the woman/beloved, recur in all the Sicilian poets and also appear in the *Stilnovisti*. As Guinizzelli states:

> E' par che da verace piacimento
> lo fino amor discenda
> guardando quel ch'al cor torni piacente;
> ché poi ch'om guarda cosa di talento,
> al cor pensieri abenda,
> e cresce con disio immantenente.[7]

(It appears that fine love comes from the true enjoyment of looking at what is pleasing to the heart; when one then looks at a precious thing, thoughts arise and desire grows immediately.)

In lyric poetry the lines of the gaze move from the male, the subject of desire, towards the woman, the desired object; the act of looking is active/masculine and stands in opposition to the passive/feminine position of being looked at.[8]

Feminist critics, in their study of cinema, have stressed the blatant absence in Western culture of positive female figures with an active and authoritative gaze. Sarah Stanbury notes that already in medieval literature the act of looking in women is censored. The woman who looks and acts transgressively is characterized as aggressive, lustful, and evil ('The Virgin's Gaze,' 1084).[9]

Feminist film critics have studied the issue of the gendered gaze in contemporary cinema and have noted that the position of the woman as spectator is 'a position often marked by an official absence, since in our culture rights to visual assertiveness and aggression belong chiefly to men' (Stanbury, 'The Virgin's Gaze,' 1084). In cinema the erotic pleasure of looking, scopophilia, is one of the most common forms of identification offered to the male spectator. A term used in Freudian psychoanalysis, scopophilia involves two modes of obtaining erotic pleasure, voyeurism and fetishism.[10] In the second mode, more pertinent to this study, woman becomes an object of the male gaze. The male subject takes pleasure in turning his fetishizing look at the woman, the passive object of desire. As Mary Ann Doane observes, in cinema there is a 'cinematic alignment of structures of seeing and being seen with sexual difference' (83). There is a certain exaggeration, a difficulty, in considering the woman who appropriates the gaze and insists on looking. When the woman looks, as in some horror films, she is being excessive and is punished for her transgression.[11] The woman is excluded from the empowering position of looking and typically takes up an exhibitionist role of spectacle, as an object to be looked at. John Berger notes that the social presence of the woman is different from that of the man; since she is reified, she becomes by definition an object to be looked at:

> Presence for a woman is so intrinsic to her person that men tend to think of it as an almost physical emanation ... One might simplify by saying: *men act* and *women appear*. Men look at women. Women watch themselves being looked at. ... Thus she turns herself into an object – and most particularly – an object of vision: a sight. (46–7)

These theoretical observations are useful in deciphering the presence of the old guardian in medieval comic poetry. The mechanisms of gendered gaze in lyrical poetry reflect those of contemporary cinema: the active pleasure of seeing and looking belongs to the poet, and the woman is thus object of the gaze. Medieval aulic lyric poetry (Sicilians and *Stilnovisti*) repeatedly presents the same dynamic. The poet derives, feeds, and explains his desire and pleasure through the sight of the woman-beloved object. In medieval lyric poetry the female eye, when it appears, does not actually see but is there only to solicit the male gaze. So the only instance of female gaze offered by lyric poetry is one that threatens to objectify the male lover but immediately retreats before the power of his desire.

Comic-realistic poetry, which opposes in style and genre the courtly Stilnovistic tradition, presents some texts where the ugly old guardian transgresses the conventional lines of the gendered gaze. The poems about the old guardian display a type of woman who is no longer the object but the subject of the gaze, although this gaze is not necessarily an erotic look at the man. The woman who looks is the guardian/custodian of the young girl loved by the poet; she is active in obstructing the male gaze. By appropriating the gaze the old woman sports the active, penetrating eye that is normally associated with the male position. The guardian's gaze is also threatening. As popular belief of the evil eye shows, the gaze of certain people can have negative/effeminizing influence.[12]

In these poems, generally vituperations, the guardian is presented as a dangerous and completely negative figure, with physically grotesque features. Old age is the quality that signals her impossibility of being the object of male desire, but it is also an indicator of her power and transgression. As in cinema, the woman who looks is depicted as transgressive, aggressive, and sometimes lustful, but she is always endowed with an unusual power and therefore is censored at various levels. The woman who looks is punished by the poet-lover, who indulges in verbal and physical abuse.

In these poetic texts the male poet who desires through sight is faced with a female presence who is no longer an object of desire and source of 'piacimento' but a subject of authority, since she exerts her power in hindering the sight of the beloved. The poet, as traditional desiring and looking subject, uses the power of his word to express his aversion to the old woman who usurps his visual privilege and contravenes conventional rules.

In the invectives against the old guardian the lines of the gaze, which normally move from the man-subject towards the woman-object, are subverted and the man is excluded from the traditional visual path. Every time the woman appropriates the gaze the outcome is negative; in a culture that censures and punishes the woman who looks, she can be represented only as a completely negative figure (evil, ugly, old, gossip). If in horror film, as Linda William concludes, the woman who looks is reflected in the monster she sees and ends up identifying with its physical deformity; similarly in comic poetry the guardian who looks is depicted as disfigured in her aged body.

The guardian deserves punishment not only because she is intent on preventing the man from obtaining his visual pleasure, but also, as noted above, because she insists on looking. The poet attacks her both with verbal abuse and by wishing upon her physical annihilation: dismemberment and destruction of a body unsuited to visual male gratification.

In the poems on the old guardian the verb 'guardare' acquires a particularly rich semantic texture. Etymologically, 'guardare' not only refers to turning the gaze, or observing, but also to guarding, defending, keeping in custody, a meaning implicit in the Germanic root 'wardon,' a term used in connection with military exercise of power, keeping guard of enemies or prisoners.[13] In aulic lyric 'guardare' is the act that triggers and feeds the 'piacimento' of the poet. In the poems on the old guardian, 'guardare' not only means looking, observing with envy and anger, guarding and watching over the young beloved, but also signals an affirmation, in etymological terms, of her own supremacy in keeping guard, preventing the poet from looking at his beloved.

Two anonymous sonnets of the fourteenth century, dubiously attributed to Cecco Angiolieri, according to Casini (208) are a *tenzone*, where the poet answers in rhyme to a burlesque proposal.[14] In both sonnets the poet is molested by the presence of an old woman caught looking. In the first sonnet the poet complains because he is pestered by a malicious, obnoxious woman, who looks at/guards his beloved.

> Tutto mi strugge l'animo una *vecchia*
> per la malizia, dond'ell'è coperta;
> quand'i' la miro, allora mi par certa
> ch' i' con le' *guardo* chi 'l bel viso *specchia*.
>
> Ell'assomiglia l'altre, come *pecchia*:
> vecchia, 'ntendete, ché m'è maggior perta;
> ché tremar fammi e prometter offerta,
> s'i' scampar posso da le sue *orecchia*.
>
> A santa Tecchia – me ne raccomando;
> ché m'hanno sempre tenuto 'n paura
> le vecchie di gran tempo: ma più questa.

Però ch'è vecchia e prosperosa e desta,
e *guata* altrui, per sua mala ventura,
e sa conoscer ciò, ch'uom va pensando. (Massera, 310)[15]

(An old woman torments my soul because of the malice that dwells in her; when I look at her it seems certain that I gaze with her at the one whose face glows with beauty. She resembles the others, like a bee: hark!, she is old and causes me most harm; she makes me shudder and accept her offers, if I can get away from her ears. I shall be grateful to Saint Tecchia; since I have always feared women of old age: and this one even more. She is old and healthy and shrewd, and she looks at others with her evil fortune, she knows what men think.)

The thematic rhyming word 'vecchia' opens the series of rhymes in '-ecchia,' repeated also in the following sonnet, which is a response in rhyme. With transgressive action the woman starts looking at the poet's beloved with him, even though her intention is different. Her sense of enterprise is punished with insult; the poet calls her malicious, a negative attribute thought typical of old women. But the transgressive potential of the old woman could be more explosive if we consider 'ché tremar fammi e prometter offerta,' an allusion to an erotic proposal addressed to the poet, who shivers in fear. This detail would connect this guardian to the guardian go-between in the pseudo-ovidian *De vetula*, who impersonates the young beloved to obtain an erotic encounter with the poet. The male poet's position of authority is endangered by the old woman, whom he fears because of her ability to know men's thoughts. The old guardian positions herself in a traditionally masculine role, in control of knowledge, of sight, and of the beloved.

In the second sonnet, a friend of the poet inveighs against the old guardian and complains about receiving the same treatment from the old woman when he looks at his beloved.

Mandarti poss'io 'l sangue, 'n una *secchia*,
sì, ched i' l'abbia per le reni aperta,
di quella *vecchia* maliziosa sperta,
che sempre farti mal pur s'*apparecchia*.

Tutto ch'i' credo ch'ella sia *parecchia*,
e spesse volte con lei si converta,
d'una, che mai non mi lasciò scoperta
la donna mia veder, tant'è *vertecchia*.

Il viso *attecchia*, – quand'i' vo *guardando*,
e solo dov'io sia lieva la testa;
Iddio non tem', e men la sepultura.

Hae anni e mesi vie più, che le mura
del Culisèo, e va ad ogni festa,
veleno e fuoco per li occhi gittando. (Massera, 310)

(May I send you her blood in a bucket, when I have opened her up by the kidneys, old malicious shrewd woman, who is always ready to harm you. I believe she is similar and often is together with another woman, who is as old and annoying and who never allowed me to see my lady in the open. When I try looking she turns her gaze, and moves her head to wherever I move; she fears neither God nor the grave. She is older than the walls of the Coliseum, and at every holiday she goes around spreading venom and fire through her eyes.)

The poet recognizes the similarity between the malicious old woman who pesters his friend and the one who harasses him, preventing him from seeing his beloved and attempting to interfere with his act of looking. The two sonnets point at the existence of a group of old women, a coterie of powerful guardians, who act for the same purpose and who are particularly abhorred by male poets. The old guardian's strength is located in her eyes that scatter poison and fire, metaphorically hinting at the power of her gaze. This detail evokes the fabulous figure of the basilisk, since this serpent-like creature of classical bestiaries was believed to kill and be killed by seeing and being seen. The power of the guardian's eye to objectify threatens the poet's subjectivity; this transgression of the old woman is punished not only with insult but here also with physical abuse, a dismemberment of the body ('Chedi' l'abbia per le reni aperta').

An author who composed texts for musical accompaniment and who shows particular hostility towards old women is Franco Sacchetti (1332–1400). Although he is best known for continuing Boccaccio's novella tradition in his *Trecentonovelle*, he composed poetry in both high lyrical and comic style. Sacchetti's poetic career opens with a work against old women, where young and old women are pitted against each other. His *Battaglia delle belle donne di Firenze* (circa 1352) is a poem in octaves structurally similar to the popular tradition of *cantari*. The poet narrates the victorious fight of the young beautiful women of Florence against the old women, who are bent on avenging Ogliente, an ugly smelly old woman killed by the young women for invading their *locus amoenus*.[16] The poem has numerous connections with the *vituperatio vetulae* of realistic poetry and with some of Sacchetti's later verse. Even though in *La battaglia* the old Ogliente is not specifically identified as a guardian, she is an intruder who forcefully enters the garden of courtly love, where the beautiful Florentine women take refuge. An aversion to aged women is stated, for example, in stanza 5 of the second 'Cantare' where the customary epithets of the comic tradition are attributed to old women: 'Le vecchie son crudeli e invidïose,/le vecchie son nimiche d'ogni bene,/ verso gli amanti sempre dispettose' (40) (Old women are cruel and envious, old women are enemies of every good, they are always spiteful towards lovers). The poem's motif, particularly old women's envy and inability to understand the needs of lovers, foretells the rage against old women found in a significant, if not copious, number of Sacchetti's *Rime*. In the ballad 'Qual diavol, vecchie, subito vi tocca,' reorienting the misogynist clichés of women's diabolic nature (as in Faitinelli) specifically towards old ones, Saccheti describes the unpleasant effect produced by the old hags on the poets in love, whose action of looking at their beloved is effectively hindered.

> Qual diavol, vecchie, sùbito vi tocca,
> quando vo' mormorate?
> Perché non contentar gli occhi lasciate?
>
> Vo' ci togliete quel tanto ch'ab<b>iamo
> agli occhi nostri in oscurarci i volti;
> e non pensate che sempre cerchiamo
> star nel veder con umiltà racolti.
> Lasciate dunque il corso agli occhi sciolti,
> tanto che apariate
> quel ch'è amor, ché non par che 'l sap<p>iate. (13–14)[17]

(What devil soon touches you old women, when you grumble? Why don't you allow our eyes to be satisfied? You take away from our eyes what we have and you obscure our faces and you do not think that we always try to keep quiet and humble in gazing. Therefore allow our eyes free course so that you may learn what is love, since it appears that you do not know it.)

In typical misogynist fashion, the poet's negative opinion about some old women is generalized to every old woman, whose behaviour is considered obnoxious. The poet's voice speaks here for all the men in love. Instead of the verb 'guardare' here the thematic word is 'occhi,' which belongs to the semantic area of looking. Sacchetti clearly illustrates the path of the gaze: the poet looks at the woman and can thereby 'contentare gli occhi' (satisfy his eyes). The insult to the old woman here is limited to her diabolic nature, but Sacchetti revisits the motif of the old guardian in the ballad 'Tra 'l bue l'asino e le pecorelle,' where the old woman obstructs the courtship of a beautiful pastorella:

> [Tra 'l bue e l'asino] e le pecorelle
> per un boschetto van due pasturelle.
>
> [Come elle vanno lo]r bestie guardando,
> così lor una vecchia cruda *guarda*
> [filando dietro a l]oro e borbotando,
> e con un fiero volto altrui *riguarda*.
> [Par ch'ella sem]pre con invidia arda,
> diavolo asembra a vederla fra elle. (107–8)[18]

(Among the ox the donkey and the little sheep, in the woods go two young shepherdesses. As they guard their herd so an old cruel woman guards them weaving and grumbling, and she looks at others with a fierce face. She seems to glow with envy; she looks like the devil among the shepherdesses.)

This ballad evokes the French *pastourelle*, a comic genre that, according to Orvieto and Brestolini, joins unnaturally the ideals of courtly love (represented by the courtly suitor/poet) and those of the lower class of the young 'pastorella.' (102).[19] In this text another person joins in the game of gazes, enriching the polysemic richness of the verb 'guardare': the shepherdesses who guard the sheep. The poet looks at the shepherdesses, while the old woman engages in a competition with the poet by looking at/guarding the 'pasturelle.' The poet's fascinated gaze at the gracious shepherdesses is disturbed by the old guardian:

> [Ma, quando a lei m'a]presso, alor s'invia
> vèr me la vecchia con la crespa pelle.
>
> [Non fo sì picciol busso, ch]e non senta,
> né tanto son di lungi, che non veggia;
> [un bavalischio par, sì] mi spaventa,

e fammi rimbucar sotto ogni scheggia.
[Diavol, a te lo do; o] tu l'aspreggia,
sì che di morte io ne senta novelle. (108)

(But when I go near her, the old woman with the wrinkled skin comes towards me. She hears any slight noise I make, she can see me from far away: she looks like a basilisk and she scares me so much that she makes me take shelter under every rock. Devil, I entrust you with her: may you trouble her so much that I may hear about her death.)

The idyllic atmosphere of the *locus amoenus*, where the 'pasturelle' live, is similar to the one in Sacchetti's first poem *La battaglia*. The old guardian appears again as an intruder who disturbs the peace and looks with envy. The transgressive attitude of the old guardian is punished through verbal abuse and through the rhetorical negative *descriptio* ('La vecchia con la crespa pelle,' 'un bavalischio pare'). The physical and moral ugliness of the old woman is highlighted by contrast with the gracious beauty of the 'pasturelle.' The old guardian imposes her authority by preventing the courtship of the 'pasturella piacevoletta.' She is caught looking, guarding, and mumbling, the latter a recurring reaction in old jealous and envious guardians, even in mothers of young girls.[20] The old woman's whole portrait is centred on her evil nature, her insensitivity to feelings of love. Particularly significant here is the comparison of the 'vecchia' with the basilisk, the imaginary deformed reptile whose distinctive feature is precisely its lethal gaze, accompanied by foul, fiery breath.[21] The poet concedes that the old guardian's aggressive gaze has a weakening effect, since he is afraid of her and forced to take shelter from her eyes ('fammi rimbucar sotto ogni scheggia').

In the final invective, the call to birds of prey to come and feed on the angry woman's body takes up a motif that is frequent in vituperations against old women:

[Ballata], truova tutti gli avoltoi
ed orsi e lupi ch'ab<b>ian forti artigli;
[dì] lor: – Merzé, i' me ne vegno a voi,
ch'a questa vecchia vo' diate di pigli,
e chi ne porti il cuor, e chi' ventrigli,
 e' corbi e' nibbi s'ab<b>ian le budelle. (108–9)

(Ballad, go find all the vultures and the bears and the wolves with strong claws; and tell them: – Please, I come to you, so that you can grab this old woman; and some may take her heart and some her stomach; and crows and kites may have her entrails.)

The same wish was expressed in Guinizzelli's sonnet 'Volvol te levi, vecchia rabbïosa,' where vultures, ravens, and falcons were summoned to tear the vecchia's body apart. From this parallelism we can surmise that Guinizzelli's invective against the old woman is also aimed at punishing a transgressive guardian, perhaps the archetype of all old guardians in comic poetry. In Sacchetti as in Guinizzelli, the guardian's attempt to use her authority and to usurp the power of the gaze is punished with bodily dismemberment. A female body that cannot provide male gratification should be dismembered and disposed of.[22]

To be sure, the guardian in Italian vernacular poetry is depicted ambiguously. She breaks the rule of the gaze, which normally excludes women from an active position of looking; she contravenes the acceptable conduct for honest women, who are supposed to avoid the look; and yet as guardian of the young girl she appears to align herself with orthodoxy, since, by preventing the love relationship with the poet/lover, she may seem to prohibit a sexual encounter and to protect the girl's honour and virginity. As stated in Adreas's *De amore*, if the pursued young woman belongs to a low social class, like the peasantry, the suitor need not respect the courtly ideals of spiritual love; for relations with peasants, after brief courtship, the final outcome is sexual intercourse.[23] If a guardian is the girl's mother or stepmother, her action can be driven by concerns about preserving virginity, but not many old ugly guardians are girls' mothers. It is hard, however, to determine what motivates the guardian's obstruction of the love relationship. Most guardians are said to be evil, dishonest, angry, and envious of young girls. Envy and jealousy are recurring feelings attributed to old guardians; hence their obstructionism seems aimed not so much at protecting a girl's reputation as at assuming control and spitefully reacting to the impossibility of themselves partaking in the game of love and desire.

Descriptive Vituperation: Guarding and Slandering in Minstrel Poetry

The motif of the old hag, guardian or other, is so pervasive that it spans from comic poetry to 'poesia per musica' and to the repertoires of minstrels and jongleurs, thereby showing how clichés about ugly old women overarch various genres and styles in a cultural continuum, which encompasses texts by affirmed authors and anonymous pieces readily circulating both in a court setting and in the market square.

Minstrels or jongleurs have left important – and yet little studied – repertoires of poetic texts that deserve our consideration. As Tito Saffioti points out, minstrels, or 'giullari,' roaming from village to village and from the court to the public square, have been largely ignored because of the ambiguity and elusiveness of their liminal and nomadic condition. The difficulty in determining paternity of the minstrel texts and the diverse and ever-changing setting for minstrels' performative poetry contribute to marginalization.[24] Saffioti, however, stresses the importance of 'giullari,' who were welcome both at court and in the public squares and functioned as propagators of news, customs, thoughts, and ideas (102). Since poetry in minstrel repertoires often appears in variations and lacks precise attribution, it is frequently considered 'popular,' 'folk' poetry, a label that carries a pejorative connotation and assumes a distinction between high and low culture. As critics have shown, 'poesia giullaresca,' as performative art aimed at a wide audience, functions as a vehicle for the circulation of both popular and literary themes. Therefore it provides a crucial cultural background for the stratification in the male/collective imaginary of clichés about ugly women. Orvieto and Brestolini observe that anonymous texts in 'repertori giullareschi' are not the product of folklore, or of the 'people'; rather, they are poetic texts that employ comic/lower, style and whose primary purpose is *lusus*, or pleasant entertainment, both at court and in the public square (101, 120). Eugenio Battisti believes that medieval 'giullari,' with their uncertain social status, and their itinerant life wandering between court and village square, contributed to the intermingling of the most diverse cultural stratifications (287).[25] In jongleur repertoires, as well as in other anonymous poetry, texts serve as repositories of both lyrical and comic themes, of high and low cultural expressions.

The *topos* of the old guardian is quite pervasive in 'poesia per musica' of the late fourteenth century. This poetry, which was accompanied by music and was meant for public performance, features many negative figures of old women, often guardians of the beloved. Alesso di Guido Donati, active in Florence in the second half of the trecento, would perform his madrigals of invective against the old guardian. In 'Ellera non s'avvitola,' where the guardian is in fact a mother, the male poet complains about the mother's strict surveillance of the 'bella zitola' (beautiful girl), and in 'In pena vivo qui sola soletta' it is the young girl desirous to get married who argues with her strict mother. The old guardian also appears as a strict mother in Donato da Cascia's madrigal 'Un cane, un'oca e una vecchia pazza,' where she is not only wrinkled but is also derogatorily called 'vecchia eretica' with reference to her religious practices, one feature that takes centre stage in the quattrocento in connection with the witch. No real punishment is mentioned for this guardian, who is simply a comic figure.[26] Donato da Cascia sets to music a madrigal that reveals many similarities between the two sonnets in the pseudo-Angiolieri *tenzone*. The same thematic word 'vecchia' appears in rhyme with 'specchia,' and also the same reference to the witch:

> Una smaniosa e insensata *vecchia*
> ha tolto in caccia 'l mie gentil amore
> con ire invidiose e con furore.
>
> Essa nel viso d'un vecchio si *specchia*,
> faccendo per piacergli astuta guarda:
> così quel mal vissuto s'ingargliarda.
>
> Per guardar la mie donna han fatto lega
> el vecchio impronto e l'arabbiata strega. (Corsi, 1047)

(A frantic and foolish old woman has kept guard on my gentle love with envious rage and fury. She sees herself reflected in the face of an old man, and keeps smart guard to please him: so that ill-disposed man gains strength. The irksome old man is in league with the angry witch to guard my lady.)

The old woman is opposed to the 'gentil amore' of Stilnovistic descent, although such grace here has undergone various changes.[27] Here too the old woman is the subject of looking, but the action is shared with an old man whom she wishes to please. This woman could be a stepmother, married to the old father of the beloved. The insulting characteristics imputed to the old woman include anger, envy, and madness. She is also called 'strega,' an epithet that will become the main focus of poetic texts in the quattrocento. The adjective 'arrabbiata,' central in Guinizzelli's 'Volvol te levi, vecchia rabbïosa,' gives further evidence that the old woman in Guido's sonnet belongs to the group of the hated guardians.[28]

The old woman as figure of authority also appears in some anonymous 'poesia giullaresca' of the northeastern region, where she is depicted as having a disgusting, excessive body. Some texts attack the old woman for her evil nature and envy and for the power of her speech. The poet attempts to disempower her through invective and with the help of rhetoric. These texts are remarkable because, despite their lack of authorship and their crude style, they display impressive rhetorical mastery, thereby confirming that anonymous and comic poetry shares the same cultural heritage as aulic poetry. In attacking the old woman, ballads and *canzonette* employ amplification, accumulation, and base language and provide detailed, orderly descriptions of the old disgusting body. These texts inflict on the old woman a verbal retribution through perfect rhetorical skills.[29] The old female is described in terms of physical repulsion, filth, and hybridity, with emphasis on an excessive, overflowing body, all features that suggest the Bakhtinian grotesque body. In *Rabelais and His World* Bakhtin opposes the features of the grotesque body to those of the classical body:[30] the classical body is closed, self-contained, static; the grotesque body is open, protruding, 'it is blended with the world, with animals, with objects' (27). It is identified with the lower bodily stratum and associated with degradation, filth, death. It is connected with 'those parts of the body that are open to the outside, ... the open mouth, the genital organs, the breasts, the phallus, the pot-belly, the nose' (26). The grotesque female figures that appear here may evoke the subversive, unruly women that Natalie Zemon Davis describes in her classic essay 'Women on Top.'[31] Although these ugly old hags are portrayed in a position of power, such a role does not allow for true subversion, or a reversal of authority; rather, any form of female empowerment is promptly vanquished by the (presumably) male poetic voice through the power of rhetoric and speech.

In *Studi di poesia antica* Tommaso Casini examines some anonymous ballads of a minstrel repertoire, in the Codex Magliabechiano VII 1070, dated around the mid-fourteenth century, which present quite harsh attacks on the old woman.[32] The poems constitute an important miniseries on the old hag, and provide an interesting sample of how different strategies, from the customary invective to rhetorical negative *descriptio*, are used as forms of retribution against the old woman's authority and her transgression.

Some poems, like the short ballad 'Do, mala vechia, lo mal fuogo l'arda,' follow the traditional scheme of the invective against the beloved's guardian and culminate in a curse; death by fire, the traditional form of punishment used for witches, appears as the apt retribution for the old guardian's obstruction. When the transgression of the old woman refers not only to the power of her eye and surveillance, but also to the authority and slander of her words, it is the poet's art of words that comes as the most appropriate form of retribution.

Medieval codes of appropriate behaviour for honest women forbid the use of both eyes and mouth. Women in public places were not supposed to look around, nor was it appropriate for them to speak. Francesco da Barberino stresses throughout his book of conduct for women, *Reggimento e costumi di donna*, the importance of women's silence, since too much speaking contributes to a woman's bad reputation: 'fenmina ch'è gran parliera / tenuta è matta e leggera' (183). In fact, silence is the coveted quality for every honest woman, and in religious, moral, and literary texts female garrulity was associated with sin and lust.[33] Silence in a woman was a sign of submission to the male authority of the father or husband. The connection between female speaking and wantonness is common throughout medieval and early modern times. The act of speaking, just like that of looking, is a male privilege, and when the woman appropriates it she is accused of sin and punished. As Stallybrass notes, 'the surveillance of women concentrated upon three specific areas: the mouth, chastity and the threshold of the house. These three were frequently collapsed into each other' (126). The closed mouth becomes a sign of chastity. Since the female body naturally tends towards the Bakhtinian grotesque (it is unfinished, outgrows itself, transgresses its own limits), the respectable woman must conform to the Bakhtinian classical body, whose signs are enclosed body, closed mouth, locked house (127).

In the ballad 'Laida vecchia stomegosa' of Casini's repertoire the 'vecchia' is presented as a slanderer, guilty of using her mouth to ruin honest women's reputations. This poem is singled out by Casini as 'più vivamente plebea delle precedenti' (218) (more vividly plebeian than the previous ones) for its crude language and graphic details. In the ballad the old woman is attacked for the power of her tongue, which is used to discredit honest women. The male poet identifies envy ('Par che invidia te consume,' line 91) as the motive for her fiery words about young women. The poem opens with an invective that targets her ugliness and vice:

Laida vecchia stomegosa,
maladeta se' tu ogni ora,
che in del mondo ní de fora
non fo mai sí mala cosa.

Quanto tu sei brutta e ria
dir non posso a parte a parte,
de bruteze tu sei dia,
d'ogni vicio tu sai l'arte; (lines 1–8)

(Ugly revolting old woman, may you be cursed at every hour, neither in this world nor elsewhere was there ever such an evil thing. I cannot say in full how disgusting and wicked you are, you are the epitome of ugliness, you know the art of every vice.)

The ballad's most striking feature, despite being an anonymous text of oral transmission, is the use of a rhetorical artifice like the negative *descriptio mulieris* in descending order, structured in an extrinsic and intrinsic portrait, to detail the physical and moral ugliness of the old gossip, whose body is inventoried from head to toe:

De la copa vien la marza,
che te colla zo del capo,
la codegna te se squarza
sí che 'l fa parer un napo;

e non voglio dir un napo,
ma el se inpliría le sechie
con quel che e[sce] da l'orechie,
che te fa tutta lodosa.

A chi piase aver sonalgi
verdi, zali, grandi e grosi,
sí recolgia quii scarcasi
che tu spudi quando tosi; (lines 13–24)

(From your neck comes pus, that drips down your head, your scalp would tear open a vase; and I cannot say a vase, rather a bucket would not be enough to contain what comes out of your ears, and that makes you all filthy. Those who like rheum, green, yellow and big should collect the one you spit when you cough;)

If rhetoric is the art of using words effectively, the poet's detailed depiction of the old slanderer's physical and moral ugliness is a fitting device to counteract the power of the woman's tongue, which threatens to damage honest women's reputations: 'Non è lengua in taverna più canina e più mordaze' (there is no tongue in the tavern that is more canine and sharp); 'Lasa star le done honeste / con la to lengua perversa' (leave honest women alone, with that perverse tongue). The epithets for the tongue reflect common misogynist clichés. The woman who uses her tongue and threatens male authority requires retribution. The entire portrait of the 'vecchia' reveals her physical and moral transgression. This woman's body crosses boundaries between the human and animal worlds. She is in fact compared to a she-dog and a sow, and she has hair on her legs, breasts, and face: 'Tu à' pelose più le lache / cun le cosse e le zenochie,' 'E te manderò un barbiero // ... tosar quele to tete, / e la barba che ne mete / a le to masele granze' (You have hairy thighs, buttocks, and knees; I shall send you a barber ... to shave your breasts and the beard which grows on your wrinkled cheeks). Her hairiness betrays masculine features that blur gender distinctions and create a further threat: 'Tu me pari un omo in volto / cun la barba a quatro page' (You almost look like a man, with that beard). The detail of the beard deserves special consideration since it recurs in several of these popular texts and leads to the figure of the wild woman, a female type who shares many characteristics with the witch, and who appears in both literature and folklore. In medieval folklore the wild woman, an animal-like quasi-primitive creature of the woods, was believed to have an exuberant sexual appetite.

Perhaps more than any other text examined so far, this physical description fits Bakhtin's definition of the 'grotesque body' that stands in opposition to the classical body portrayed in high literature. In the grotesque body Bakhtin identifies the combination of human and animal traits and the open, penetrable body with its excrescences, orifices, protuberances, a body that overflows and is described in its excessive physicality, with an emphasis on eating and drinking and other bodily eliminations, as well as copulation and dismemberment. In this ballad most of the old hag's bodily orifices are mentioned, and all of them are overflowing: ears, nose, and eyes are described in their openness and are dripping, her anus is said to be full of stinking manure. The openness of the old woman's other orifices is metonymic for her open stinking mouth: 'Te puza più la bocha / che non fa mile carogne' (your mouths reeks more than a thousand corpses). The foul smell coming from her mouth clearly reflects the foul language she can use, but also evokes the bad odour of Rustico's 'buggeressa.' This old woman violates the boundaries of acceptable behaviour not only with her unruly tongue but also her excessive drinking and habit of frequenting the tavern: 'Tu à la golla como sponga / da trincar vin e vinaza' (your throat is like a sponge from drinking wine and grape seed). Andrew Cowell, in a study of French comic literature of the Middle Ages, has shown that the tavern is a locus of transgression where all the evil of medieval society is found.

The ballad's *congedo* reinforces the sense that at the core of the old woman's desecration lies her transgression in using mouth and speech. When the ballad is invited to spread the negative word about the 'vecchia,' the most appropriate curse is that she may lose her language and that her scandalous tongue may fall off: 'che Dio te dia tal fersa / che tu perdi ogni lenguazo // ... Ballatina mia lizadra/ ... de cantar non far finita / le malici' e sue bruteze; / fin a tanto che se sveze / quela lingua scandalosa' (May God give you such a blow that you may lose your language ... My gracious ballad ... continue to sing about her malice and her ugliness, until her scandalous tongue falls off).

Deserving of a special place in Casini's collection is the ballad 'La vecchia d'amor m'à biasemata,' a particularly ancient one (early fourteenth century).[34] Here is heard a loud and clear female voice: the poem features a female poetic persona speaking out against an old guardian.[35] If for women the act of speaking goes against the codes of socially accepted behaviour, it is already problematic to accept as valid what the poetic female persona is advocating in the ballad.[36] Indeed, the issue of the female voice in anonymous or male-filtered texts is under debate by both literary scholars and historians.[37] Jane Burns, who studies anonymous French fabliaux with female protagonists, poses the question of whether or not it is possible to hear a real independent woman's voice when it is the anonymous fabliau narrator who makes the woman speak (92).

The ballad (most likely composed by a male author and transmitted orally in different variations by minstrels during public performance) reveals ambiguities with regard to the female voice. That voice here appears to share in the dominant mentality that punishes guardians; the poem is structured as a lament and an invective by the young woman kept in confinement by her strict guardian. It is revealing that here a double standard applies to the act of female speaking. The author's voice is projected upon the young woman, who, contravening the rule of silence, speaks out and espouses the usually male, aggressive message against the guardian/slanderer. The old woman is herself being slandered for guarding the girl and for contravening the rule of feminine silence: the 'vecchia' in fact is said to be replete with 'mal dir[e].' In the first part of the ballad the woman invites her male lover to stop visiting her to avoid the old hag's reactions ('non pasar per la mia contrata,' line 2), and complains about the abuse she suffers at the hands of her custodian; in the second part the woman inveighs against the old guardian and in turn inflicts verbal abuse. The young woman depicts her guardian as cruel ('Perché m'ài così incolpata, / crudel vechia rinigata?' lines 7–8; Why did you accuse me like that, cruel renegade old woman?)

and extremely harsh ('et à me tanto lagniata / ch'i' son tucta sfigurata,' lines 13–14; she has tormented me so much, that I have lost my usual appearance), as well as incapable of understanding love, one theme encountered frequently in Sacchetti. The polysemy of the act of looking is evident here:

> La vechiarda rinalda, scarfalda
> m'aguarda quando [tu] m'adochi;
> mal fugarda, rutarda, bifarda,
> musarda, che volto e che ochi! (lines 4–6)

> (The malicious, bad, old woman stares at me when you look at me; annoying, dissolute, mocking, idle, old woman, what a face and what eyes!)

The guardian returns the look of the lover – here just the silent receiver of the girl's laments – and obstructs the male gaze with her powerful eyes. The purpose of the guardian is to protect the young woman's reputation, which in her opinion is compromised ('et dice che m'à trovata/con uom stare a la celata,' lines 18–19; 'dice che so' svergognata,' line 25; she says that she found me alone with a man; she says that I am shameless). After the lament, the young woman faces the guardian directly and proceeds to the invective. The presence of a female voice does not change the rhetorical strategies used to depict the old guardian. Invective and verbal abuse fall on the moral and physical attributes of the 'vechia.' Many negative qualities echo common misogynist clichés. The old woman is malicious, cruel, indecent, and devoted to ornamentation, which makes her look like a ridiculous prostitute.

> Com morsechia l'orechia, una vechia
> stortechia si mette per gioia;
> la bertechia ingordechia smordechia;
> scannecchia e la par una troia (lines 39–42)

> (When she adorns her ears, she wears old twisted earrings: that greedy ape bites shamelessly, and she grinds her teeth like a bitch)

The word 'bertechia,' a regional version of 'bertuccia,' evokes the ape in Muscia and the classic misogynist *topos* of women devoted to the art of ornamentation and who are considered prostitutes.[38]

The verbal abuse inflicted by the young woman on the guardian includes an accusation of witchcraft ('striga e sbirfa indovina,' line 45) and the curse levied is death by fire, the preferred method of disposing of witches. The disgusting physical details are reiterated to denigrate the aging, misshapen woman:

> O sannuta, dentuta, grabuta,
> spaluta, gran noia mi fai;
> [o] barbuta, berruta, grognuta,
> gozuta, tu mal ci starai:
> io so' sí amaistrata
> che tu rimarrai scornata.' (lines 51–6)

(Tusked, toothed, hunched, stocky old woman, you annoy me so much; oh bearded, snouty, mug, with a big throat, you shall suffer: I am trained so well that you shall be scorned.)

The ugly old guardian is defined by her deformed, beastly, almost masculine body. The hybridism of the old woman's gender again signals her transgression. The presence of the rhymes in '-echia,' and the thematic word 'vecchia' rhyming with 'orecchia,' reveal the connection between this text and the pseudo-Angiolieri *tenzone*. The old guardian's loquacity hints at her wantonness. She is called 'soza vechia' and 'troia' (dirty old woman, bitch). The adjective 'barbuta' points to the figure of the hairy wild woman that in folklore was believed to inhabit the woods. In her study of sexual difference and the construction of gender in the Middle Ages, Joan Cadden points out that prominent body hair signified masculinity; moreover, hairiness was associated with sensuality and lust.[39] Below I discuss the implications of the wild woman and her sexual exuberance in connection with the witch.

In the ballad's finale the young woman reveals the strength and intelligence that she can muster to oppose the powerful guardian: 'io so' sì amaistrata/ che tu rimarrai scornata.' This text pits the young woman in love against the old guardian and proposes two strong female figures that represent two generations defending their values. This guardian is constructed by a female voice, but the female speaking subject is not endowed with an independent voice; her voice is appropriated by the dominant voice. In fact, this guardian's portrait is effected using the same rhetorical techinques found in poems expressing the dominant male voice, and it fits the conventions and social constructions of female old age examined so far.

Another anonymous text that should be considered in connection with Casini's ballads is the *canzonetta* 'D'una vechia ch'è zilosa.' This poem, also from northeastern Italy, is dated between the end of the fourteenth and the beginning of the fifteenth century.[40] The *canzonetta* sums up many motifs on the ugly woman I have considered. It opens with an invective against the old guardian, who obstructs the poet's love for his beloved:

> (D')una vechia ch'è zilosa,
> la qual m'à sì tolto a peto,
> la me crede far dispeto
> per tenir mia dona ascosa.
>
> Questa bruta vechionaza
> che m'à tolto sì graveza,
> de[h] g[h]e vegna el strangoione! (lines 1–7)

> (One old woman is jealous, she has it in for me so much, that she thinks to spite me by keeping my lady concealed. This ugly old hag who is so hostile to me, may she choke!)

This woman uses both her eyes and her tongue to assert her power. She is a gossiper called 'sgargaiosa' (chatterbox, line 20) whose power of speech is symbolized by an open mouth and big tongue: 'quando el vien che la favela, / l'apre quela sua bocaza, / l' à più d'un palmo de lenguaza' (when she speaks, she opens that big mouth, she has a tongue a span long; lines 49–51). The male poet's retribution upon the old woman again is effected through the art of rhetoric. In this *effictio ad vituperium* the parts of the female body are described in detail, with particular emphasis on the face. The old woman is hairy and has a beard, her breath is foul and her face wrinkled.

> Là sì stranio visazo
> che la me fa pur paura,
> ...
> La me par un omo quaso,
> perch'è la femena barbuda;
> ma chi la vedes[s]e nuda
> a mo' d'un orso l'è pelosa.
> ...

Ma chi la sente lo matino
g[h]e puza el fiato da can vechio,
la se va a mirar in spechio
e si se tien tropo ponposa.

L' à quel suo viso afaldato
che par proprio una gonela,
l' à quel volto regrignato (lines 25–6, 33–6, 41–7)

(She has such a strange face that she scares me ... she almost looks like a man, because she is a bearded woman; but if you see her naked she is hairy like a bear ... but if you see her in the morning her breath stinks like an old dog, she looks at herself in the mirror and she thinks herself so splendid. Her face is so wrinkled that it looks like a pleated skirt, she has a pug face)

The old woman's hairiness and animal-like appearance (she is compared to mutton, bear, and sheep) again reveal a transgression of boundaries. As the description proceeds, the accumulation of masculine traits climaxes in the poet's conviction that she might actually be a man ('la me pare un omo quaso,' line 33). The old hag's masculine features are particularly disturbing to the male poet, since gender distinctions have collapsed in her.

Many depictions of ugly women in popular poetry include the epithet 'strega.' In Donato da Cascia's madrigal and in two anonymous ballads the woman is called a witch. In this *canzonetta* the old woman appears not as a witch proper, but as the popular variation the 'Befana,' an old hunchbacked woman who was believed to ride the skies on a broom and drop down chimneys to visit children on the night of the epiphany: '[qu]ando vien che i puti zase,/[la] vien zó per le cadene,' lines 65–6. One connecting element in Casini's repertoire and in this poem is the bearded/hairy aspect of the old woman. This feature is typical of medieval folklore about the wild woman who lives in the forest and who is associated with lust.

Richard Bernheimer, in his classic study on medieval folklore and popular tradition, claims that in medieval demonology witch and wild woman were the same thing (35). Tracing the origin of this figure, Bernheimer identifies the ancestors of the wild woman in the Lamia of Greek antiquity, a blood-sucking, child-stealing female demon; in the Lilith of Jewish mythology; and in the first Eve of biblical tradition – all figures who embody feminine negativity and power.[41]

In the Middle Ages, according to Bernheimer, many texts make Lamia coincide with *strix*, that is, the witch or Italian 'strega.' The Lamia and the witch also have points in common with the wild woman. In medieval folklore the wild woman is believed to have a distinctive physical aspect that evokes some of the old women encountered so far: she is hairy, sometimes has an enormous body, has a wrinkled face, and appears naked but fully covered with thick hair; since she inhabits the forest and woods she typifies an individual at the boundaries, who can assume transgressive behaviour. In some depictions of the wild woman her disgusting physical appearance is compounded by drooping breasts dragging on the ground, so long as to be thrown over the shoulders, a feature that in medieval sculptures defines the personification of Luxuria or Lust.[42] In the wild man's and woman's hunt, a medieval popular ritual of the Alpine regions, the wild person is compared to a bear and often the hunt is extended to a horde of individuals, including women, who are likewise wild and hairy. As Bernheimer (50–84) notes, the wild man's hunt in its prehistoric past was a gathering of ghosts guided by a female goddess; later on, this ritual gave rise to the witches' sabbath. In medieval times the wild horde was part of the Carnival and Epiphany festivities, where sexual inversion (woman-on-top) and gender blur would typically include men disguised as wild beasts or grotesque wild females, often performing wanton gestures.[43] The Epiphany and Carnival are also associated with the figure of the 'Befana,' the old ugly woman who is also called 'striga'or 'marantega.' Today the effigy of the 'Befana' is still burned in city squares on the last day of the Carnival. The distinctive feature of the wild individual seems to be exuberant sexuality.[44]

The wild man as a bear or hairy person has significance for the anonymous poems, where the ugly woman is depicted as hairy and is compared to a bear. Moreover, in both 'D'una vechia ch'è zilosa' and 'Laida vecchia stomegosa' the old woman with a hairy body is disturbing to the poetic persona because she looks like a man or a bear. Thus the depiction of the female grotesque body in anonymous poetry allows us to connect the old woman with both the witch and the wild woman, figures that reinforce transgression as sexual excess, a powerful use of eyes and tongue, and gender hybridity.[45]

The examined anonymous texts of the fourteenth and fifteenth century provide compelling evidence of the stratification of literary, mythological, biblical, and folklore motifs that merge the figure of the old woman, as guardian/gossip, with the witch and the wild woman; all these types show that the male imagination envisions ugly femininity as transgression and authority. Empowered by vision and speech, driven by wild or demonic forces, the old ugly woman subverts conventional power relations, blurs gender distinctions, displays hybridism and therefore spells danger, and requires punishment or retribution through verbal abuse, invective, and annihilation.

The literary motif of the old guardian was quite dominant up to the fifteenth century and even later. We find it, for instance, in Bernardo Giambullari (1450–1529), active at the court of Lorenzo de' Medici and famous for further developing poems on the model of *Nencia*. Giambullari has a 'Ballata contro le vecchie invidiose' where, as in the jongleur's ballad 'La ve'chia d'amor m'à biasemata,' the female voice (here it is the daughter-in-law speaking out) is used to launch an invective against old women. Giambullari exploits the usual misogynist themes (calling old women envious, evil, jealous, vindictive) and follows the rhetorical rules of the descriptive portrait. The young daughter-in-law's attack is addressed against all mothers-in-law and invokes the ballad itself to become bearer of the ill-omened message. This ballad, like Sacchetti's, is centred on the juxtaposition between the beautiful young woman and the evil ugly old guardian:

> Queste vecchie grinze e nere
> sono schiatta di cicale
> che sempre commetton male;
> peggio vorrebbon vedere.
>
> Le son tutte d'una buccia
> di dir mal delle pulzelle;
> l'hanno visi di bertuccia,
> grinza e bigia hanno la pelle; (169)

(These old wrinkled dark women descend from chatterboxes, they always do evil; and worse, they like to stare. They are cut from the same stone, they all talk badly about young girls; their faces are like Barbary apes, wrinkled and grey is their skin;)

Typical of the *descripito vetulae* is the wrinkled face. The reference to the 'bertuccia,' both a type of monkey and an epithet for a gossipy woman, is a recurring element in the old hag (it had already appeared in Muscia's sonnet), and the anger in old women dates back to Guinizzelli.

In the finale, as in other poems, the ballad is called upon to spread the word about the malevolent old guardians, so that they can soon be buried in hell.

The Witch in Burchiello and Giovan Matteo di Meglio

During the quattrocento comic-realistic poetry re-elaborates the motif of the ugly woman and enriches it with new elements. The ugly woman seems to be the female figure that best embodies all masculine fears and anxieties about women in positions of authority or women acting beyond the boundaries of the conventional space assigned to them. Two figures that emerge more clearly in the fifteenth century are the witch and the prostitute/procuress. These female types, definitely less prominent in the Italian medieval tradition except tangentially in anonymous poetry, become key figures of ugliness and transgression in the Renaissance.[46]

Poetic production on the old woman spreads from Tuscany, with Domenico di Giovanni (1404–48) nicknamed 'Burchiello;' post-burchielleschi such as Giovan Matteo di Meglio (1427– ?1481); Antonio Cammelli, called il Pistoia (1436–1502); and culminating with Poliziano.[47] The Tuscan examples use consolidated *topoi* such as vituperation and employ them to attack new feminine types such as the witch and the prostitute/procuress. Needless to say, all these female figures are the embodiment of transgression. The Latin tradition of Horace, Ovid, and Martial partly accounts for the rediscovery of the figure of the prostitute/witch in the quattrocento. In Ovid's *Amores* (book 1, 8) the invective is directed against Dipsas, an old prostitute/bawd (*lena*) whose magic power and excessive drinking are highlighted; in Propertius's *Elegies* (book 4) the old woman is Acanthis, a semi-bald prostitute whose magic arts are used to help young women attract their lovers. However, aversion to witches/prostitutes in the fifteenth century can also be attributed to the socio-historical and religious climate of open hostility against such women. As we saw in chapter 1, the motif of the witch and prostitute is not very dominant in medieval comic-realistic poetry, where the main focus is on evil character, repulsive physical appearance, or ornamentation. The emergence of female figures like the witch and the prostitute in fifteenth-century poetry, each as synonym of the other, reflects not only the influence of the Latin classics but also the historical situation, marked by mounting hostility towards witches. The witch, seen with suspicion by Latin poets, was already present in medieval popular imagination, perhaps best embodied by the figure of the sorcerer; but after the fourteenth century, when the church officially recognized the witch as an existing person guilty of heresy and of having sexual relations with the devil, obsession with and aversion to witches increases.[48] Sigrid Brauner, in her study on the construction of the witch in early modern Germany, assesses the pivotal role played by papal inquisitors Kramer and Sprenger's *Malleus maleficarum* (1487) in developing the first gender-specific concept of the modern witch (26). The *Malleus*, an enormously influential text, singles out women as witches and associates their sin with lust. The witch threatens the social order with her wanton sexuality, and witchcraft is aimed at rendering men impotent. The witch also challenges established authority by dominating men with her sexuality and displaying arrogant self-assertion; she undermines divine order symbolized by the subordination of women to men. Chiara Frugoni, who focuses on a socio-historical perspective, attributes the hostility towards witches in Italy to the religious and moral influence of preachers like Bernardino da Siena (382).[49]

In *Demon Lovers*, the most recent contribution on demonology and witches in early modern Europe, Walter Stephens offers a more current interpretation of the obsession with witches that dominated Europe from the fifteenth century onward. While confirming the misogynist stance of the *Malleus maleficarum*, Stephens claims that witchcraft and the preoccupation with witches became so prevalent through the work of witchcraft theorists, who needed to maintain the existence of witches in order to demonstrate the power of Christian faith to vanquish them.[50] Stephens's fascinating work opens new avenues in the study of demonology but does not diminish the misogynist impact of witchcraft theorists, who still used women – deliberately constructed as transgressive and sexually unruly – as the inevitable scapegoats and most suitable candidates for witchcraft.

Biographies of witches mentioned their excessive sexual appetite and their degenerate relations with the devil. Witches were by definition old and ugly. According to a medieval proverb found in Slavic areas, 'Ogni vecchia è una strega' (Every old woman is a witch) (Bonadiman, 61). The witch enters fifteenth-century poetry through the mediation of 'poesia giullaresca' and poetry for music, although this version of the witch is in fact more aligned with popular folklore and with the figure of the wild woman.[51] As noticed, the epithet 'strega' appears in some of the texts of the trecento: in the anonymous ballad 'La vecchia d'amor m'à biasemata' the witch is called 'striga,' and in Donato da Cascia's madrigal 'Una smaniosa e insensata vecchia' she is 'arrabbiata strega.'

The *Feminist Encyclopedia of Italian Literature* devotes an entry to the witch and pairs this female type with the prostitute and sometimes the widow. A witch is a type of woman who resists conventional definitions and endangers the patriarchal system. She does not fit the traditional male categories of virgin or wife, and she is socially and physiologically impossible to control, 'subject only to the uncontained desire of ... [her] socially "unmarked bodies"' (356). The unmarked body is associated with monstrous content; hence the fury against the witch's body both in historical reality, when the witch is publically burned at the stake, and in literary texts, where the curse levied involves bodily destruction.

Florentine barber Domenico di Giovanni (1404–49), 'Burchiello,' was the first to adopt the 'sonetto caudato' ('sonnet with a tail'), an expanded version of the traditional sonnet, to inveigh against old women. Antonio Lanza (*Polemiche e berte*, 174) sees in Burchiello's poetry considerable innovation derived not only from elaboration of the medieval comic tradition, but also and more importantly from real-life experience and from the environment of lower-class Florence in which he lived. Burchiello's invectives against old women are considered an expansion on medieval literary *topoi*. Marti (*Cultura e stile*, 217) views Burchiello as the essential connecting link between Cecco Angiolieri and Renaissance comic poet Francesco Berni. The poet composed two sonnets on the old woman as witch: 'Vecchia ritrosa, perfida e maligna' and 'Ardati il fuoco vecchia puzolente.' His aversion to old witches reflects the socio-cultural atmosphere of furore against witches:

Vecchia ritrosa, perfida e maligna,
inimica d'ogni ben, invidiosa,
e strega incantatrice e maliosa,
trista, stravolta, che se' pien di tigna.

Barbuta se' più folta che gramigna,
gli occhi e 'l naso ti colan senza posa,
puzzati el fiato, sdentata rabbiosa
se ridi pari un diavol che digrigna.

E tanto è velenosa la tua vista
che ciò che miri corrompi per paodo,
che ... angel non ... pua ... o salmista.

Ma io mi voglio di te un colabrodo,
che sempre mai t'ha fatto viver trista,
e pagner ... se m'hai fatto frodo.

E di questo mi godo,
perchè da te si fugge tutta gente,
per lo tuo marcio conno puzzolente. (Messina edition, 45)

(Old riotous, wicked, and evil woman, enemy of every good, envious, enchantress witch and sorceress, mean, contorted, you are full of ringworm. Your beard is thicker than weeds, your eyes and nose drip constantly, your breath is foul, toothless mad woman if you laugh you look like a devil grinding his teeth. Your sight is so venomous that you spoil everything you look at, neither ... an angel nor a psalmist can. But I want to poke you like a colander, so that you may always live in sadness, and ... since you cheated me. And I enjoy the fact that all people run away from you, because of your rotten stinking cunt.)

The old malodorous woman with dripping nose and oozing eyes reminds us of Beroe and of the old hag in 'Laida vecchia stomegosa,' whereas the foul smell most certainly evokes Rustico Filippi; the adjective 'rabbiosa' was inaugurated by Guinizzelli. The old woman's moral defects repeat the usual misogynist elements: maliciousness, envy, wickedness. Burchiello's attitude towards the witch in this sonnet, and in his other one on the same topic, reflects the historic treatment of women accused of practising witchcraft: male rage against the witch focuses on the body, depicted in its repulsiveness and cursed with physical destruction ('Ma io mi voglio di te un colabrodo'). Physical repulsiveness is epitomized by the foul and rotten genitalia ('marcio conno puzzolente') that here again hints at the woman's sexuality. The adjective 'barbuta' connects this text to the popular ballads, where the witch was an incarnation of the wild woman, another figure connoting excessive lust.

The second sonnet contains another violent attack against the witch, a person accused by the church of heretical practice:

Ardati il fuoco, vecchia puzolente,
che non ti resti mai di pensar male,
di resia seminando le tuo scale,
poiché moneta non trai dalla gente.

Cieca ti fai, Die ti faccia dolente:
fussinti tratti gli occhi e messi in sale
et io fussi di te il micidïale
acciochè fussin le tue fiamme spente.

Lupo cervier non ha il veder sottile
come tu sottilezi raguardando,
né da sì picciol buco tanto umile.

Pigliar diletto forte sospirando
per te agrizzando il volticel vecchile:
col borbottar mimarti lagrimando.

Al fuoco racomando,
o vecchia strega, o malitiosa ghiotta,
ladra, ruffiana, maladetta potta. (Zaccarello edition, 172–3)[52]

(May fire burn you, old stinky woman, you never cease to think badly, you scatter heresy on your steps, because you cannot get money from people. May you go blind, may God make you miserable: may your eyes be plucked and put under salt and may I be your killer so that your flames can be quenched. A deer wolf has no such a sharp vision as you have when you look and guard nor does it come from such a small opening. One can take pleasure with strong sighs by looking at your wrinkled old face frowning: one can imitate you by grumbling. I entrust you to the fire, old witch, malicious and glutton, thief, bawd, wretched cunt [toad].

Disgust in this portrayal centres on the old woman's bad smell, a traditional element in medieval vituperations.[53] The accusation of heresy bears witness to some of the historical religious roots inherent in the image of the witch. The persecution of heretics that had marked the Middle Ages finds its Renaissance incarnation in the witch, associated not only with social and moral transgression but also with religious deviancy. The connection between heresy and possession of power by women has been shown by Bloch (*Medieval Misogyny*, 31). As Stephens (*Demon Lovers*) argues, sacraments were a crucial point of contention for heretics who opposed eucharistic orthodoxy and were known for sacramental desecration; for this reason Stephens considers the witch to be a new kind of desecrating heretic, but more dreadful than the ones active in the Middle Ages.[54]

In Burchiello's sonnet the emphasis is on the old hag's act of looking and on the sharpness of her gaze, and adequate punishment for her infraction seems like a Dantean 'contrappasso': the poet wishes that the witch may go blind, that her eyes be plucked out of her face and put in salt. As Stephens informs us, salt was often used as a substance to counteract demons' and witches' *maleficia* (*Demon Lovers*, 252). In this poem the invective of the opening verses reappears in the last stanza, where the last verse presents some discrepancy in various editions. In Zaccarello's edition the final invective has 'maladetta potta,' whereas in the Messina/London edition the last verse is 'Ladra, ruffiana, maledetta botta.'[55] The use of 'botta' (toad), instead of 'potta' (sexual organs), highlights the multivocal function of the old woman. As a witch she is defined by her excessive sexuality – where her entire being is reduced to her sexual organs – but she may also be portrayed as a toad, one of the possible incarnations of witches.[56] The witch is also called 'ruffiana' or procuress, a woman who is or used to be a prostitute, a figure most commonly found in Giovan Matteo di Meglio and Poliziano.

Despite Burchiello's quasi-neglect in modern criticism, his legacy was particularly influential on Tuscan poetry, which is conventionally termed 'post-burchiellesca.' In the limited poetic output of Florentine Giovan Matteo di Meglio (approximately thirty poems), the invective against the old woman, the witch, and the procuress figures prominently. Giovan Matteo, like Burchiello, uses the *sonetto caudato*. For Lanza (*Freschi e minii*, 267) Matteo's poetry displays the influence of both Burchiello and Angioleri and adds 'un'esasperata ricerca di immagini e di suoni d'un verismo crudo e talora rivoltante' (267) (an exasperated search for crude and revolting images and sounds).[57]

The sonnet 'Vecchia azzimata, richardata e vizza' is a violent invective against the old woman, wherein accumulation, harsh sounds (emphasis on '-izza' as variation on the '-uzza' endings of Cavalcanti), and obscene language contribute to an aberrant depiction of feminine old age:

Vecchia azzimata, richardata e vizza,
nata di più albumi e più veleni
che tutt'altri animal' bruti terreni,
ereticha, maligna et mare di stizza;

lupa gholpina, rozza, et chagna in izza,
ipocrita, strebbiata et sanza freni,
nel tuo 'nferno molt'alme a morte meni:
ghuai a quel ch'a sseghuirti il chor dirizza!

Pubblicha mamma di toro e di verro,
discesa di progenia vile e strana,
pazza, hubbrïacha, villana e bastarda;

nata di bestia, chalzata di ferro,
putta honesta et sollecita ruffiana,
pront'al mal fare, al ben pigra e 'nfingharda.

Malïosa e bugiarda!
quel ch'ell'à fatto 'l fa et fallo fare,
et dove fugge 'l topo si fa dare. (49–51)

(Withered, made-up, dolled up old woman, born of more concoctions and poisons than any other ugly animal on earth, heretic, evil and a sea of anger; rough offspring of a she-wolf and a fox, raging she-dog, hypocrite, painted and out of bounds, you lead many souls to death into your hell: woe to those who raise their heart to you! Promiscuous mother of a bull and a boar, descended from strange and low progeny, crazy, drunk, rude bastard; born of a beast, with chained feet, honest prostitute and solicitous procuress, ready to do evil, slow and lazy to do good. Witch and liar! what she did she does and has done, and she has her hole filled where the mouse lives.)

Giovan Matteo opens with the traditional misogynist attack on the use of make-up and proceeds to completely dehumanize this old woman, who is associated with perhaps one of the richest collection of animals to be found in such works. Both Burchiello and Giovan Matteo compare the witch with the wolf or wolf-like animal. Stephens (*Demon Lovers*) explains that witchcraft theorists strongly associated wolves with witches because these animals devoured their infants just like witches were accused of killing young babies (285). Also, the comparison with the fox betrays the activity of witchcraft, since this animal was considered one transformation of the witch. Where Rustico Filippi wrote of the ability of the 'buggeressa' to generate a fox ('in corpo credo figlinti le volpe'), Matteo ups the ante and claims a genetic origin from animals ('nata di bestia'), confirming the danger that lies in a hybrid figure crossing the boundaries of the human and animal worlds. The reference to excessive drinking evokes both Latin examples of Ovid and Propertius and the anonymous minstrel ballads of the trecento. Giovan Matteo's poetry presents old women as lustful and obscene, and the closing lines here have a clear sexual double entendre. The conflation of the old hag/witch with a prostitute and procuress ('putta honesta et sollecita ruffiana') is Giovan Matteo di Meglio's trademark and becomes a common theme in sixteenth-century Italy.[58] In many poems Matteo uses the adjective 'maliosa,' which is considered a synonym of 'witch.' In the sonnet 'O chalandrona' the witch who takes part in the sabbath is called 'stregonizza,' 'maliosa,' and 'maestra di fatture.' The witch's sexual appetite is described with such crudeness that it finds a match only in some Latin antecedents, such as Horace's epode 12.

> Socchorso d'ogni frate e ttregendiera,
> vulva arrabbiata, in chui la foia è 'ntera,
> anzi arsīone, e di drieto e davante. (55)

(Helper of every friar and sabbath's witch, angry vulva, whose lust is great, whose heat is in front and back.)

In the sonnet 'S'tu volessi un doppio errore' (107), 'strega rinbanbita' (imbecile witch) is the epithet used for the woman who insists on using cosmetics and apparel to improve her appearance; the traditional misogynist polemic against women and make-up is paired with the motif of old age and witchcraft. Matteo's hostility to old women is intensified in the canzonetta 'De! Udi un po' novella,' where the woman is 'grinza e vizza' and acts as procuress to her own daughters. This poem is a public denunciation of the depravity of a mother/bawd and her prostitute daughters who have a different lover for every day of the week.[59] Matteo di Meglio adds to the *topos* of *vituperario vetulae* not only the figure of the witch, already present in Burchiello, but also the lewd prostitute/procuress.

Among the so-called post-burchielleschi the invective against old women is also used by Antonio Cammelli (1436–1502), called il Pistoia. Cammelli, a native of Pistoia, lived at various courts of the Po valley and was in contact with the Sforza and Este families, particularly with Isabella d'Este of Mantua, to whom he intended to dedicate his collection of *Sonetti faceti*.[60] Although the poet spent most of his life outside his native Tuscany, his creative vein reflects the burlesque, caricatural genre as well as Burchiello's style. Cammelli uses the *sonetto caudato* first employed by Burchiello. The woman targeted in the poem is a widow, another female figure difficult to accommodate in the conventional definitions of femininity allowed by the patriarchal system. The widow can easily be accused of witchcraft and is handled by the male poet with a mixture of ridicule, hostility, and invective. The *sonetto caudato* 'Il viene una imbrunata vidoetta' inveighs against a widow of noble family with rotten flesh and a wrinkled and dirty face:

74   The Ugly Woman

Il viene una imbrunata vidoetta,
ch'ha quarantasette anni o manco un poco;
largo, brigata! orsù, datigli loco,
tanto ch' el passi via la sua carretta!

Guardate occhietti come la civetta!
che regina de scacchi posta al gioco!
Lei pare un carboncin mezzo di foco;
o che bel donnellin creato in fretta!

Che belle carne purpurine e rancie!
Quando lei aguzza quel bocchino istrano
fa mille crespatine ne le guancie.

Lei par la fanticella di Vulcano,
un giardinel dove nascon le ciancie,
porta per gala un bocchettino in mano.

Adesso parla piano,
or si nasconde, or cenna, or ride, or guarda,
mostaccin bel da lavargliel di farda.

Va via, che 'l foco t'arda,
putrida volpe ancor viva rimasa
per vituperio de sì nobil casa. (104)

(Here comes a dark widow, who is forty-seven years old or thereabouts: make room brigade! Come on, make space, for her cart to move on! Look at those little eyes like an owl: what a chess queen set in the game! She resembles a charcoal in the fire: Oh what a nice little woman created quickly! What beautiful flesh purple and rancid! When she strains her odd little mouth a thousand wrinkles appear in her cheeks. She looks like the lady of Volcano, a garden where gossip grows; she carries in her hand a little purse as ornament. Sometimes she speaks softly, sometimes she hides, or nods, or laughs or watches, her face is so pretty that you want to bathe it in spit. Go away, may a fire burn you, putrid fox not dead yet a disgrace to such a noble family.)

This text is perhaps the only one where a precise anagraphical detail of feminine old age is given: the widow is forty-seven years old, not far into middle age for us in modern times, but probably on the verge of decrepitude in the late quattrocento. The sonnet is a mixture of vituperation and paradoxical praise ('che bel donnellin creato in fretta!') and shares some elements with the rustic parodies of *Nencia da Barberino* and *Beca da Dicomano*, for example, in the use of diminutives ('occhietti,' 'bocchino strano,' 'donnellin') typical of rustic poetry.[61] Unlike rustic poetry, this sonnet is addressed to a woman who is neither young nor the poet's beloved. In a derisive tone the author invites a 'brigata' to move over and make space for the lady: because the woman here is neither beautiful nor young, space is given for her to quickly disappear from male sight, since she cannot satisfy the male gaze (rather, she is caught in the act of looking, with no further consequence attached to it). The final vituperation evokes the medieval tradition, including bodily annihilation. The references to death by fire and to the owl, and the epithet 'putrida volpe' (filthy fox) – one of the transformations of the witch – confirm that the 'vidoetta' belongs to the long list of witches of fifteenth-century poetry. The owl, whose Latin name is *strix*, evokes the link between the nocturnal bird and the 'strega.' Cammelli forgoes obscenity and the lust of the prostitute, which were the trademark of Giovan Matteo di Meglio, but still penalizes this woman for her middle age and physical noncompliance with the models of feminine perfection. The derision and annoyance of the male poet are publicly acknowledged by the 'brigata,' most likely a group of male gazers, whose only wish is to get the ugly widow out of their sight as soon as possible. As noted above, the widow is often equated with the witch, or more generally with a category of women who resist conventional definition in the patriarchal system; she is no longer married and no longer a virgin, and therefore in patriarchal society she is viewed with suspicion and perceived as a possible threat. In fact, in this sonnet it is said that she contaminates the nobility of her lineage, and she is called the shame of her family.

The Old Prostitute: Angelo Poliziano

The prostitute is a woman who offers sex outside of marriage and seeks monetary compensation for her services. She is transgressive by definition and is relegated to the margins of society. A woman who is in charge of sexual and economic exchanges is scandalous, dangerous, and feared by men, even more so when the description of her body reveals old age and physical ugliness instead of beauty and youth.

In Angelo Poliziano's poetic output the old prostitute appears both in vernacular and in Latin. This female type is the subject of the ballad 'Una vecchia mi vagheggia' and of the Latin ode 'In anum.' In both poems Poliziano assumes the poetic persona of the victim of the ugly prostitute's advances. In his vernacular work Angelo Poliziano reveals a special openness to popular tradition, low comic style, and contemporary popular Tuscan poetry. The ballad 'Una vecchia mi vagheggia' provides another poem in the rich tradition of texts on the old woman, but the harsh tone of the invective is replaced by humour and derision.

Mainstream criticism reads both of Poliziano's texts on the prostitute as *lusus*, a playful game on a traditional literary motif. However, a reading of *lusus* simply as laughter and light escapism veils the sense of anxiety hiding behind Poliziano's text. In Bakhtin's interpretation of Carnival, for example, *lusus* and laughter provide an interlude, a permitted time and space for relief from the feelings of fear and oppression that burdened medieval people.[62] Understood this way, *lusus* betrays more serious concerns about the underlying causes of male poets' fear of and obsession with the 'vecchia.' Poliziano's comic treatment of the old prostitute reflects his anxiety about a female figure who transgresses the codes of proper behaviour and decency and who obliterates the fascination with/veneration of female youth at play in some of his most famous poetry.[63] In the ballad Poliziano focuses on a particularly upsetting event in which an old ugly woman takes the initiative and engages in courtship of the poetic persona. The poet reacts with abhorrence, scorn, and humour and attempts to neutralize the disturbing circumstances by sharing his experience with a sympathetic audience:

> Una vecchia mi vagheggia,
> vizza e secca insino all'osso;
> non ha tanta carne adosso
> che sfamassi una marmeggia.
>
> Ell'ha logra la gingiva,
> tanto biascia fichi secchi,
> perch'e' fan della sciliva
> da 'mmollar bene e pennecchi:
> sempre in bocca n'ha parecchi,
> ché 'l palato se gli 'nvisca;
> sempre al labro ha qualche lisca
> del filar ch'ella morseggia.

Ella sa propio di cuoio,
quand'è in concia, o di can morto,
o di nidio d'avoltoio:
sol col puzzo ingrassa l'orto
(or pensate che conforto!),
e fuggita è della fossa;
sempre ha l'asima e la tossa
e con essa mi vezzeggia.

Tuttavia el naso le gocciola,
sa di bozzima e di sugna,
più scrignuta è ch'una chiocciola:
po,' s'a un tratto el fiasco impugna,
tutto 'l suga come spugna,
e vuole anche ch'i' la baci.
Io la sgrido: 'Oltre va' giaci!';
ella intorno pur matteggia.

Non tien l'anima co' denti,
ch'un non ha per medicina;
e luccianti ha quasi spenti,
tutti orlati di tonnina.
Sempre la virtù divina
fin nel petto giù gli cola;
vizza e secca è la suo gola,
tal ch'un becco par d'acceggia.

Tante grinze ha nelle gote,
quante stelle sono in cielo;
le suo poppe vizze e vote
paion propio ragnatelo.
Nelle brache non ha pelo,
della peccia fa grembiule;
e più biascia che le mule,
quando intorno mi volteggia. (106–7)[64]

(An old woman longs for me, she is withered, skin and bone; there is not enough flesh in her to feed a little worm. Her gums are worn out from chewing too many dried figs, this produces the saliva to moisten well the

78   The Ugly Woman

flax: she always holds so much in her mouth, that her palate becomes slimy; in her lip there is always some piece of the threads that she bites. She smells just like leather when it is tanned, or like a dead dog, or like the nest of a vulture: her smell is enough to grease the field (now, think, what a comfort!) and she has escaped from the grave; she always has asthma and a cough and she endears me with it. Her nose is always dripping, she smells like grease and lard, she is more twisted than a snail. If she grabs the flask, she drinks all of it like a sponge, she even wants me to kiss her. I reproach her: 'Come on, go away!' and yet she acts crazy around me. She cannot hold her soul by the teeth, since she only has one for medication; her eyes give out no light, and are full of tartar. Divine spirit drips down to her chest; her throat is so withered and dry, that it looks like a woodcock's beak. There are as many wrinkles in her cheeks, as there are stars in the sky; her withered and empty breasts look like worn out fabric. In her pants there is no hair, her belly can be made into an apron; she champs more than mules when she circles around me.)

Delcorno Branca traces precisely the Latin and vernacular antecedents at play in this ballad (191–2), but finds the true model in Poliziano's negative *descriptio mulieris* in the ode 'In Anum.' The language in the ballad is rich in borrowings from medieval realistic poetry. The old woman is 'vizza' like the 'vecchiuzza' of Niccola Muscia, and her 'puzzo' recalls Rustico's 'buggeressa'; the dripping nose and the eyes 'tutti orlati di tonnina' are a reminiscence of Beroe, whereas the adjective 'scrignuta' immediately calls to mind the 'scrignutuzza' of Guido Cavalcanti, a poet particularly revered by Poliziano. The ballad centres on the transgressive attitude of the old hag who courts the poet. The act of contemplating the poet with pleasure, summed up in the verb 'vagheggiare,' in Delcorno Branca's words 'verbo per eccellenza del galateo amoroso' (196) (verbs by definition of the love/courtly etiquette), is in itself an oxymoron. An ugly, old, and disgusting woman who is associated with such an activity can only call up abhorrence, rejection ('Io la sgrido: 'Oltre va' giaci!'), and laughter in the male subject. Her advances are not limited to the 'vagheggiare'or 'vezzeggiare' but go so far as to request the poet's kisses ('e vuole anche ch'i' la baci'). As Lois Banner points out, it was not an unknown practice for aging women to hire young men for sexual purposes, when they could no longer attract men on their own (172). Yet the independence and self-assertiveness displayed by this female figure are disturbing to the male poet. The narrator's response to the old hag's advances is one of total rejection, and yet the detailed and meticulous description of her private parts ('poppe vizze e vote,' 'nelle brache non ha pelo, / della peccia fa grembiale') would indicate first-hand experience rather than vivid imagination.[65] Although the text does not openly call this old woman a prostitute, her explicit requests, along with some other transgressive behaviour, point in that direction. Excessive drinking, for example ('s'a un tratto el fiasco impugna, / tutto 'l suga come spugna'), was typical of prostitutes. As Lyndal Roper has shown in her historical study, prostitutes regularly frequented taverns and were devoted to excessive drinking.[66] The activity of spinning, in proverbial tradition a typical occupation of retired prostitutes, reinforces the identification of this old woman as a prostitute.[67] The 'vecchia' is not called witch in the poem, but her acts of spinning and drinking implicitly link her with the witch as she appeared in the Latin tradition. In Ovid's *Amores*, for example, the old prostitute Dipsas not only drinks to excess but also knows all the arts of witchcraft.[68] This ballad is a variation on the traditional descriptive vituperation against the disgusting old hag; as in Cammelli's sonnet, the poet/narrator is conversing with an imaginary audience invited to participate in her mocking.[69]

Poliziano again assumes the persona of the persecuted male in the Latin ode 9 'In Anum,' a text particularly indebted to Horace's epode 12. Contrary to the ballad, here the emphasis is on the old woman's excessive lust and on 'l'aspetto ributtante e libidinoso della vecchia' ('the revolting and lustful aspect of the old woman') (Delcorno Branca, 194). 'In Anum' fits more comfortably in the genre of the *vituperatio vetulae*, since from the opening line the poet invokes the power of the verses to help him elude the obscene old woman. Here disgust and the minute description of physical ugliness are closely linked to classical models and medieval Latin rhetoric (e.g., Beroe):

Huc huc, jambi! Arripite mi jam mordicus
Anum hanc furenti percitam libidine,
Tentiginosam, catulientem, spurcidam,
Gravedinosam, vietam, olentem, rancidam. (*Opera Omnia*, 271)

(Here, here iambs, get off my teeth the furious old woman, excited, lustful, in heat disgusting, flaccid, malodorous.)

Disgusting physical appearance is also defined by the corpse-like body of the old prostitute, described as 'cadaverosam' and then 'nec jam anus sed mortua' (not quite old but rather dead). Such animals as the sow, dog, and donkey are preferable to this filthy old woman. Charlet sees many echos of Vendôme's portrait of Beroe but notes the prominence of the old woman's lewdness.

As critics point out, this text can be linked by opposition with the Latin ode 'In Puellam'; it is its negative counterpart. The 'puella delicatior' is presented through a detailed canonic description of feminine beauty and youth, whereas the 'anum tentiginosam' is depicted as disgusting and decayed, with details and cumulative force that correspond to the degree of obscenity and excess in the woman's behaviour.

Both in the vernacular ballad and in the Latin ode the disgusting old prostitute is attempting to seduce the poet, provoking his abhorrence. Old age, lust, and seduction constitute a particularly unsettling combination to the male imagination. Poliziano must have been particularly disturbed by aging, decaying women since his most famous Italian poetry is a glorification of feminine youth, beauty, and modesty. The portrait of Simonetta in *Stanze per la giostra* (particularly stanza 78) as well as some of the ballads (most famously 'Ben venga maggio') pay homage to female virginity, beauty, and youth. Male attraction and desire derive from youth, physical beauty, and conformity to accepted social and moral behaviour.[70] The patriarchal system cannot envision any role for the older woman, particularly with respect to her sexuality; rather, after fertility has faded sexuality is relegated to the margins of society, to a space characterized by indecency, excess, and disgust.

The disgusting and transgressive old prostitute attempting to satisfy her sexual appetite continues to upset male poets well into the sixteenth century. Niccolò Franco (1515–70) composed a revolting and obscene sonnet describing 'Una vecchiazza, ch'è tutta canuta,' an ugly old hag who is 'vizza e rancia' and who, despite her repulsive appearance, successfully manages to have sex with the poet by enticing him with money.[71] Disgust, ridicule, disdain are common male reactions to the unthinkable phenomenon of the old woman seeking to satisfy her sexual drive. In Giovan Matteo di Meglio, Poliziano, and Franco the old woman who is actively trying to initiate a purely sexual encounter with the poet must be relegated to the imaginary space of the transgressive, the marginal, and the physically ugly.[72]

chapter 3

The Portrait of the Ugly Woman in the Renaissance: The Peasant, the Anti-Laura

Parodoxical Praise

During the sixteenth century depictions of female ugliness develop along two distinctive lines. Under the influence of quattrocento poetry, the invective continues against the old woman, particularly as a lascivious prostitute or procuress, typified in Niccolò Franco and Ariosto's 'Lena.' At the same time a new trend emerges in the representation of female ugliness: the mock or paradoxical encomium. In Renaissance poetry the ugly woman is no longer discriminated against for her moral laxity and age difference, but for her social class. With the onset of Renaissance secularism, the male poetic imagination is less obsessed with indecency, immorality, or the disturbing old woman. Even without the distinctively medieval bias against age, female ugliness remains a marker of transgression; now, however, it is aesthetic rather than moral transgression. Deviance is understood as infringement on the canon of female beauty established in the late fourteenth century and accepted during the Renaissance by the dominant classes and their culture. Ugly women are no longer vituperated for their disgusting old body and lust, nor attacked for the power of their eyes or speech, but praised – though mockingly – for sporting bodily features and manners in contrast to the models of ideal beauty glorified in the courtly codes of Renaissance culture. The unattractive women of Renaissance poetry, found primarily in rustic poetry, are depicted as socially marginal and aesthetically transgressive; they appear as Other for belonging to non-dominant social groups (peasants), for living at the geographical margins, and for subverting the ideals of female beauty espoused by hegemonic culture.[1] The peasant's body, described in its disproportion and excess, contravenes the highly codified norms of the Renaissance classical body, based on principles of perfection, balance, proportion, and refinement propounded by literary models. The representation of excessive female bodies serves two purposes: as a satire of the manners and behaviour of lower social classes and as a critique of conventional literary female portraits and their rigid stereotyping. Interestingly enough, paradoxical encomia of nonclassical female bodies are created by male poets who belong neither to the aristocracy nor to the peasantry they portray. These individuals often occupy a liminal position; they are outsiders who may be independent or sponsored by the aristocracy, and they often have some connection with the countryside/periphery of which they know the customs, habits, and cultural values.

Ugly women also appear in anti-Petrarchan mock encomia, which challenge the clichés of female beauty in lyrical poetry and depict the anti-Laura, a fragmentary and grotesque female figure. Rather than being genuinely interested in portraying literary women in less idealized and more realistic terms, poets who practise anti-Petrarchism are more inclined to exploit the new genre for ideological purposes, thereby using female ugliness as a vehicle for a literary agenda in which the woman continues to be an object, and a negative one at that.

In Renaissance rustic poetry female ugliness is depicted with precise characteristics, which in Silvia Longhi's view amounts to a new and distinctive literary convention (*Poeti*, 938). Thanks to the increased use of longer metric formats (octave and *capitolo*), physical descriptions become more elaborate and detailed; the extrinsic *descriptio* is more complete than in medieval examples, which were often confined to the limited space of the sonnet.[2] The consolidation and diffusion of feminine literary beauty in a stereotyped canon affects the way the other side, female ugliness/Otherness, is represented.

Ugly women in the Renaissance appear in the context of paradoxical praise, considered a form of *lusus* where, as Longhi states, 'humble content is unnaturally joined with "epic" style' (*Lusus*, 141); it is a witty game where amusement derives from commending the most insignificant and least commendable things. Despite their apparent superficiality, paradoxical encomia display high literariness, being parodies of verbal homage to the lady, a literary genre that had become so pervasive and standardized as to be accepted as a universal literary model. The mock encomium derives from the adoxographic tradition of classical times; it was a rhetorical exercise widely practised by sophists and revived in the Renaissance by Erasmus's satire *Praise of Folly* (1508).

The paradoxical encomium in vernacular poetry is best represented in the form of burlesque *capitolo*, the 'terza rima' of which Francesco Berni was the first advocate, soon followed by Giovanni Mauro, Agnolo Firenzuola, Giovanni della Casa, Benedetto Varchi, Anton Francesco Doni, Lasca, and Pietro Aretino. Paradoxical encomia chose as subject such things as madness, the plague, the urinal, or the broad bean, all things that common sense considers insignificant, negative, or disgusting, but that are defended and praised in these works, often because they lend themselves to sexual double entendre.

The mock encomium of the woman is the rhetorical mode preferred in early modern times to describe in laudatory terms a female type that does not share the aesthetic qualities of conventional literary beauty; rather, it turns the norms of the descriptive portrait upside down. In the Renaissance, female beauty and ugliness are presented as antithetical; ugly women are women whose attributes reverse the rules of the canon, but no moral judgment on them is pronounced, nor are they the subject of attack and invective. Paradoxical encomia of women are couched in ambiguity. On the one hand they attempt to criticize the excessive conventionality of literary beauty; on the other hand they mock the uncouth manners of country people and their distortion of the dominant paradigms of female perfection.

Parody in Rustic Poetry

As we discussed in chapter 1, parody entails the idea of palimpsest, the rewriting or remaking of a strong literary model. Parody involves transgression, the breaking of rules valid in a certain literary system. It originates as the antithesis of official cultural models and offers a world turned upside down. Parodistic texts are non-mimetic forms of artistic expression because they do not imitate nature but instead distort existing literary models. Only a strong model can become the object of parody. According to Almansi and Fink, the easiest to parody are 'the least eclectic, the more repetitive authors; the ones who are connected with a privileged obsession such as Petrarch' (26)

In order to account for the mechanisms that lie behind the development of the Renaissance mock encomia of literary woman (praise of the ugly woman), we need first to take a look at the stereotyped models of feminine beauty that became established in literature by the sixteenth century. Francesco Petrarca and Giovanni Boccaccio are the two authors who contribute the most to the formation and fixation of the conventions of feminine literary beauty.

As Giovanni Pozzi observes, in classical antiquity physical beauty was presented through the description of the woman ('Il ritratto, 8); however, the systematic use of elements in the framework of a canon occurs by the end of the Middle Ages and continues into the Renaissance. In the late Middle Ages the representation of woman's physical beauty acquires systematic descriptive precision and becomes a canon.[3] Pozzi refers to the descriptive technique used in literature to represent feminine beauty as a 'canone delle bellezze' (canon of beauty). Within the canon Pozzi distinguishes two subcategories: the 'canone breve' (short canon) and the 'canone lungo' (long canon). The short canon produces a full view of the person by highlighting selected parts of the face (eyes, hair, mouth, face) valued for their brightness, and another adjacent detail (hand, neck, breast). Light and colour are considered the primary sources of beauty. The long canon allows for a detailed bodily description from head to toe, focusing on the order, form, and proportion of body parts. Here proportion and brightness conflate to create the model of perfect beauty.[4]

With Petrarch and Boccaccio the descriptive system becomes more rigid and the distinction between long and short canon more clear. Petrarch concentrates on the short canon, preferred by the lyric, whereas Boccaccio specializes in the long canon, more suitable for narratives and epic romance. Boccaccio's extended praise of Emilia's beauty, described at the moment of her wedding in the temple of Venus, in the epic romance *Teseida* (circa 1339–41), along with the portraits of the six nymphs in the *Comedia delle ninfe fiorentine* (circa 1342) are considered paradigmatic models of literary female beauty. Boccaccio portrays woman with a systematic descriptive technique centred on the perfection of the body. The rhetorical *descriptio* follows the norms of medieval *Artes dictandi*. As noted in chapter 1, rhetoricians such as Matthew of Vendôme and Geoffrey of Vinsauf placed special importance on completeness and descending order in the descriptive technique. In Boccaccio's portraits it is not the individual characterization that matters, but the adherence to norms of beauty. As Renier notes (111), Boccaccio's female descriptions are all minutely analytical and nearly identical, and his depiction of feminine beauty comes closer to Renaissance principles. In *Teseida* the portrait of Emilia, inventorying the canonical parts of the female body from head to toe, extends to over eighty lines:

Era la giovinetta di persona
grande e ischietta convenevolemente,
e, se il ver l'antichità ragiona,

ella era candidissima e piacente;
e i suoi crin sotto ad una corona
lunghi e assai, e d'oro veramente
si sarian detti, e 'l suo aspetto umile,
e il suo moto onesto e signorile.

Dico che i suoi crini parean d'oro,
non con treccia ristretti, ma soluti,
e pettinati sì, che infra loro
non n'era un torto, e cadean sostenuti
sopra li candidi omeri, né foro
prima né poi sì be' giammai veduti;
né altro sopra quelli ella portava
ch'una corona ch'assai si stimava.

La fronte sua era ampia e spaziosa
e bianca e piana e molto dilicata,
sotto la quale in volta tortuosa,
quasi di mezzo cerchio terminata,
eran due ciglia, più che altra cosa
nerissime e sottil, tra le qua' lata
bianchezza si vedea, lor dividendo,
né 'l debito passavan, sé stendendo.

Di sotto a queste erano gli occhi lucenti
e più che stelle scintillanti assai; (*Tutte le opere*, 652)[5]

(The damsel was of a suitably tall and slender body, and if antiquity tells true, she was most candid and pleasing; and her tresses beneath a crown were long and full-bodied, and truly could be said to be made of gold, and her aspect was humble, and her movement upright and noble. I say that her tresses seemed gold, not tied back in braids but falling loose, and combed that not a single knot was in them, and they fell on the support of her shining white shoulders, and never before or after was hair of such beauty seen; nor did she wear over it anything but a crown, which was greatly esteemed. Her brow was ample and spacious, and white and level and very delicate, beneath which in a twisting arch terminating almost in a half circle were two eyebrows, more than any other thing most black and fine, between which one discerned a broad whiteness separating them, nor did they pass due measure in their extent. Beneath these were shining eyes and sparkling much more than a star;)

The descriptive portrait continues for another seven stanzas and painstakingly details each part of Emilia's perfect body: the nose, the rosy and well proportioned cheeks ('guance ... né magre fuor di debita misura'), the small mouth and slender lips ('bocca piccioletta,' 'labbra sottili'), pearly white, well-proportioned teeth ('denti ... si potean somigliare / a bianche perle ... si ben proporzionati'), little chin, white throat ('mento piccolino'), full long neck well seated above rounded shoulders ('pieno era il collo e lungo,' 'ben sedente / sovra gli omeri candidi e ritondi'), firm breasts, sturdy arms and long hands ('braccia sue grosse,' 'lunghe le mani'), slender fingers, slender and compact waist in good measure ('Le dita sottili,' 'era in cintura / sotile e schietta con degna misura'), her hips well formed and her feet small ('nell'anche grossa e tutta ben formata,' 'il pié piccolin'). This ideal of beauty is based not only on colour and brightness, but also on measure, proportion, and grace of the female body parts. Boccaccio's Emilia, along with the six nymphs in *Ameto*, are models of literary female portraiture for the coming centuries to imitate.

Petrarch contributed to the consolidation of the short canon in his *Canzoniere*. Laura provided the model of physical perfection and moral dignity in lyrical poetry, gaining the status of the universal paragon of beauty and elegance for centuries of lyrical poetry in Italy and abroad. Although Laura possessed the features that every woman of high rank and perfect grace should have, her body was never described in a full and detailed portrait. As critics noted, her *descriptio* is fragmentary and selective. In the sonnets and short metric formats, her portrait includes only certain parts of her face: golden curly hair ('Chiome bionde e crespe,' 227), rosy cheeks ('candide rose con vermiglie,' 'Guance ch' adorna un dolce foco,' 127), rosy lips, pearly teeth ('Bella bocca angelica, di perle piena e di rose,' 200), and shiny eyes ('Dolce lume uscia degli occhi suoi,' 106). In longer poems we sometimes catch a glimpse of Laura's other noble parts: youthful breasts ('Bel giovenil petto,' 37), gentle arms ('Braccia gentili,' 37), white thin hands ('Man bianche e sottili,' 37), and slender feet ('Più bei piedi snelli,' 348).[6]

Renaissance high literature, imbued with Neoplatonic philosophical doctrine, contributed to an affirmation of the concepts of love and beauty. As a hegemonic form of culture, high literature gradually placed more emphasis on physical beauty as an outer manifestation of inner beauty. For women in particular, beauty becomes a necessary complement to moral virtue. Beautiful women as recipients of Platonic love were extolled as objects of perfection within the boundaries sanctioned by the canon. It was in the rarefied elegant ambience of Renaissance aristocratic courts that the conventions of feminine beauty and decorum were sanctioned by authorities such as Pietro Bembo and Baldassar Castiglione.[7]

Parallel and counter to this aristocratic world of perfection, refinement, and power is the world of the lower classes, the ill-mannered peasants or labourers who live in the Italian countryside, in the peripheral mountain or valley regions, and who come in contact with the cultural establishment. Rustic poetry portraying the simple life of the peasants has a long tradition dating back as early as the thirteenth century that can be traced in Boccaccio's *Decameron* and *Ameto*.[8]

Before it became a learned form of amusement at Lorenzo de' Medici's court in the *Nencia da Barberino*, rustic poetry or 'poesia rusticana' circulated in the Tuscan countryside and, according to Marchetti, had already developed its distinctive idiomatic language through the songs of the rustic poets. Marchetti stresses the impact of the medieval comic-realistic tradition on rustic poetry (63). As noted earlier, comic-realistic poetry in vernacular infringes upon the canon of *Stilnovismo* and gives a non-idealized representation of the woman. The woman is no longer an angelic, immaterial creature but now a realistic figure. Medieval realism takes a rustic shape in the popular literature of village people. The earliest rustic production did not display the distinctive satirical flavour that is found in the later texts, possibly because it was produced anonymously within its own social milieu. With the stanzas added to the *Nencia*, and with Luigi Pulci's *Beca da Dicomano* (after 1470), rustic poetry begins to display a more parodistic tone. Thanks to the fortune of rustic poetry in the Laurentian circle, this genre became quite successful during the Renaissance and as late as the seventeenth century, when it reached its stylistic perfection.[9]

Rustic poetry finds its literary sanction with the *Nencia da Barberino*. This work in octaves was attributed to Lorenzo il Magnifico and is dated around 1470.[10] Although in its spin-offs critics detect progressive deterioration in content and style and a shift to more popular forms, they also note the lasting fortune of this poetry, which establishes a true literary genre with numerous offshoots and comic remakes such as Luigi Pulci's *Beca da Dicomano*. If the *Nencia* was indeed written by Lorenzo, it is most likely one of his first works. The poem imitates the rustic language of the peasants in the Tuscan countryside of the Mugello, the area where the Medici family originated. The *Nencia* narrates Vallera's love for a young peasant girl. Vallera, who longs for the beautiful but distant girl, expresses his feelings with such awkwardness, in comparison with the refined sophistication of lyrical poetry, that the result is comic.[11] Among the motifs explored in the poem is praise of Nencia's beauty.[12] In the *Nencia* humour arises out of the habits, behaviour, and language of the peasants, whose words often have an obscene double entendre. Critics note that the rough and simple life of the country people is viewed as comical when observed from a distance by the aristocratic circles. The cultural and political establishment based in the city centre, who promote the highest forms of refinement and cultivation, juxtapose their values to those of people living in the country, at the periphery; the rough attitudes and manners of the 'villani' serve to reaffirm, by contrast, the cultural and political hegemony of the aristocracy living in the centre.

Nencia's descriptive praise is only slightly parodistic and comic. The comic effect is evident in the shift towards a more realistic poetic tone, which disrupts the canons of lyrical tradition. There are some trivial similes in the praise of Nencia:

> Non vidi mai fanciulla tanto onesta,
> né tanto saviamente rilevata;
> non vidi mai la più leggiadra testa,
> né sí lucente, né sí ben quadrata;
> con quelle ciglia che pare una festa,
> quand'ella l'alza ched ella me guata;
> entro quel mezzo è 'l naso tanto bello,
> che par propio bucato col succhiello.
>
> Le labbra rosse paion de corallo,
> e àvvi drento duo filar' de denti
> che son più bianchi che que' del cavallo:
> da ogni lato ve n'à più de venti; (*Poesie*, 57–8)

(I never saw such honest girl, so well raised, I never saw such a graceful forehead, so shiny and nice and well shaped; and she has two eyebrows [eyes] that are a beauty, when she raises them to look at me; and in the middle is her nose so pretty, that it looks molded by a gimlet. Her red lips are like coral, and inside are two rows of teeth that are whiter than the ones of a horse, and on each side she has more than twenty;)

The parodistic effect derives from the contrast between 'denti' (teeth), a canonic element of the *descriptio*, and the noun 'filar' (rows), which lowers the tone of the description. Likewise the simile with the horse is extraneous to the lyrical tradition, but perfectly legitimate in the context of peasant life. Orvieto sees in the *Nencia* the introduction of parodistic, desecrating elements in the descriptive praise (107).[13] This process is carried to its extreme in Pulci's *Beca da Dicomano*. Luigi Pulci (1432–84), who was sponsored by the Medici, expanded on the tradition of *Nencia*, inaugurated by his friend and master Lorenzo, and adapted it for more open comical effect. In the *Beca* the antifrastic process completely annuls the conventions of the descriptive canon of feminine beauty:

> La Beca mia è solo un po' piccina
> e zoppica ch'appena te n'addresti;
> nell'occhio ha in tutto una tal magliolina
> che, s' tu non guati, tu non la vedresti;
> piloso ha intorno a quella suo bocchina
> che proprio al barbio l'assomiglieresti,
> e com'un quattrin vecchio proprio è bianca
> solo un marito come me le manca. (*Opere minori* 139–40)

(My Beca is only a bit small and she limps but you can barely notice it; in her eye there is a little stain and if you do not pay attention, you wouldn't notice it; she is hairy around her little mouth and she really looks like a barbel, and she is as white as an old penny, the only thing she lacks is a husband like me.)

The diminutives, rather than foregrounding the gracefulness of the female body, stress the deformities that produce the comic portrait of Beca. Beca is praised for her limp, for her stained eyes, and for her hairy lips: all irregularities that subvert the concept of beauty as perfection, typical of the beloved in high lyrical style. The emphasis on Beca's white complexion, a canonic element in the lyrical portrait, produces here a comical effect in the trivial comparison with the worn-out bleached coin ('quattrin vecchio').

The popularity of Nencian and rustic poetry in the cinquecento makes it a viable genre for authors such as Niccolò Campani, Francesco Berni, Anton Francesco Doni, Pietro Aretino, Michelangelo Buonarroti, and his grand-nephew Buonarroti il Giovane.[14]

Praised Ugliness/Otherness: The Peasant in Strascino, Berni, and Firenzuola

In rustic poetry some *capitoli ternari* deserve particular consideration for their treatment of praised ugliness. Predictably, it is in the anti-classicist tradition of the irregulars, authors who belong to neither the aristocratic elite nor the lower classes, that we find examples of the paradoxical praise of feminine beauty. Niccolò Campani (called 'lo Strascino of Siena,' 1478–1523), Francesco Berni (1497–1535), and Agnolo Firenzuola (1493–1543) all used the *capitolo ternario* to produce mock encomia of the beloved in the rustic genre. Strascino's *Rime* include two *capitoli* 'Delle bellezze della dama,' Berni's *Rime burlesche* include a 'Capitolo alla sua innamorata' (circa 1522–23), and Firenzuola has a *capitolo* 'Sopra le bellezze della sua innamorata' (1549).[15] The *capitolo ternario* or 'in terza rima,' the most common metric format of comic/burlesque poetry in the sixteenth century, paradoxically derives from classic texts such as Dante's *Commedia* and Petrarch's *I Trionfi* and is exploited by Berni and all composers of comic poetry.[16]

In the mock encomia the female verbal portrait is a parody of the long canon. The *capitoli* in praise of the beautiful peasant share the conventional themes and language of the Nencian tradition, but they depart from the model in that they use the *capitolo* rather than the traditional *rispetti* (eight-line stanzas) or ballad, and they push the portrait of the beloved to extreme deformity. In these *capitoli* the long canon offers a detailed description of female body parts, generally in descending order. A deliberate transgression of the canon is produced through various strategies. Infringement on the canon is effected through the language, similes, and body parts discussed. Parody of conventional verbal portraits of the 'canone lungo,' such as Boccaccio's, and distortion of the Nencian model in rustic poetry result in what Longhi defines as

> esasperazione deformante, che trasforma la descrizione dell'amata in termini rusticali – oggettivamente comici, ma positivi nelle intenzioni di chi parla – nel ritratto di donna brutta e ripugnante: una nuova e distinta convenzione letteraria. (*Poeti*, 938).[17]

> (deforming exasperation, which transforms the description of the beloved in rustic terms – objectively comical, but positive in the intentions of the speaker – in the portrait of an ugly and repulsive woman: a new and distinctive literary convention.)

The new literary convention for portraying the ugly woman finds its roots in Campani's two *capitoli*, which for Longhi are essential to explain Berni's and Firenzuola's verbal praise of their beloved.

Any description of the woman's beauty for purposes of praise, be it serious and positive or comical and negative, distorts the female body image through manipulation and fragmentation. As Ellen Zetzel Lambert has noted, Lessing's essays (*Laocoön*) on verisimilitude in visual and verbal arts had already pointed out the dismembering effect of verbal representations over pictorial ones (37). Even if words force us to see an image piece by piece, literary artists can nonetheless create a painterly effect of a body seen as whole. In Zetzel Lambert's view, when writers choose not to portray a physical body as a whole, as often happens in female verbal portraits, it must be for a precise and desired effect: dismemberment and objectification.[18] The negative descriptions of the beloved's body found in rustic mock encomia share the same effect of dismemberment and objectification with their positive counterparts. Objectification and fragmentation, in fact, seem to be the common destiny that male lyricists and parodists have in store for the female literary portrait. Strascino's depictions of the 'dama' in his paradoxical encomia well illustrate the fragmenting technique and its grotesque effects.

Niccolò Campani composed two *capitoli* 'Delle bellezze della dama' about the peasant beloved. This Sienese middle-class author, nicknamed 'lo Strascino' possibly for a physical disability that forced him to drag his feet ('strascinare'), was very popular in his time and is mentioned in Castiglione's *Cortegiano* as a professional comedian whose art consists of 'vestirsi da contadino in presenza di ognuno' (dressing up as a peasant in front of everybody). Strascino owes his fortune to the character of the peasant that he would perfect as a professional independent actor during his stay in Rome.[19] Campani and other comedians active in Siena in the first decades of the sixteenth century, traditionally considered by mainstream critics as the pre-Rozzi, are identified by Cristina Valenti as 'comici artigiani,' a group of middle-class artisans with dramatic aspirations, who contributed to the creation of a semi-popular form of theatrical entertainment for city dwellers and aristocratic circles (11).[20] Peasants and the 'contado' offer Strascino suitable subject matter for entertainment and performance. Most of the 'comici artigiani' use their comic inclination at the expense of the peasants, whose lifestyle, language, and attitudes are satirized and ridiculed.

Valenti (55) clearly identifies the liminal position of an artist like Campani, whose poetry oscillates between the Carnivalesque transgression of popular culture and classical-humanistic values of the courtly model. Strascino brought his comic art and improvisation from Siena to Rome, where he entertained at aristocratic private functions and at the papal court. Campani achieved his fame by donning the clothes of the awkward peasant, who is pitted against the middle-class city dwellers of Siena. He sang and improvised on the repertoire of rustic poetry using the cithara and the lute. Strascino the character and the actor became very successful during his time, and was engaged by the most prominent courts.[21] Comic craftsmanship allowed Campani and other 'comici artigiani' to create shows meant for performance and entertainment outside the cultural context of origin: rather than being performed in city festivals in Siena, Campani's pieces about peasants were packaged for court divertissement and private elite fetes. Although his main works are plays, Strascino's repertoire included capitoli in terza rima.[22] In the *capitoli*, which Valenti considers tools acquired during his Sienese apprenticeship before moving to Rome, the peasants are represented with their non-hegemonic values, which are portrayed negatively. The rustic poems reflect the Bakhtinian concept of the grotesque body. As mentioned in chapter 2, for Bakhtin the classical, closed, and finished body opposes the grotesque body, which is marked by excess and openness; in the grotesque body the emphasis is on parts that are open to the outside, such as the open mouth, the genital organs, and the breasts. The classical body, static and self-contained, is identified with the 'high' official culture of the Renaissance, and the grotesque body, irregular, protruding, and changing, with 'low,' non-hegemonic culture.[23] While for Bakhtin the grotesque body of non-official culture hints at renewal and social transformation, in Campani the depiction of the grotesque female body produces an inversion of aesthetic values, but does not effect a true subversion of the status quo, nor does it suggest social change or advancement for the woman. As Barbara Spackman has noted for the grotesque depiction of woman in Macaronic poetry, this female grotesque is not an incarnation of the unruly woman, of the empowered woman on top, as Zemon Davis's and other studies of the female grotesque have suggested.[24]

Valenti sees in the techniques of the rustic culture, which Campani uses, a repository of artistry to entertain the courts: degraded language; reversed speech; the invention of sexual, physiological metaphors; and creation of situations focused on excess (55). Strascino's two *capitoli* in praise of the Lady, meant for musical accompaniment 'ad cytaram,' are both mock encomia. Longhi (*Poeti del cinquecento*, 938) has emphasized the importance of these poems for the invention of a distinctive literary convention in the portrayal of female ugliness; Strascino's poems were the model for Berni, Firenzuola, and Mauro. The first *capitolo*, 'Da poi in qua ch'io m'ebbi a innamorare,' opens with the typical tones of lyrical poetry: the lament, the classic symptoms of love sickness, the throbbing heart, the tormented sleeplessness:

> Da poi in qua ch'io m'ebbi a innamorare,
> sempre mi son sentito il batticore,
> chè più non dormo e non posso vegliare.
>
> Almanco fuss'io un bel cantatore,
> ch'io le potessi dir l'animo mio
> a chi m'incalappiò co 'l suo splendore; (192)

(Ever since I fell in love, I have been feeling the heartthrob, and I can neither sleep nor stay awake. At least if I were a good singer, I could open my heart and speak to the one who enchanted me with her splendour;)

Although the poet expresses his inadequacy to the task of the poetic encomium, he then moves on to verbal homage to the 'dama.' All these conventional motifs of lyrical poetry, already employed by the peasants in Nencian poetry, mark a sharp contrast with the rustic setting of the *contado*. The peasant, on his way home after hoeing a field of muskmelons, catches a glimpse of the miller's daughter:

> Avendo un dì sarchiato il poponaio,
> mi ritornavo a casa al mio solìo.
>
> Io riscontrai la figlia del mugnaio:
>
> di fatto ch'io te l'ebbi sbilerciata;
> Tutta addobbata com'un bel pagliaio. (192–3)

(One day after hoeing the musk-melon field, I was returning home all alone. I met the miller's daughter: as soon as I had taken a look at her, all so adorned like a nice haystack.)

The poem introduces two distinctive representatives of the country social make-up: the peasant and the miller's daughter, both of whom are ridiculed. According to Ulysse, millers were actually among the most hated of the *contado*, so it is not coincidental that the woman depicted in grotesque tones belongs to this group.[25] The woman, whose skirt is lifted ('La ne veniva alla ritonda alzata'; she had her skirt rolled up) allows the peasant to take a look at otherwise concealed body parts. Evoking what Bakhtin calls the logic of the world *à l'envers*, typical of the Carnival and of folk festivities, the verbal portrait is executed literally upside down, since it starts from the feet and proceeds upwards:[26]

> La mi mostrava que' due bei pedoni,
> che ognun pareva una zolla scalbata.
>
> Un po' più su l'aveva due gamboni
> dritti, distesi, come due calocchi,
> bianchi, ulivigni, come due tizzoni.
>
> Va' poi più su; l'aveva due ginocchi
> che ognun pareva una cipolla intera,
> ed odoravan come due finocchi. (193)

(She was showing me her two big feet, that looked like tilled sod. Slightly upwards were her two big legs straight and long like two poles, white, olive-hued, like two firebrands. Moving a bit higher up she had two knees each one looking like a whole onion, and they smelt like fennel.)

The peasant proceeds upwards in his inventory of the female body parts he sees, mentioning legs, knees, buttocks, and thighs, but stops short of giving more details about the intimate parts, best left to the imagination: 'Pensa quell'altra cosa com'ell'era' (Think how that other thing must have been). The similes must have had a comic effect in a cultivated audience, who would have recognized and enjoyed the exaggerations and sexual innuendos, but also the more subtle transgressions of the canon, such as the inclusion of body parts absent from the long canon, such as knees, navel, hips, and ears. The portrait of the beautiful woman, with such emphasis on detail, is in fact an assemblage of body parts, a mixture of disproportion and excess in the female body. Similes effect a debasement of the refined models of classicist literature: the oversize arms, crooked hands, the blister-like breasts, the neck too long.

> Due fianchi, come mantici soffiavano,
> grandi e badiali come l'ha il bue;
> e come il lardo al sol che luccicavano.
>
> Le pocce le vid'io intrambedue,
> che come due vesciche eran gonfiate;
> come alla capra penzolavan giue.

Le braccia aveva lunghe e sperticate;
rimunitoccie, con non troppa rogna;
le man come un rastrello roncinate:

il collo lungo come una cicogna
la bocca larga come una bureggia;
e 'l mento se lo rade per vergogna. (194)

(Her two hips were huffing like bellows, big and large like an oxen's; and they were shining as lard in the sun. I saw both her breasts, they were swollen like blisters; and drooping like in the goat. Her arms were long and dragging; they did not have too much scabies; her hands were hook-shaped like a rake: her neck was long like a stork's, her mouth is wide like a sack, she shaves her hairy chin out of shame.)

The lady's ugliness is that Otherness which derives from infringement on the canonical rules: disproportion of bodily members, stressed by the pervasive use of the augmentative ('pedoni,' 'gamboni,' 'ginocchioni,' 'corpo grande'; 'le man come un rastrello roncinate'; her hands were crooked like a rake) and from disgusting corporal details ('tutta pelosa'; 'le pocce ... come due vesciche eran gonfiate'; 'le braccia ... con non troppa rogna'). Here we note the ambivalence towards this female Other. Ridicule and disgust are mixed with a certain attraction to the peasant woman, who repulses but also stimulates the sense of sight and the other senses too. As critics have noted, Renaissance burlesque poetry often establishes a direct link between food items and sexuality.[27] Here some parts of the peasant's body are likened to food. Her knees smell like fennel, her hips shine like lard, her cheeks are compared to cottage cheese. In fact, at the end of the poem the lover fantasizes about the erotic effect of touching some of her body parts:

Considerate questo giglio d'orto!

O com'io debbo spegnere i miei danni?
Sol toccando tai cose è 'l mio conforto,
s'io posso poi lavar la carne e i panni. (195)

(Consider this lily of the garden! Oh, how can I soothe my pain? Only by touching those parts can I have some comfort, only if I can then wash flesh and clothes.)

The depiction of the peasant female body reveals the transgressive relation that subtends the representation of the Other, embodied in the lower social class. As Peter Stallybrass and Allon White note, 'Repugnance and fascination are the twin poles of a process in which a *political* imperative to reject and eliminate the debasing "low" conflicts powerfully and unpredictably with a desire for this Other' (4–5). Strascino's poem reveals the ambiguous attraction/repulsion towards the Other (woman/peasant) pinpointed by Stallybrass and White. On the one hand, voicing the values of the upper class for which this poetry is intended, the *capitolo* elicits ridicule of and disgust towards the female Other, a body image that does not conform with the rules of the canon and is depicted as repulsive. On the other hand, the excess, the disproportion (signaled by pervasive use of augmentatives), the gastronomic metaphors, and the sexual innuendos hint at a female body that excites erotic desire. A similar mechanism is at play in Strascino's second *capitolo* and, as we shall see below, also in Berni's 'Capitolo alla sua innamorata.'

Strascino's second poem for the 'dama' opens as a commendatory conversation with the beloved:

> Tu mi pari oggi la deia Driana,
> tu se' più fresca che di maggio un maio,
> tu matti Elena e la fata Morgana.
>
> Hai quel capoccio che pare un pagliaio,
> quegli occhi strafulgenti bianchi e neri,
> che mi stralucon quanto un lampanaio (196)
>
> (You look today like Goddess Diana, you are fresher than a may tree branch, you exceed Helen and Morgan Le Fay. You have that big head which looks like a haystack, those shiny black and white eyes dazzle me like a chandelier)

This poem depends more than the previous one on the Nencian tradition. The text is replete with borrowings from *Nencia* and to some degree from Pulci's *Beca*. In Strascino the verbal portrait focuses on the deviation from canonical rules through the rhetorical use of augmentatives and diminutives to convey the distortion of the peasant's body with respect to the models of literary female beauty. If augmentatives stress the disproportion and abundance of the female body and its Carnivalesque attractiveness, the use of diminutives simply reflects a different set of aesthetic values.[28]

Quei cigli come archi da tinieri,
e quel nasin tanto ben bucherato,
che pare un sampognin da far cristeri:

i denti a filo come uno steccato;
e quel bocchin par quel d'un campanello;
la lingua pare il battaglio attaccato:

quel bel mentino auzzo e tondarello,
che me 'l par mille volte aver veduto
in casa su l'acquaio su 'l piattello. (196–7)

(Those eyebrows are like casks' handles, and that little nose has such nice holes, that it looks like a clyster bag: her teeth are as straight as a fence; and that little mouth is as round as a bell; her tongue seems like the clapper. That little pointy round chin, I seem to have seen it many times at home in the little dish by the kitchen sink.)

The inventory of the lady's body parts follows here the traditional descending order but stops at the chest. The purpose of the encomium, as in Berni below, is the proposal of marital/carnal union and depends on the lover's assets and ability to please the 'dama,' all recurring motifs in Nencian poetry. The poet's choice to include the tongue in the verbal portrait immediately hints at the subversive nature of the poem; inner parts, like the tongue, are always excluded from the classical body but appear in this grotesque portrait.

The sight of the peasant's body produces in the rustic lover erotic fantasies of intercourse, where again the referent is the pleasure of food.

O s'io mettessi un po' quel becco in mollo,
ancor direi d'un'altra tua bellezza
che l' ha 'n un lato, e non vuo' dirlo, e sollo.

Quando ci penso sento una dolcezza
Che avanza al mondo ogn'altra melodia,
E mêle, e fichi, e latte, e uva mezza. (197)

(If I could wet my beak I could describe another of your beauties that you have on one side, that I do not want to say, but I know it. When I think about it I feel a sweetness that surpasses any melody in the world, and apples, and figs, and milk, and ripe grapes.)

The verbal praise is aimed at gaining the favour of the beloved for the purpose of carnal union, rather than a formal marriage. The *descriptio* is instrumental to the second part of the poem, where the lover proposes to the beloved and boasts of his physical qualities and special abilities, all motifs of the Nencian tradition. In addition to the marriage proposal, the poem includes the offer of material goods and even a trial period in which the 'dama' can personally put to the test the lover's abilities. Here the metaphors focus on the man's working skills, with overt sexual allusions centred around the image of the land/woman, which the peasant can skilfully till/work to her satisfaction.[29] Although the text echoes the *Nencia* in both language and metaphors, the portraits of Nencia and of the 'dama' differ significantly. *Nencia*'s minor departure from the classical canon is magnified in the *capitolo*, where the beloved is a figure who ambiguously challenges the audience/reader in an oscillation between attraction and repulsion.

Besides the elements in the peasant's *descriptio* that are generally perceived as repulsive, like arms with scabies or drooping breasts, these poems produce a comic effect that results from comparing the woman's body parts with objects that, within the aesthetic ideals of hegemonic Renaissance culture, are perceived as inappropriate. In Strascino's *capitoli* many similes are drawn from the agrarian setting surrounding the peasants, and as such would not have appeared ridiculous to the peasants themselves; rather, it is the perception from above, from the viewpoint of hegemonic aesthetic conventions imposed on the reader by the author co-opted by those values, that makes us laugh and scorn the beauty of the 'dama.'

In his essay on the biological basis of Renaissance aesthetics John Onians, in addition to noting the cultural forces at play in Renaissance aesthetics, argues for a set of 'mechanisms which are better understood in natural than cultural terms – that is, as biologically driven' (12). Although Onians's observations are intended to apply to art in a broad sense, and indeed are directed towards expressions of hegemonic culture, his idea of the impact of nature and biology on the formation of aesthetic values can give some insight into the similes peasants would naturally use to describe their beloved in Campani's poetry and rustic poems in general. In both Strascino's *capitoli*, the beloved's blonde hair is compared not to canonical gold but to a haystack ('Hai quel capoccio che pare un pagliaio'); the knees are round like onions and fennel.[30] Such objects, which are intended to be perceived as comic, belong to the countryside environment; rather than conventions, they are part of nature, whose impact would have contributed to a different concept of what is beautiful.[31]

In Strascino the description of the peasant woman, as representative of a lower social order, unveils the ambivalence of hegemonic culture towards the female Other; the 'dama' is subjected to ridicule and loathing but creates the necessary polarization that reinforces the superior culture and its supremacy over the culture of the Other. The dominance here is double: that of being a woman and at the same time a peasant, of belonging to the dominated gender and to an inferior social group. The female grotesque body then produces infraction and inversion, but not true subversion, since it does not allow the woman to escape male dominance.

Strascino's *capitoli* are the essential *trait d'union* with Berni's poems to his 'innamorata,' of which they share the metric format and even the number of verses: both of Berni's capitoli consist of sixty-one lines, like Strascino's. Among Renaissance authors of comic poetry Francesco Berni occupies a central position as the initiator of 'stile bernesco,' the characteristic burlesque style that takes his name. Berni was a deeply influential and yet very contradictory figure. Although he was surrounded by the refinement of the papal court and started his literary apprenticeship with sophisticated Latin verse, he affected an unlettered persona and composed almost exclusively comic burlesque literature ranging from parody to caricatures and violent verbal attack.[32] With his taste for witty, bizarre, scurrilous, and paradoxical themes, Berni was also the most notable opponent to Renaissance *Petrarchismo*. Berni's vernacular models are quattrocento Tuscan poets such as Burchiello, Cammelli ('il Pistoia'), the rustic Lorenzo de' Medici, and Poliziano, authors he came to know during his early years in Florence.[33] Berni popularized the paradoxical encomium in *capitoli* where, with evident double entendre, he celebrates needles, meat jelly, eels, bubonic plague, chamber pots, and other such things. As critics pointed out, what Bembo was to high poetry Berni was to comic verse.[34] His themes and style were widely imitated by numerous followers and immediate friends such as Agnolo Firenzuola and other poets who belonged to the Roman burlesque Academy of the Vignaiuoli.[35]

Of Berni's two *capitoli* for his 'innamorata' in rustic style, it is the first one that pays verbal homage to the peasant beloved. Following the model of *Nencia* and Strascino's rustic poetry, the 'Capitolo primo della sua innamorata' mocks the *topos* of descriptive praise of the beautiful lady.[36] This *capitolo* offers a portrait of the beloved that reveals a disproportionate female body:

> Quand'io ti sguardo ben dal capo a' piei
> e ch'io contemplo la cima e 'l pedone,
> mi par aver acconcio i fatti miei.
>
> Alle guagnel, tu sei un bel donnone,
> da non trovar nella tua beltà fondo,
> tanto capace sei con le persone.
>
> Credo che chi cercasse tutto 'l mondo
> non troveria la più grande schiattona:
> sempre sei la maggior del ballo tondo. (*Rime burlesche*, 253)

(When I look at you from head to toe and contemplate the tip and the base, I think I know my stuff. By Lord, you are a beautiful big woman, there is no bottom to your beauty, since you are so capable with people. I believe one could search the whole world without finding a girl bigger than you: you are the best in the round dance.)

The influence of the Nencian tradition, already noted by Longhi ('Le rime,' 263–5), is pervasive in this text, but here the subversion of the canon reaches a degree that the *Nencia* never did. However, Berni does not follow exclusively the conventions of 'poesia nenciale.' Among other elements at play, Longhi points out the parody of Petrarchan poetry, which emerges in the learned references to the beloved as the great plant that gives shelter to the lover-poet.[37] The text serves as a critique of the excessive conventionality of female verbal portraits in contemporary high literature. The sexual innuendos in the poem also contribute to the radical shift towards the representation of the lower spheres of love. As in the *Nencia* and in Strascino's poems, love is all-physical and the verbal praise is a coaxing technique aimed at marital/carnal union.

Although the physical portrait is sketchy and not a complete long canon, Berni shows full awareness of the descriptive technique adopted in conventional verbal portraits in high literature. The descending order is condensed in the opening gaze from head to toe (from 'capo' to 'piei'). The comic effect is produced throughout by the use in rhyming position of augmentatives, which produce a deformed image of the woman, whose deviancy from canonical balance and proportion is defined by excess. The Tuscan expression 'schiattona' is used in relation to a young and robust 'innamorata,' whose breasts are compared to wine flasks and whose full portrait is the one of a 'donnone,' an extremely big woman. The measures of the peasant's 'innamorata,' viewed as excessive from the viewpoint of aristocratic classicism, are a source of laughter and denigration of the inferior social class. Besides the anti-Petrarchan mark and the use of Nencian *topoi*, what makes this *capitolo* interesting is again the ambiguous presentation of female ugliness/Otherness. The nature of the encomium betrays ambivalence towards such supposed ugliness. Is this excessive woman really ugly and ridiculous in her disproportion, or is she not in some way an Other who is both repulsive and attractive? On the one hand, Berni expresses the hegemonic laughter of the higher class, which mocks and rejects the rough manners of the peasants and their unconventional concept of beauty; on the other hand, the large physical proportions of this female portrait, with its Bakhtinian grotesque features, bring to light the attractive and seductive side of the peasant woman. The physical abundance of the 'villana' symbolizes her strength, sensuousness, and fertility. The fascination and desire that this feminine Other elicits is evident in the way the poet looks, and the male reader is made to look, at her body. The abundant sight stirs not only visual pleasure but also sensual fantasies involving other senses such as touch and taste, which are systematically left out in hegemonic literary discourse. The particular emphasis on touch and taste, where hunger and thirst become synonymous with sexual appetite, pervades the entire poem.

> Quando io ti veggio in sen que' dui fiasconi,
> oh mi vien una sete tanto grande
> che par ch'io abbia mangiato salciccioni;
>
> poi, quand'io penso all'altre tue vivande,
> mi si risveglia in modo l'appetito
> che quasi mi si strappan le mutande. (253)
>
> (When I see your breasts as big as flasks I feel as thirsty as when I eat sausage; and when I think about your other parts, my appetite grows so much that my pants almost tear off.)

So the low-class peasant is presented to the intended audience, the aristocratic circles to which Berni would read or recite this poem, as ridiculous, excessive, disgusting perhaps, but also, in Stallybrass and

White's terms, transgressively attractive, as the female body becomes both palpable and palatable.

After Strascino and Berni, Agnolo Firenzuola also takes on the mock encomium of the beloved's beauty in the *capitolo ternario* 'Sopra le bellezze della sua innamorata,' proving that the new literary convention is enjoying considerable diffusion. A defrocked monk who lived most of his life outside Florence, Firenzuola includes this *capitolo* on the beloved's charms in his *Rime* (1549), a collection of poems that range from traditional Petrarchan lyric to satirical and comic compositions in bernesque style.[38] Firenzuola seems equally at ease with Renaissance classicism, with the comic tradition of Tuscan quattrocento, and with bernesque poetry. Critics have noted Firenzuola's lesser accomplishment in comic poetry in comparison with Berni (Maestri, 95). In 'Sopra le bellezze della sua innamorata,' inspired by Strascino and Berni's *capitoli*, Maestri sees a falling short of the sensuousness of Berni's model. However, Firenzuola's poem deserves careful consideration. Like Berni's, it mocks the lofty style of *Petrarchisti*; moreover, it is an exercise in self-parody, since it subverts the features of feminine beauty of which Firenzuola himself had become the most accomplished promoter after writing his treatise *Celso* (1541). Firenzuola's *Dialogo delle bellezze delle donne*, or *Celso*, is considered the most complete and authoritative description of ideal feminine beauty in the sixteenth century; it uses a descriptive/prescriptive technique where celebratory tones mask a tendency towards domination and fragmentation of the female body.[39] The treatise, disguised as an act of praise and homage to women in classical high literary tones, produces a female image that is the reverse of the one in the *capitolo*, but is equally fragmentary and negative. In both works the female body is partitioned and divided through descriptive technique. The abundance of parts and details hardly constitutes a whole image. Indeed, the beauties of Firenzuola's lady in the *capitolo*, as a negative image of the woman, can illuminate the deceptive nature of verbal descriptions for the purpose of praise. Encomia and mock encomia of woman's beauty both produce negative distortions of the female body image.

In Firenzuola the woman's body stirs desire, but is perceived as dangerous and needs to be controlled; the fragmenting descriptive technique enables Firenzuola to dominate the woman's body and contain his sexual impulses. Dismemberment and objectification are at play in both Firenzuola's poem and treatise. The dialogue, in two parts, attempts to define universal beauty and seeks to create the perfect beautiful lady. As the conversation of the various interlocutors progresses the task becomes more challenging, and the passage from theory to practice reveals that the beautiful woman by definition exists only in the imagination. She is a chimera, an impossible achievement. The features of the chimera are in perfect accordance with the canon. She possesses Petrarchan splendour (golden curly hair, rosy cheeks, ruby lips, etc.) and the proportion of Boccaccio's models: 'I capegli adunque, secondo che mostrano coloro che ne hanno alcuna volta su per le carte ragionato, vogliono essere sottili e biondi e or simili all'oro, ora al mèle ... crespi, spessi copiosi e lunghi' (765) (The hair, then, according to what writers have said about it from time to time in their works, should be fine and blonde, sometimes similar to gold, sometimes to honey ... wavy, abundant, long lustrous).[40] The body must be lean and of the right proportions ('i membri svelti e destri, che li mostri ben collocati e con debiti spazii e rettamente misurati,' 767). Eyebrows must be thin and short and her eyes blue or brown and full. Ears must be of medium size, and as for the nose, 'chi non ha il naso nella total perfezione, è impossibile che apparisca bella in profilo' (776) (it is impossible for a woman without a totally perfect nose to appear beautiful in profile) (57). The treatise continues this portrait with exacting descriptive technique and proceeds in precise order until the entire body of the chimera is painstakingly described. The dignified ambience of the dialogue and the conventions of classical literature naturally entail that the private parts of the female body should not be mentioned, since what the eye cannot see is best left to imagination.

This digression on Firenzuola's *Celso* allows one to see that the *capitolo* is both an inversion of the canonical discourse on female beauty sanctioned in the dialogue and a redeployment of the same fragmenting technique at play in *Celso*. In the *capitolo* Firenzuola challenges his own precepts by presenting a female type whose physical features subvert the rules established in the dialogue.

> Prima de' suoi capei vo' raccontare,
> che paion proprio due matasse d'accia
> poste sovr'una canna a rasciugare.
>
> Che dirò io di quella allegra faccia,
> che lustra, come fa lo stagno vecchio,
> netto con uova peste e rannataccia?

E di qua e di là tiene uno orecchio
più bello assai di quel del mio secchione,
ch'io comperai l'altr'ier dal ferravecchio.

La testa sua pare un pan di sapone,
e quei suo'occhiolin due fusaiuoli,
dipinti a olio, e tinti col carbone.

Manichi son le ciglia di paiuoli:
il naso è come quel del mio mortaio,
la bocca ha come i popon cotignuoli.

Le gote en come rape di gennaio:
la gola è grossicciuola, e proprio pare
di rame una mezzina in su l'acquaio. (962–3)

(First I want to talk about her hair, which looks like two skeins of raw yarn placed on a lattice to dry. What shall I say then of that happy face, which shines like old tin, polished with beaten eggs and ashes? And on either side she has ears much more beautiful than those of my big pail, that I bought the other day at the tinker's. Her head looks like a bar of soap, and those little eyes are like two spindle discs, oil-painted, and dyed with coal. Her eyebrows are like pail handles: her nose is like the pestle of my mortar, she has a mouth like a musk-melon. Her cheeks are like turnips in January: her throat is large, and looks just like a copper jug on the sink.)

By using rustic poetry Firenzuola follows Berni and Strascino's lead and merges a serious *topos* (*commendatio pulchrae puellae*) with a comic poem. Emphasis is on the descending order of the *descriptio*, which inventories the body parts in extreme detail. The *capitolo* and the *Dialogo* both give a description of the woman's body, but for different purposes. In the *Celso* the *descriptio* is prescriptive and celebratory. It attempts to establish a universal model of perfect beauty and to pay homage to female beauty, while in the *capitolo* the verbal portrait is parodistic and disparaging. However, both texts resort to the same fragmenting technique: a minute inventory of the female body. In *Celso* the depiction of the female body generates sexual desire in the male reader/viewer, which is repressed and controlled through fragmentation. In the *capitolo* the laudatory description is paradoxical since praise hides abuse. The female body is fragmented, ridiculed – through disgusting similes – and violated, when the poetic voice expresses his desire to bite the woman's breast. Both texts use the same descriptive technique of division to control the woman's body. The body parts examined in the two works are the same. The dialogue, given its larger format, is the more complete.[41] The poem, being composed in lower style, does mention the private parts, which were censored in the treatise. In the *capitolo* such parts stimulate taste and touch rather than visual pleasure:

> Non son sì buone là per San Martino
> le nespole, o le pere carovelle,
> né così dolce il vin del botticino,
>
> là come i' credo che sian dolci quelle.
> Ma lasciam queste cose corporali,
> che basta sol toccarle pelle pelle. (963)

(Medlars, or sweet pears are as not as good at Saint Martin's feast nor is the wine in the little flask so sweet as I believe are sweet those [peasant's private parts]. But we shall leave these corporal things, that one only needs to touch with his skin.)

As in Berni and Strascino, here again the urge to reject the non-canonical female Other and her grotesque body conflicts with sexual desire for her.

In *Celso* beauty consists of proportion, balance, elegance, and delicate colours, whereas in the *capitolo* alleged beauty is disproportion, marked by the use of augmentatives ('poccioni,' 'braccione'), lack of colour ('capei ... matasse d'accia,' 'faccia ... come stagno vecchio,' 'gote en come rape di gennaio'), and absence of the very attributes that Firenzuola sanctioned in the dominant aesthetic canons of the *Dialogo*.

Since the poem presents a reversal of the ideal portrait of the lady in the dialogue, Firenzuola not only transgresses the canon and parodies the *topoi* of Petrarchism but also pokes fun at his own canonical discourse. The mockery of the peasant's homage to beauty indicates that Firenzuola, like other authors of rustic poetry, observes country behaviours and attitudes with amusement and distance, rejects the aesthetic values of this social class, and yet cannot hide some attraction for the excessive and disproportionate body. Since most of Firenzuola's work fits comfortably in the context of Petrarchism and Neoplatonism, comic poetry and parody are just a temporary escape into a comic genre that was becoming hugely popular after Berni's lead.[42] The grotesque 'innamorata' of the poem is clearly a reversal of the beautiful chimera, but the two portraits unveil two faces of the same reality; fragmentation and domination of the female body are evident both in hegemonic culture, the high spheres of classicism, and in the reversed world of the peasants. The poet achieves distance and control through objectification, dismemberment, and ultimately abuse. If the sexual excitement over the female body is more contained and yet very present in the *Dialogo*, in the *capitolo* there is an oscillation between attraction and revulsion, desire to possess and impulse to abuse.[43] In the poem some body parts, as in Berni and Strascino, are associated with food (mouth like melon, cheeks like turnips, arms soft as a cabbage, genitalia sweet like pears and wine), and the woman's body is the locus of sexual attraction, excited through the senses of taste and touch. When describing the breasts, one of the woman's most erotic parts, the poem verges on abuse:

> Lucon quei duo poccion come due ampolle:
> ché s'io potessi starvi sopra un giorno
> a mio bell'agio due ore a panciolle,
>
> i' darei certi morsi lor dattorno
> che parria ch'ella fosse una schiacciata
> con l'uve secche, uscita allora del forno. (963)

(Her two big breasts shine like two cruets; if I could lie on top of them for a day, and linger there two hours to my pleasing, I would bite them so that they would look like a flat bread with raisins, fresh from the oven.)

The description of this body part is tinged with sadistic, aggressive undertones – inherent in the desire to bite and bruise the breast – that betray a male urge to abuse the female body.[44] Firenzuola's 'Capitolo sopra le bellezze' can be read as a critique of literary female representations such as the chimera in the *Dialogo*, where the female figure is completely removed from reality. However, conventional and paradoxical praise present the female body as the locus of male ambivalence vis-à-vis sexual attraction to the woman. In Firenzuola's discourse of beauty, which ranges from the established conventions of hegemonic culture (*Dialogo*) to the subversive realm of peasant aesthetics ('Capitolo' in its choice of the peasant class), the woman is presented as an object of male power. In the 'Capitolo' as in the *Celso*, a precise and detailed physical description of the woman results in fragmentation and partitioning that produce objectification and control, in the *capitolo* becoming abuse of the female body. Once again the non-hegemonic expression of female beauty, with its preference for the excessive, grotesque female body, effects an inversion of aesthetic values but does not result in true subversion or liberation of the woman, who continues to remain an object.

Transgression on the Margins: The Disgusting Other

In the repertoire of mock encomia of the woman's beauty, female ugliness/Otherness, from *Nencia* to Berni's and Campani's 'dama,' is embodied in the representative of a lower social class, which serves as the negative pole necessary to reinforce the concept of beauty and the aesthetic values of hegemonic culture. The rustic poems are ambivalent towards the non-canonical woman: the female Other, personified in the peasant, causes ridicule and disgust but may also stir attraction and a sexual desire for plenitude, as is evident in Strascino, Berni, and Firenzuola.

The more marginal is the group represented in rustic poetry, however, the more repulsive becomes the description of the female body. The literary convention of descriptive female ugliness identified in Campani, Berni, and Firenzuola tends towards extreme degradation as we shift towards the social and geographical margins. Some texts within the genre of the paradoxical encomium of the woman's body well deserve to be called poems about the disgusting female Other. When the very peripheral classes in the socio-geographical spectrum are represented, there are female descriptions where repulsion completely overcomes attraction. It is here that Renaissance mock encomia intersect with the tradition of medieval vituperations. Women associated with porters ('facchini') and mountain women are depicted in paradoxical praise with utmost disgust.

In Renaissance Italy, 'facchini' and mountain residents were considered perhaps the most vulgar and uncivilized of people; porters and mountain dwellers were closely connected, since 'facchini' in early modern Italy originally descended from mountain and valley regions to find work as servants in the urban centres of northern and central Italy. Their uncouth manners and rough language became a literary cliché. In poems by Pier Antonio Stricca Legacci and Giovanni Mauro, as well as in the anonymous 'Stanze in lode della donna brutta,' ugly women on the margins are depicted with ultimate abhorrence. The poet's disgust towards the marginal female Other derives not only from the physical disproportion and lack of civility, but also from bodily filth and uncleanliness, which singles out the vulgar low in opposition to the bodily purity of the elite.

The 'Capitolo rusticale contando le bellezze de la sua inamorata,' catalogued as anonymous at the Biblioteca Trivulziana and partially quoted by Merlini (115) as an example of rustic poetry in praise of female flaws disguised as beauties, appears to overlap with Pierantonio Stricca Legacci's 'Capitolo alla Villana contando le Bellezze della Dama,' listed by Valenti among the poems in the collection of *Strambotti et Capitoli alla Villana* by Pierantonio Stricca Legacci, published in Siena in 1546.[45] Legacci, like Campani, is a middle-class artisan actor included by Valenti among the Sienese 'comici artigiani.' Although little is known about Legacci's life, he boasts a rich but largely unknown repertoire of rustic comedies. Ulysse (383) notes the prominent position of Legacci, along with Strascino, among the early sixteenth-century Sienese artists for his extensive dramatic production. Legacci wrote the greatest number of plays among the Sienese 'comici artigiani.' Despite scanty information about the author or his possible audience, Valenti assumes that his spectators could not be limited to the citizens of Siena and that his work must be composed for the elite of large cultural centres like Rome and Florence. If Legacci's 'Capitolo alla Villana' indeed is the same as the anonymous 'Capitolo rusticale' first discovered by Merlini, it belongs to the repertoire (*strambotti* and *frottole*) for musical performance on the cithara and the lute ('ad cytharam,' 'ad leutum') and serves as a comic exercise at the expense of the lower classes.[46]

Unlike in Campani or Berni, the 'Capitolo rusticale' presents a female Other who is not a peasant in her native countryside setting praised, though paradoxically, by a fellow countryman; the 'inamorata' bears many characteristics of the peasant, except that she is found in the urban setting, where most likely she was transplanted to find work. This 'beauty' is said to be particularly suitable for 'fachini' or porters, hardworking people who were more marginal than peasants and, as noted, were a favourite target of satire among other city dwellers and higher classes. Merlini had already noticed that the process of urbanization of mountain people in the main cities produced a particular hostility among city dweller towards the newcomers, with their uncivilized manners and rough language.[47] The satire against the 'villani,' which began with the mild humour of Lorenzo's *Nencia*, spread and intensified its negative tones in the rest of Tuscany, particularly in the area of Siena, and in regions of northern Italy too. The female grotesque that results from pseudo-Legacci's verbal portrait is the product of what Stallybrass and White define as 'displaced abjection,' a process whereby '"low" social groups turn their figurative and actual power, *not* against those in authority, but against those who are even "lower" (women, Jews, animals, particularly cats and pigs)' (53).[48] Here the poetic voice is directing the attention of men in need of a 'dama' (the same epithet used by Strascino in the *capitoli* for the beloved) to this 'manza bellona' ('manzotta' is a Tuscan expression used for a heavily built woman),[49] a grotesque female type who, according to the author, arouses interest among the 'fachini,' ('in piazza tra fachini/di null'altro che lei non si ragiona'; in the square, one talks only about her), the porters in the city market square, who are not peasants but city dwellers ('è propio un boccon da cittadini'; she is a good catch for city dwellers). The poem's humour, then, targets 'fachini' and 'cittadini,' proving that the intended audience of such poems is the elite, who would have enjoyed the scornful treatment of servants (perhaps former peasants) transplanted to the city. The poet states his intention to praise the woman's beauties from head to toe, feature by feature, as is customary in a canonic verbal portrait, with equally fragmenting results. However, the praise evokes the highest level of disgust, making the inventory of her 'beauties' a blatant paradox. The physical details of the female body hark back to some medieval elements, such as old age and white hair:

> Bianchi e' cape' come una ciminea,
> succidi, lendinosi, arroncicati
> come son gli oncini d'una statea.
> ...
> E' denti ha radi et pochi ve n'enteri
> e non vaglion tra tutti un bolognino
> tanto son rotti, barbeggiati et neri.
> ...
> Le spalle l'ha ossute et smisurate
> rognoso lorde che son tanto belle,

(Her hair is white like a smokestack, filthy, lousy, curled up like the hooks of a scale ... her teeth are sparse and broken, and they are worth only a 'bolognino' so black and filthy and full of tartar ... her shoulders are bony and out of proportion, they are so beautiful that they are full of scabies and dirt.

Her body is also said to be wrinkled and withered ('vizo e grinzoso'). Rather than the fresh young peasants of rustic poetry, these details are a reminder of medieval old hags. This *capitolo* mixes medieval features of female ugliness with elements of rustic poetry. The 'inamorata' has eyes similar to those of rustic 'villane': 'Un occhio all'a stravisa biancho et nero' (One eye is crooked, black and white); and her arms are similarly disproportionate: 'Le braze ha sperticate come antenne' (her arms are as big as poles).

The paradoxical encomium follows the descending order of the long canon but reaches a degree of disgust unparalleled in the Renaissance *capitoli* examined so far. The defining element of the woman's ugliness is not so much her disproportion and deformity (crooked eyes, big nose, wide throat, large arms and shoulders, deformed hands), which echo the features of peasants, but rather her dirt and filth. The lice-ridden hair ('cape ... succidi e lendinosi'), the lurid body, marred by mange ('Le spalle l'ha ossute et smisurate / rognoso lorde'), and the uncleanliness of the 'inamorata' evoke disgust towards the urbanized poor, the most marginal social group, whose filth defines by opposition the social purity and civility of the higher classes.[50]

The paradoxical praise is set in the context of market-place trade. The rhyming words 'fachini,' 'cittadini,' 'bolognini' (a type of currency here assumed as the amount the poet pays to the 'dama,' who is probably a servant), and the reference to lever scales ('statea') indicate a setting different from the countryside evoked by Berni, Campani, and Firenzuola. According to Stallybrass and White, the market centre of the city is a site where come together 'categories usually kept separate and opposed: centre and periphery, inside and outside, stranger and local, commerce and festivity, high and low'; it is a place where 'limit, centre and boundary are confirmed and yet also put in jeopardy' (27–8). The market-place setting in this *capitolo* reflects precisely such conflicting attitudes towards people on the margins, and towards foreigners and outsiders; the 'innamorata' is said to have the eyes of a foreign cat ('paion pur que' d'un gatto forestiero'), perhaps a reference to her status as newcomer in the city. The absence in this female portrait of comparisons with agricultural products (vegetables or fruit), so pervasive in rustic poems and which allude to the sensual or erotic appeal of the woman, proves that here the ambivalent feeling of attraction/repulsion towards the 'villana' is not present at all; here disgust for the woman's decrepitude and filth prevails.

'Facchini' and the disgusting details about uncleanliness and old age are also featured in the anonymous 'Stanze in lode della donna brutta' examined in detail at the end of this chapter. The first indication of the connection between the two poems, despite many dissimilarities, is the date and region of publication. The 'Stanze' appeared in Florence in 1547, one year after the publication of pseudo-Legacci's 'Capitolo' in Siena, most likely for the Carnival celebrations, since for the 'Stanze' we have the exact day and month of publication, February 12, definitely Carnival season.

Giovanni Mauro also wrote a mock encomium about the disgusting Other; in his *capitolo* about mountain women the opposition between the civilized elite and the dirty, boorish mountaineers is particularly evident. Mauro (1490–1536), a noble from Friuli, moved to Rome early in his life and there worked for various members of the local aristocracy. According to Longhi, despite virtual neglect by scholars, Mauro should be viewed as one of the most important authors of burlesque poetry after Berni (*Lusus*, 34). Along with Berni, Firenzuola, and della Casa, Mauro belonged to the Roman Academy of the Vignaiuoli. His 'Capitolo delle donne di montagna' is an epistle addressed to Giovanni della Casa, with whom Mauro was a close friend during the 1530s, the time this poem was composed.[51] Mauro, on assignment at Rocca Sinibalda, in the mountains of Latium, describes the women of the mountain village. The region of Sabinia defines a geographical area that, for Mauro and his addressee, represents the point of maximum distance from the congenial ambience of Roman *bien vivre*, beautiful courtesans, elitist refinement, and social purity.

> Io vi discriverrò, messer Giovanni,
> di queste gentildonne di montagna
> le fattezze, l'andar, l'abito e i panni;
> le quali acqua stillata mai non bagna (*Poeti del cinquecento*, 904)

> (I shall describe, Mister Giovanni, the features, the gait, the dress and clothing of these gentlewomen from the mountains; they are never touched by distilled water)

The 'donne di montagna' fit well in the category of the disgusting Other. Living in such a remote geographical area, seemingly untouched by civilization, the women are covered with dirt.

Ma come la Natura tutte quante
di pura terra fe,' così sen' vanno
di quella ornate dal capo alle piante; (904)

(As Nature made all of them of pure dirt, so they go around decorated with it from head to toe;)

Since they are always tending animals, they are said to assume subhuman aspect. Ornamentation and make-up, which in medieval texts were considered a source of suspicion and evidence of the woman's evil nature, have become symbols of civilization and refinement in opposition to the roughness and filth of mountain women. The element of dirt, stressed in the bodily representation of the marginal female Other, reinforces the poet's agenda to impose the hegemonic position of the elite, and to revile the vulgar for their lack of cleanliness, civility, and decorum. Here the female Other is depicted through revolting physical details ('e i capei folti, bosco da pidocchi, / e gli denti smaltati di ricotta,/e le poppe, che van fin a'ginocchi'; thick hair is a forest of lice, the teeth are covered with cheese, and their breasts fall down to their knees), which confirm the condition of filth in which these women live. Perhaps because of their work herding, mountain women have developed the sturdiness of horses and donkeys, and indeed they have horseshoe feet, says Mauro; in short, they have acquired animal-like features: 'Pie' da cavalli che non posan mai./E par ch'abbian ferrati gli talloni / a guisa di somari e di cavalli' (906) (Horse feet that never rest. They look like they have horse-shoed heels like donkeys or horses). Otherness in the denizens of the peripheral mountain areas is completely devoid of that subtext of erotic attraction that can be found in the rustic *capitoli* of Strascino, Berni, and Firenzuola. The sight of mountain women not only fails to excite any sexual attraction, but is said to extinguish any lustful impulse: 'E sì strane bellezze nei volti hanno, / che sospirar Amor e gir dolente/col capo chino, e la lussuria, fanno. (904–5) (They have such strange beauty in their faces that they make Love sigh in sadness and lower the head of lust). The detail of lice-ridden hair, a recurring element in Mauro, in pseudo-Legacci, and in the 'Stanze,' seems particularly offensive to male poetic imagination, perhaps because it concerns the hair, the female body part that, as noted above, in classical lyric tradition epitomizes female beauty and seductiveness.[52] It is not just the appearance and the dirt of mountain women that is ridiculed and described with disgust, but also their uncivilized manners and even their names. The poem is addressed to the future author of *Galateo* (1558), the most prominent Italian tract of its day on good manners and civility. As Stallybrass observes, the Renaissance develops a new canon that distinguishes correct techniques for care of the body and establishes social purity; the process of bodily differentiation – outward bodily propriety, enclosure of the body, and cleanliness – allows the social elite to separate themselves from the vulgar (124–5). The filth and uncivilized habits of the 'donne di montagna' highlight their vulgar status, in contrast to the refined manners and social purity of the elites embodied by Mauro and della Casa:

> Voi [Della Casa] morireste di rider la festa,
> quando sen' vanno a messa la mattina
> con le mutande de' mariti in testa. (*Poeti del cinquento*, 907)

> (You would laugh a storm to see them on holidays, when they go to mass in the morning wearing their husbands' underpants on their head.)

The marginality/incivility of this socio-geographical group is evident in the most integral aspect of their culture, one that appears completely alien to the poem's author. Mauro also indulges himself on the women's names, considered too odd to show any Christian origin.[53] Moreover, for their ugliness and lack of civility the mountain women are directly opposed to Roman courtesans, with whom Mauro and della Casa were particularly familiar during the 1530s.[54]

In conclusion, mock encomia in rustic poetry parody the traditional concept of feminine beauty. The portrait of the beloved displays various levels of transgressions of the canon and produces some grotesque images. The grotesque is the result of authors in liminal position assuming the elitist standpoint of their aristocratic audiences and mocking the inadequate manners of peasants, porters, and mountain dwellers. Parody also targets the stereotypical conventions of feminine portraiture in high literary tradition. Paradoxical encomia employ the rhetorical technique of the *descriptio* and, by using trivial language and vulgar and allusive similes, they reverse descriptive order and transform the serious into the comic, perfection into deformity. Female ugliness is no longer expressed, as in the Middle Ages, in portraits of old age with attendant invective, and moral contempt, but in ridiculous images of women who subvert the models of perfection and proportion promoted in Renaissance classicism. Strascino's two 'Capitoli' in rustic poetry inaugurate a distinctive convention in the representation of the ugly woman that becomes widespread in the poems of Berni, Firenzuola, pseudo-Legacci, and Mauro.

Every instance of detailed feminine physical description results in a form of fragmentation and partitioning of the body that leads to objectification and domination, be that in canonical portraits in homage to women's beauty or in mock encomia. Along with the derision and ridicule of paradoxical female portraits, there emerge instances of the Bakhtinian grotesque, particularly in the representation of the peasant. When poets writing for upper-class audiences praise country women, their position is ambivalent: they display scorn for a female Other that disrupts the hegemonic canon, but they also reveal transgressive attraction towards the Other. The plenitude and abundance of excessive female bodies arouse sensuous desire for both visual and tactile pleasure. Ridiculing peasant culture and its aesthetic principles enables hegemonic groups to reinforce their values and cultural supremacy, by stressing the clash between high and low concepts of female beauty. Rustic poems expose a conflicting feeling, a mixture of scorn and disgust, together with a desire for the low-class peasant woman and her Otherness. When the low can no longer inspire attraction, the affirmation of hegemonic values of canonical female beauty prompts male poets to the representation of ugly women as abhorrently base, dirty, and uncivilized. The women depicted as disgusting Others are those who belong to the margins, such as country women transplanted to the city and associated with 'facchini,' or mountain women observed from the refined vantage point of urban elites. Here some elements of medieval tradition reappear. This disgusting female Other, depicted as old, wrinkled, malodorant, and filthy, rather than protecting from the danger of love's illness like Cavalcanti's 'scrignutuzza,' extinguishes any erotic impulse or lustful thought.

Anti-Petrarchism: The Anti-Laura in Berni, Doni, and Aretino

Poetry in Petrarchan style thrived during the Renaissance thanks to the practice of imitation. Further sanction of Petrarchism came about when Venetian cardinal Pietro Bembo glorified Petrarch's poetry and vernacular as a canonical model of lyrical style in his *Prose della volgar lingua* (Venice, 1525). *Antipetrarchismo* encompasses all those sixteenth-century authors who were strongly critical of Petrarchism and the glorification of Petrarch's poetry during the Renaissance. The *Antipetrarchisti* targeted vapid and trite imitation of the Petrarchan mode in lyrical poetry, addressed not so much to Petrarch's lyrical style, as to its sixteenth-century imitations. The Petrarchists used the strong and authoritative model of Petrarch's lyric poetry, and in the worst cases brought about its impoverishment and exhaustion. Berni, as inventor of the bernesque genre, is considered the main opponent of Petrarchism.[55]

Anti-Petrarchan poetry is generally viewed as *lusus* but, as Silvia Longhi explains, in paradoxical discourse *lusus* allows for criticism of accepted values, the pleasure of expressing dissenting opinions under the pretense of laughter (*Lusus*, 178). From this perspective, in paradoxical encomia of the ugly woman, *lusus* proves to be a missed opportunity for criticism about the representation of women in literature, since the image of the ugly woman, produced in the inverted female portraits, produces no liberating or valid alternative to the stereotyped ideals of feminine beauty.

In his 'Chiome d'argento,' an anti-Petrarchan mock encomium, Berni delivers a pointed attack on Pietro Bembo's sonnet 'Crin d'oro crespo.' Bembo's role as propagator of Petrarchan imitation led Berni to compose a sonnet that for Longhi establishes a 'dialogo antifrastico ... con i due sonetti bembeschi del perfetto amore' ('an anti-frastic dialogue ... with Bembo's two sonnets on perfect love,' *Poeti*, 848). In general, Berni's criticism was directed against the contrived style and commonplaces of the *Petrarchisti*; however, 'Chiome d'argento' targets Bembo's sonnet precisely in both style and content. Berni's paradoxical praise highlights the exhaustion of the clichés of female literary figuration and urges a revision of the canonical model. In this sonnet in praise of his lady, Berni critically addresses the traditional figurative representation of the beloved.[56]

> Chiome d'argento fino, irte e attorte
> senz' arte intorno ad un bel viso d'oro;
> fronte crespa, u' mirando io mi scoloro,
> dove spunta i suoi strali Amor e Morte;
>
> occhi di perle vaghi, luci torte
> da ogni obietto diseguale a loro;
> ciglie di neve, e quelle, ond'io m'accoro,
> dita e man dolcemente grosse e corte;
>
> labra di latte, bocca ampia celeste;
> denti d'ebeno rari e pellegrini;
> inaudita ineffabile armonia;

costumi alteri e gravi: a voi, divini
servi d'Amor, palese fo che queste
son le bellezze della donna mia. (103)

(Hair of fine silver, shaggy and twisted / Tastelessly around a beautiful face of gold: / Wrinkled brow, gazing at which I pale, / Whereon Love and Death break their arrow points. // Shimmering eyes of pearl, beams turned away / By every object unequal to them; / Eyebrows of snow, and you, which move my heart, / Fingers and hands, delightfully thick and short. // Lips of milk, large azure mouth, / Teeth of ebony, rare and wandering, / Unheard of, ineffable harmony; // Manners haughty and ponderous; to you, divine / Servants of Love, I now make plain that such / Are the charms of my lady.)[57]

Berni mocks the *topos* of descriptive praise of the beautiful lady. The parts of the woman's body mentioned here are the canonical ones found in Bembo and, generally, in any literary woman of Laura's lineage: hair, forehead, eyes, mouth, lips, teeth, hands. Since Bembo is the direct parodic target, there are direct lexical borrowings from his 'Crin d'oro crespo'; words like 'oro,' 'neve,' 'perle,' 'armonia' appear in both texts, indicating a subtle work of manipulation. Berni's list humorously juxtaposes the canonical metaphors with inappropriate body parts. The equivocation produces a comic effect and undermines the logical link between members of the metaphors. The traditional comparison between gold and hair conveys the idea of beauty through colour, brightness, and preciousness. But if gold is shifted to a comparison with the woman's face instead of her hair, and pearls are metaphors for her eyes, they are no longer the attribute of a beautiful lady. Instead they become metaphors for a yellow face and oozing eyes, possibly due to illness or old age; likewise, snow attributed to eyebrows instead of the forehead, and ebony to teeth, evoke the old age and unattractiveness of the lady. Silver is not only a less precious metal, defying the concept of absolute perfection normally associated with the lady's attributes, but also indicates grey hair and the aging woman, thereby contrasting with the stereotype of the beloved's eternal youth and reviving the medieval cliché of female unattractiveness in connection with old age.[58] Berni's transgressive operation is remarkable because parody is produced by using the very attributes and figurative components of the Petrarchan model and then mismatching them. The poet challenges the conventional mode of representation of feminine beauty in love poetry by adopting a method similar to the one used in the anagram, a technique whereby all the elements of Petrarchan beauty are rearranged in unusual order. With this procedure, Berni not only reminds us of the normative beauty from which this woman deviates, but also alerts us to how easily fixed standards of beauty, and the valuations on which they are based, can be unsettled. Linguistically, 'Chiome d'argento' presents a minimal transgression of the canon and, by shifting the metaphorical attributes to inappropriate parts of the lady's body, turns beauty into ugliness, the Petrarchan lady into the anti-Laura. Berni's 'amata' stands counter to models of conventional feminine beauty and anticipates unorthodox choices of women's figuration in baroque poetry.[59]

Anton Francesco Doni also engages in a critical discourse with Petrarchan poetry, as is evident in his sonnet 'La mia donna ha capei corti e d'argento.' Doni (1513–74), of a Florentine family of humble origin, is also an eccentric figure in Renaissance Italy. Because of his bizarre and unstable temperament he found it particularly difficult to accept the conservative rules of court life.[60] Recent critical work has underscored Doni's role as model of an intellectual working outside the traditional Renaissance cultural centres of the court and the church.[61] As free spirit and radical, Doni, like Berni, attacked Petrarchism and its excessive stylization in the representation of feminine beauty. The introduction to his *Madrigali satirici*, a collection of lyrical poems in anti-Petrarchan style, contains a letter that reveals Doni's feelings towards *Petrarchisti*:

> Ho poetato per burlarmi del mondo, e per farmi beffe d'alcuni scattolini d'amore, i quali non sanno uscire di – *Madonna io v'amo e taccio* – e – *S'io avessi pensato* – e simili ciabatterie, oggimai così fruste come le cappe de' poeti.[62]

> (I composed this poetry to mock the whole world and to poke fun at some love poets, who cannot compose anything different from – *Madonna I love you and I say nothing* – and – *If I had thought* – and other similar silly things, that nowadays are as worn out as the poets' cloaks.)

Doni clearly states his intention to mock the *poeti petrarchisti* and, in particular, targets their most vacuous clichés.

In *I marmi* (1552–3) Doni presents a series of unrelated dialogues that take place on the marble steps of Florence's Duomo. The dialogue's interlocutors include real people, personifications, and even talking statues, who discuss various topics ranging from gossip to injustice in Florentine society.[63] In part 3 of the second volume, in the 'Ragionamento dei sogni degli academici peregrini,' is the anti-Petrarchan sonnet 'La mia donna,' intended as an extravagant dream fantasy. Doni parodies the portrayal of the woman's beauty as canonized by the *Petrarchisti* and produces his own version of the anti-Laura.

> La mia donna ha i capei corti e d'argento,
> la faccia crespa e nero e vizzo il petto,
> somiglion le sua labbra un morto schietto
> e 'l fronte stretto tien, ben largo il mento;
>
> piene ha le ciglia giunte e l'occhio indrento,
> come finestra posta sotto un tetto;
> nel riguardar, la mira ogn'altro obietto
> che quella parte ove ha il fissare intento;
>
> di ruggine ha soi denti e poi maggiore
> l'uno è dell'altro e rispianate e vote
> le guance, larghe, prive di colore;
>
> ma il gran nason che cola, in fra le gote
> così sfoggiatamente sponta in fuori
> ché chi passa s'imbratta, urta e percuote.[64]

(My lady has short and silvery hair, her face is wrinkled, her breast is black and withered, her lips resemble those of a dead man, and her forehead is narrow, her chin is wide; her eyebrows are full and united; and her eyes are sunken, like a window placed under a roof. When she looks she sees every object except the one where her eyes are fixed; her teeth are rusty and one is bigger than the other, and her cheeks are flat, empty, wide, and colourless; but her big dripping nose sticks out so prominently between her cheeks, that whoever goes by, gets dirty, irritated, and beaten.)

Doni's indebtedness to Berni's poem is quite remarkable: this poem is notable for its metrical and thematic affinity with Berni's. The lady's silver hair is the first detail of the *descriptio* in both sonnets, and her eyes are described by both as crooked. Expanding on Berni's inversion of the Petrarchan model, Doni adds the transgressive element of short hair. Since every lady in lyrical poetry from Laura onwards has long, curly hair, praising a beloved with short hair challenges the convention. The sonnet also mentions the lady's nose, big and dripping to boot; the inclusion of this part of the face, normally omitted by the *Petrarchisti* and always ignored by Petrarch, indicates a deliberate intention to disrupt the canon.[65] The most transgressive aspect of the portrait is the presence of facial features not normally included in the short canon (nose, chin, cheeks) – absent even in Berni's sonnet – and the introduction of inappropriate elements, such as disgust at the aged body, with 'rusty' teeth and withered breasts. The catalogue of Doni's 'bruttezze' subverts classical elements such as proportion and balance. As Firenzuola prescribed in his *Celso*, proportion is essential to the Renaissance figuration of perfect feminine beauty. Instead it is disproportion that here reigns: the canon prefers the chin to be small and the forehead wide, whereas this woman has a narrow forehead and wide chin. Perfect eyebrows should be well separated; instead, they are united. Colour and brightness, essential elements connoting beauty, are replaced by dark tones, lack of colour, and a cadaverous look.[66]

Unlike Berni, Doni inserts a considerable amount of inorganic material, which makes this sonnet stylistically less perfect: the vocabulary is a hybrid mixture of Petrarchan and realistic language, which points to the medieval tradition of comic-burlesque poetry, where the counter-figure of the 'amata' was the old hag, with a wrinkled and disgusting body. Doni employs some *topoi* of the medieval comic tradition of the old hag. The dripping nose, the withered face and dark breast, the 'rusty' teeth evoke Beroe. The lady's teeth, encrusted with tartar, evoke Rustico Filippi.[67] Among fifteenth-century burlesque poets who indulge in *descriptio* of the woman's ugly body, Burchiello is certainly the most congenial to Doni's bizarre temperament. Burchiello's invectives against the old woman were very familiar to Doni, who was the author of a commentary on Burchiello's *Rime* published in Venice by the press of Marcolini in 1553. Doni provides an interesting example of the convergence of the Renaissance parody of *Petrarchismo* and Medieval comic-realistic poetry on the old hag.[68] The dark complexion of Doni's poem may be an element that baroque poets found congenial for their altogether different poems in praise of the dark lady.

In Berni and Doni's sonnets we witness a return of the old woman as subject of poetry, but not of the attacks that were so common in medieval sonnets. Here the genre is the paradoxical encomium, where what is presented as the beautiful lady is disgusting and old. The old age of the woman is not the real focus of these poems, but is inherent in the detail of the silver hair, on which Doni expands, reviving some elements of the medieval tradition.

The lady's hair and its colour spark the mechanism of inversion of the Petrarchan model of beauty. As Milena Montanile observes, the physical feature that best epitomizes feminine beauty in classical literature is the golden hair of Laura and later of countless examples of classical literary beauties.[69] So Berni, and Doni after him, begin the reversal of the Laura type by targeting the beloved's hair; remarkably, they draw the metaphor 'argento' for the hair directly from *Canzoniere*, where Petrarch used it to describe the aging Laura in sonnet 12.

Both Berni's and Doni's sonnets convey the same ideological message: a criticism, through parody in the form of mock encomium of Petrarchism and of the excessive conventionality of feminine beauty in literary practice. Although their transgressive operation challenges conventional modes of the representation of women's physical appearance, it does not in any way liberate Renaissance literary woman, beautiful or ugly, from the inevitable reification and fragmentation of the descriptive technique. Berni's and Doni's critiques of stereotypical depictions of feminine beauty have little to do with genuine concerns about the discrepancy between literary and actual beauty in women of the time. The praise of the female body and the easy reversal of the beautiful and young into an old and ugly woman is merely a pretext for a literary polemic over stylistic and poetic clichés, confirming the misogyny of the two poets. In the paradoxical encomia there is no real interest in freeing the image of the literary woman from the objectifying strategies of classicist poetry; rather, the other face of the beautiful Petrarchan lady is the equally fragmentary and grotesque anti-Laura.

If Italian Renaissance poetry does not escape the fixed scheme of praise and anti-praise of the woman, neither does French or Spanish literature. In France the level of objectification and fragmentation of the female body reaches its peak in the genre of the anatomical blazon and its comic reversal, the counterblazon, inaugurated by Clement Marot, both reducing the woman to one single fragment of her body. In Spain the critique of Petrarchism focuses on the woman's old age and draws on the many clichés of medieval invectives against the old hag.[70]

Pietro Aretino adopts his own demystifying approach to representing women's beauty in some anti-Petrarchan poems of his early years, later incorporated in the *Sei giornate* (1534–6), his two-part dialogue on prostitution. After assessing that a career as a whore is the best choice for young Pippa, in the second dialogue, *Dialogo nel quale la Nanna insegna a la Pippa*, veteran courtesan Nanna indoctrinates her daughter into the arts and dangers of the profession.[71] The second and third day of the

The Ugly Woman in the Renaissance   121

Dialogo include several poems in anti-Petrarchan style.[72] They reflect Aretino's hate for the *Petrarchisti* and are conceived as a mockery of love's affectation, with none of them specifically focusing on the verbal portrait except one madrigal in the second day. Here Nanna warns Pippa about the tricks that men play on women in the profession. As an example, Nanna narrates the misadventures of Monna Quinimina, a woman of easy virtue, whom a suitor had first beguiled with Petrarchan praise and then humiliated with mock-encomium. The cynical suitor is a poetaster of the hated Petrarchist type, who ridicules Quinimina's boasted poetic knowledge, by praising her beauty in less than flattering terms. The madrigal is a serenade sung by the suitor, who can pass off a burlesque distortion for an original Petrarchan poem because of the woman's inability to discern a proper Petrarchan encomium.

> Per tutto l'or del mondo,
> donna, in lodarvi non direi menzogna,
> perché a me e a voi farei vergogna.
> Per Dio che non direi
> che in bocca abbiate odor d'Indi o Sabei,
> né che i vostri capelli
> de l'oro sien più belli,
> né che negli occhi vostri alberghi Amore,
> né che da quelli il sol toglie splendore,
> né che le labbra e i denti
> sien bianche perle e bei rubin ardenti,
> né che i vostri costumi
> faccino nel bordello andare i fiumi:
> io dirò ben che buona robba sète,
> più che donna che sia;
> e che tal grazia avete
> che, a farvelo, un romito scapparia.
> Ma non vo' dir che voi siate divina,
> non pisciando acqua lanfa per orina. (286)[73]

(For all the gold in the world, my lady, in praising you I wouldn't lie, because I would shame you and me. By God I wouldn't say that you have in your mouth the smell of Indian or Arabian perfumes, nor that your hair is more beautiful than gold, nor that in your eyes resides Love, nor that the sun draws its splendour from them, nor that your lips and teeth are white pearls and beautiful shiny rubies, nor that your manners would invert the course

122   The Ugly Woman

of rivers: I shall say that you are good stuff, better than any other woman; and that you have such grace that a hermit would run away rather than making it with you. But I do not want to say that you are divine, since you do not pee scented water but urine.)

The scoffing negation of clichés about the woman's physical features effects a dethroning of the Laura type and deconstructs the Petrarchan goddess-like image of the beloved. As shown in the finale, this poetic strategy does not grant any dignity to the woman; the simile of the last verses ('non pisciando acqua lanfa per orina') produces a debasing effect that fully reveals Aretino's misogyny.

The technique of defining the lady by negation is experimented on later in William Shakespeare's *Sonnets* (1609). Sonnet 130 to the Dark Lady bears remarkable similarities to Aretino's madrigal:

> My mistress' eyes are nothing like the sun,
> coral is far more red, than her lips red,
> if snow be white, why then her breasts are dun:
> if hairs be wires, black wires grow on her head:
> I have seen roses damasked, red and white,
> but no such roses see I in her cheeks,
> and in some perfumes is there more delight,
> than in the breath that from my mistress reeks.
> I love to hear her speak, yet well I know,
> that music hath a far more pleasing sound:
> I grant I never saw a goddess go,
> my mistress when she walks treads on the ground.
>   And yet by heaven I think my love as rare,
>   as any she belied with false compare. (97)[74]

Shakespeare attempts to bring the lady's goddess-stature down to earth with moderate humour, but departs from Aretino's crude tones in the finale, where disgusting details are supplanted by an authentic and yet positive depiction of a realistic woman. Interestingly, the infringement on the clichés of the beloved's hair is less dramatic in Aretino's than Shakespeare's poem, where 'black wires grow on her head,' and therefore the beloved's hair is black. This element illustrates Shakespeare's affinity to Italian baroque poetry and its fascination with the dark lady, as we shall see in the following chapter. If Aretino indeed had an influence on Sonnet 130, Shakespeare managed to transcend the narrow perspective of *Antipetrarchismo* and provide a sample of a more realistic homage to woman's beauty, which survives the anti-Petrarchan attack.[75]

'Stanze in Praise of the Ugly Woman'

An anonymous poem published in a book from Doni's printing shop in 1547, the 'Stanze in lode della donna brutta' deserve our attention as a text that until now has been virtually ignored by scholars. Lacking paternity and being as inconsistent and nasty to the woman as other texts with unclear authorship have so far proven, it appears as a pastiche of the themes and motifs on the ugly woman that we have encountered. Moreover, it is the only text in this book that openly proclaims as its subject matter the 'ugly woman.'[76] This poem reworks some themes of Doni's sonnet, recycles some anti-Petrarchan material from Berni's 'Chiome d'argento,' hints at the Nencian tradition, reworks some motifs of pseudo-Legacci's *capitolo*, and recycles some medieval comic-realistic and misogynist clichés. These twenty 'stanze' in 'ottava rima' deserve consideration in the history of the genre that has been delineated because they are the ultimate example of ugly verses on the ugly woman. Ugliness is promised right from the title, which does not pretend, like many mock encomia, that ugliness is beauty. One could suspect that the ugly woman is a rhetorical embodiment of ugly poetry, and yet, even so, the woman is used merely as a vehicle for negativity and ultimate aberration. The 'Stanze in lode della donna brutta,' a patchwork of language, themes, and styles leading to parody, appear here in their entirety for the first time since their first publication.[77] This poem is a mock encomium wherein motifs of baroque poetry are beginning to emerge. The comic-realistic and anti-Petrarchan styles are intertwined in a mixture of Renaissance parody, medieval vituperation, and pre-baroque witticism.

The textual inconsistencies begin with the metrical format. The tradition of the *capitolo* or sonnet, preferred for Renaissance mock encomia, is abandoned for octaves, the meter used in 'poesia nenciale' and in romances of chivalry.[78] The twenty stanzas offer a portrait of the ugly woman that shows some similarities to Doni's verse. It could be surmised that the 'Stanze' were composed by Doni himself or by someone close to his circle. The praise originates from the poet's desire to soften the haughty lady's cold and distant attitude towards the poet, a traditional *topos* of lyrical poetry.

> Donna, il cui viso rincagnato e piatto
> et di varii color vecchia pittura:
> che perché 'l naso il ciel lungo v'ha fatto,
> et le poppe di sotto a la cintura,
> et le man da fachin gli occhi di gatto,
> troppo altiera ven' gite e troppo dura:
> udite le dolcissime parole
> del vostro Amante, che lodar vi vole. (I, 6–8)

(Woman, with a flat pug face, old picture of various colours: since heaven made your nose so long, and your breasts drooping to your waist, and your hands like a porter, your eyes like a cat, since you are too haughty and too hard, listen to the sweetest words of your Lover, who wishes to praise you.)

The motif of the lady as marvel ('Ben volse / ... empir d'alto stupore il secol nostro/Natura, quando vi compose e il viso,' II, 1, 2–3, Nature wanted ... to fill with great marvel our century when she shaped your face) becomes comical since marvel and wonder are a source of laughter ('materia di riso') caused by a face 'più sereno e candido ch'inchiostro' (more clear and white than ink). The element of marvel immediately points to the baroque 'meraviglia,' the pivotal instrument of Giambattista Marino and the baroque lyricists' new poetics, as discussed in chapter 4. Mythological figures, used profusely in lyrical poetry as comparison for the lady's divine beauty, here are marked by negativity; this woman is equated to the Furies and the Fates, the most feared and disgusting mythological monsters:

> Che né Aletto, Tisiphone, e Megera,
> né Atropo anchor, né Lachesi, né Cloto
> o se altra furia v'è più scura e fiera,
> o mostro per horror più chiaro e noto
> certo non ha di voi più brutta ciera. (III, 1–5)

(Neither Alecto, nor Tisiphone, nor Megaera, neither Atropos, nor Lachesis, nor Clotho or any other Fury is darker and fiercer than you, a monster more eminent and famous for its horror certainly does not have an uglier aspect than yours.)

Transgression of the Petrarchan model comes from the juxtaposition of the opening celebratory tone and the rest of the poem, where unrelenting dispraise culminates in the invective against the ugly woman in the last stanza.

> In questo tempo pregherò Natura
> ch'in ciò almen mi contenti e sodisfaccia
> che come vi fe' brutta oltra misura,
> così infelice e misera vi faccia. (XX, 1–4)

(In the meantime I'll pray Nature, so that my wishes may be satisfied and fulfilled, and as Nature made you ugly beyond measure, it may also make you miserable and unhappy.)

By shifting from praise to invective within the same composition, the text merges two genres that so far were kept separate: medieval vituperation and Renaissance paradoxical praise.

The length of the poem is well suited to a long canon, but the *descriptio* neither respects the descending order nor provides a complete inventory of the body. As a short canon this text transgresses basic rules. It includes inappropriate body parts such as the nose, always banned from Petrarchan tradition, and deliberately selected in Doni's sonnet. The 'donna brutta' is described with metaphors that subvert the concept of beauty based on light and brightness. Darkness is the prevailing tone of the woman's appearance: her face is like ink and her teeth are as dark as ebony. Parody, as in Berni's and Doni's sonnets, lies in the deliberate disruption of semantic relations in the similes: 'neve' (snow), traditionally used to designate the snow-white face of the woman, is used for eyes and hair, producing the transformation from *pulchra puella* to old hag. In Berni's sonnet 'neve' was used for the eyelashes; here it shifts to the eyes as a whole, and 'ebeno' (ebony) is used for teeth, just like in Berni. Aesthetic transgression arises also from the disruption of the rules of proportion, the ones that normally subtend the long canon. Deformity by excess deliberately targets some body parts: long nose, heavy hands ('man da fachin'), drooping breasts ('poppe di sotto a la cintura'), mouth exceedingly wide ('bocca larga'), large and heavy feet ('piede lungo e greve'). Other than the metric format, there are very few traces of Nencian and rustic tradition. The mouth, which was previously described as very wide, shortly afterwards is called 'bocchino' with a diminutive common in Nencian poems. More than *Nencia*'s measured laughter, the referent is the scornful attitude of rustic poetry towards the 'facchini.'[79] As in pseudo-Legacci's and Mauro's *capitoli*, this woman fits the type of the disgusting Other, an old and revolting person who is filthy and full of lice and ringworm: 'Chi mira i crin, dirà son de pidocchi / questi e di tigna pur certo un bel bosco.' (V, 5–6) (Who looks at your hair shall say that with lice and ringworm it forms a nice forest). The body, language, and manners of a 'fachino' ('un parlar spiacevol, e fachino') make this woman a representative of individuals on the geographical margins, who are reviled for their class inferiority and incivility. Many elements hark back to the comic realistic medieval tradition. The foul mouth ('Sentono un odor in quel bocchino, / che par che s'apra un puzzolente vaso' VI, 6–7; they smell an odour in the little mouth, that is like a stinky vase), the oozing eye, the 'viso rincagnato,' bony body, are all features that date back to Beroe and medieval invectives against the old hag.

Like Mauro's 'donne di montagna,' this disgusting woman is said to be a remedy against love and lust. Stanzas 14 and 15 revisit medieval misogynist prejudice against women's make-up and the belief that menses would make women poisonous to plants: 'muoion l'herbette, così sono offese / da non so che, ch'a voi vien ogni mese' (XIV, 7–8; Herbs die and are affected by that thing which happens to you every month).[80] This contradictory figure with withered body and yet still menstruating is perhaps akin to the pregnant old hag that in Bakhtin is the emblem of the female grotesque, but is devoid of the positive regenerating force Bakhtin finds in the grotesque body. Unlike Nencia, the 'donna brutta' is ugly because of her old age, as in Berni's and Doni's sonnets, but also and foremost because she is disgustingly filthy, as in pseudo-Legacci and Mauro.

This poem plays an important role as a *trait d'union* with baroque poetry. It is here that the poet exploits the motif of the woman's dark face and body: 'Non venne di paese aspro e remoto/Mora giamai con così horribil faccia' (III, 6–7; Never came from harsh and unknown country a dark woman with such a horrible face). This mention of the Moor ('mora'), traditionally referring to an individual coming from Africa, most often from Mauritania or Ethiopia, implies not just the gender/class/civility discrimination seen towards peasants and mountain women, but also the racial one, regarding visible minorities.[81] In stanza 18 the poet reinforces the woman's ugly appearance by stating that she could find a match among Ethiopians or midgets: 'ben sarebbe d'huopo/a dar sì bella donna per mogliera/a un bel marito, a un Nano a un Ethiopo' (It would be appropriate to give such a beautiful woman as wife to a handsome husband, to a midget, or an Ethiopian). Pairing

Ethiopian, Moor, and midget is significant, since it connects female ugliness not only with the racial Other but also with the exotic, the bizarre, or, to borrow from Mary Russo's instances of 'female grotesques,' to the freak (an oddity of nature such as the midget, Siamese twins, the giant, etc.), which in the nineteenth century appeared as a spectacle at various venues such as fairs, carnivals, and circuses.[82] In baroque poetry these same categories of women become the subject of witty poems about unconventional and outlandish beauty rather than ugliness. The motif of the dark woman, which here appears along with the one of the medieval old hag, of the anti-Laura, of the disgusting Other, is the most innovative element in this perplexing and generally disturbing poem. As I show in chapter 4, baroque poetry reworks the theme of the dark lady and makes it, not the subject of invective or dispraise, but the source of marvel and witticism.

Despite their lack of authorship and the already established convention of poetry on the ugly woman, the 'Stanze' dare to present themselves as a universal model to follow in the depiction of ugly things:

> Chi la fame o l'invidia, o la Quartana
> ritrar volesse od altra brutta cosa
> a mirar voi gli occhi e la mente volga;
> da voi la forma e 'l bel dissegno tolga. (IV, 5–8)

(Who wishes to portray hunger, envy, or Quartan fever, or any ugly thing, should turn their eyes and mind to you; from you they should take the shape and the beautiful design.)

The paradox of this paradoxical encomium, with its lack of unity, its inconsistencies and aberrations, lies perhaps in the inability of such bad poetry to portray the woman, be she ugly or not.

chapter 4

New Perspectives in Baroque Poetry: Unconventional Beauty

From Ugliness to Unconventional Beauty

Baroque poetry in Italy was completely absorbed in its task of renewal and detachment from Renaissance Petrarchism. Yet as Asor Rosa noted, baroque taste was not born in an act of conscious and sharp break from tradition.

> Il sentimento e la ricerca del nuovo, che pure costituiscono elementi primari del gusto barocco, debbono essere intesi e valutati in un quadro complesso di relazioni, in cui il fattore della continuità e della tradizione non pesa meno delle istanze di rinnovamento. (*La lirica del seicento*, 3)

> (The desire and search for novelty, which are indeed primary elements of baroque taste, must be evaluated within a complex context of relations, where continuity and tradition are as important as instances of renewal.)

Seicento poetry reacts against the most exhausted and trite clichés of Petrarchism and explores new poetic avenues in its attempt to surprise and excite marvel through daring and unthinkable metaphors. Giambattista Marino, the key figure in the Italian Baroque, espouses the poetic of 'meraviglia' as a rhetorical tool to express the excellence of new poetry, which includes the bizarre, the unusual, and the witty.[1] The search for novelty in late Renaissance and baroque literature produces a vast and rich output of texts on unconventional beauty, rather than on ugliness, in high rather than comic style. With the shift from Renaissance to baroque poetry female ugliness is no longer expressed in the invective of the comic-realistic, nor in paradoxical praise of the peasant.

Baroque poetry promotes new aesthetic values, where ugliness no longer figures as an absolute category in sharp opposition to beauty. In the seicento beauty and ugliness come closer together and provide a vast area for the representation of the literary woman. Getto has noted that a typical feature of the baroque *canzonieri* is the 'predicazione multipla, numerosa, e in certo modo inesauribile della donna' ('Multiple, numerous and, in a sense, inexhaustible predication of the woman,' 'Introduzione,' 22). This leads to an interest in aspects of femininity that were so far excluded from lyric poetry.

In an effort to integrate imperfection with the idealistic tradition of high lyrical style, seicento poetry reinvents the verbal homage to the lady and turns it into a praise of unconventional beauty. Along with Petrarchan tradition, sixteenth-century bernesque and paradoxical poetry provide sources for woman's verbal homage in baroque poetry; the themes of comic and serious poetry converge to create a hybrid form of lyric, all focused on showing the poet's virtuosity and witticism. At first glance baroque poets seem committed to representing literary women more realistically than their predecessors, to transcending class barriers by electing to extol common women, maids, labourers, and so on; and yet their poetry is highly ambiguous.[2] Depictions of imperfect and unconventional female beauty are not just an attempt to be more realistic, true to nature, or less elitist; they fully reflect baroque poets' tendency to feed their imagination through the vast repository of both the Petrarchan and anti-Petrarchan/comic traditions. Attributes that in idealized female representations were considered undesirable are presented as attractive; this ploy allows the poets to display their deftness in exploring arduous and unthinkable combinations of beauty and deformity. To praise tainted or unconventional beauty, the poets exploit Petrarchan style and realistic/burlesque subject matter, effecting thematic reversal.

Praises of imperfect beauty abound in 'Lirica marinista' and appear as more or less deviant variations on the Petrarchan model, with copious sonnets and madrigals. Baroque poets are attracted to the love theme and, in an effort to discard perfect Petrarchan beauty, take up the challenge of commending women with physical defects. The beautiful can include a midget ('bella nana' in Giovan Leone Sempronio), a stutterer ('bella balbuziente' in Scipione Errico, 'bella tartagliante' in Paolo Abriani, and 'bella balba' in Giuseppe Salomoni), a woman with a limp ('bella zoppa' in Abriani, Antonio Bruni, Salomoni, and Alessandro Adimari), with a hunchback ('bella gobba' in Adimari and Bruni and the 'bella scrignuta' in Salomoni) – perhaps a subtle revisiting of Cavalcanti's 'scrignutuzza' – or cross-eyed ('bella guercia' in Marcello Giovanetti and Adimari), which echoes Berni's cross-eyed beloved in the sonnet 'Chiome d'argento.'[3] The desire to elude the illustrious conventions of the love lyric leads to a subversion of the ideal representation of woman, often possible by adding just one bodily detail, a missing tooth for example ('bellissima donna cui manca un dente' in Bernardo Morando), which can disarrange the perfect order of female beauty sanctioned in the Renaissance. Male poetic imagination is populated with all possible forms of tainted beauty; this fascination for the no-longer-perfect woman stands in opposition to Renaissance Neoplatonic idealization, which is particularly evident in the Petrarchan lyric. Despite the juxtaposition between the Renaissance idealization of woman's perfection and the baroque's praise of female ugliness and deformity, the woman's position in lyric poetry does not change. She continues to appear as the object at disposal of male poets' various agendas.

The collection *Tersicore* (1637) by Alessandro Adimari, a Florentine poet active in the first half of the seventeenth century, provides an eloquent sample of baroque poets' obsession with feminine tainted beauty and their determination to make the homage to woman's beauty as arduous and conceited as possible.[4] Adimari's *Tersicore* has been dismissed by critics like Mario Praz as the product of the worst 'concettismo' and as proof of the inability of baroque poetry to transcend the limits of wit and conceit to achieve that Romantic feeling of sympathy with and participation in the lot of human disfiguration or physical deformity.[5] As indicated by the full-length title of the collection – *Tersicore o vero scherzi, e paradossi poetici sopra la beltà delle donne fra' difetti ancora ammirabili, e vaghe* (Florence: Amadore Massi e Lorenzo Landi, 1637) – Adimari moves in the realm of paradox and joke, which mark the Florentine/Tuscan tradition of bernesque and jocose poetry. Moreover, Adimari attempts to do what Renaissance mock encomia would not: affirm women's beauty despite their defects and physical flaws. Antonio Belloni called *Tersicore* bizarre but not witty and 'apoteosi quanto mai risibile – ma che non fa ridere, anzi irrita ed esaspera – del deforme del ripugnante, dove l'aberrazione diventa addirittura delirio' (68) (ludicrous apotheosis – which does not make one laugh [but] rather irritates and exasperates – of deformity and repugnance, where aberration becomes delirium).[6] Adimari's systematic inventory of defective beauties includes some women of flawed character – the 'bella sdegnosa' (disdainful and beautiful), 'bella insensata' (foolish and beautiful), 'bella incostante' (fickle and beautiful), 'bella dispettosa' (spiteful and beautiful), 'bella astuta' (shrewd and beautiful), 'bella sciatta' (shabby and beautiful), 'bella bugiarda' (beautiful liar) – but it enumerates in more detail physical blemishes and irregularities, all of which are alleged not to undermine the woman's beauty. The catalogue includes 'bella piccola' (beautiful small woman), 'bella gobba' (beautiful hunchback), 'bella zoppa' (beautiful with a limp), 'bella guercia' (beautiful cross-eyed), 'bella muta' (beautiful dumb woman), 'bella sorda' (beautiful deaf woman), 'bella rognosa' (beautiful with mange), 'bella calva' (beautiful bald woman), 'bella cieca' (beautiful blind woman), 'bella butterata' (beautiful pock-marked woman), 'bella negra' (beautiful black woman), 'bella con un occhio' (beautiful woman with one eye), 'bella sfregiata' (beautiful and disfigured woman), 'bella macchiata' (beautiful and stained woman), 'bella sterile' (beautiful and sterile woman), and, to conclude, 'bella morta' (beautiful dead woman), just to mention the most emblematic examples.[7] The poem that most eloquently illustrates Adimari's goal in this collection is the sonnet 'bella totalmente brutta' (beautiful and totally ugly), which presents the most daring and unheard-of challenge for the lyrical poet, a genuine homage to the ugly woman:

> Qui sì, che non potrà lingua mortale,
> con quanti furon mai colori adorni,
> pingere al senso altrui debile, e frale,
> che dove tolto fu l'abito torni,
>
> e pur tu Brutta in fin dal tuo natale
> fra mille di Natura oltraggi, e scorni,
> negro il sen, torto il naso, occhio ineguale,
> di più d'un cuore a trionfar ritorni.
>
> Quell'occulto vigor, quel tuon, quel brio,
> quel, ch'io ridir non so d'alta virtute,
> rapiscon l'altrui vista, e 'l pensier mio.
>
> La triaca così fra l'arti mute
> di mummie, e serpi, e sangue, e tosco rio,
> un composto divien, che dà salute. (109)

(Here, no mortal tongue shall be able to paint, with whichever adorning colours, to the feeble and frail senses, something that could restore what was taken away, and yet you ugly woman ever since your birth, among many ravages and scorns of Nature, with black breasts, crooked nose, squinting eye, you come to triumph over many a heart. Such hidden vigour, such thunder, such liveliness, that high virtue which I cannot say, ravish my thoughts and other people's sight. Likewise theriac, among silent arts, becomes a mixture of mummies, snakes and blood and evil poison, that gives health.)

Such female ugliness is said to be attractive because of the mysteriously powerful, lively presence of this woman, which has managed to ravish the poet's thoughts. Female ugliness is a mere pretext, then, which excites the intellect and acts like theriac ('triaca'), a disgusting concoction that, despite its pestiferous ingredients, restores one's health. This poem marks the departure from Renaissance paradoxical praises such as the 'Stanze in lode della donna brutta,' where the woman was described in her physical ugliness and presented as completely devoid of power to erotically attract the male poet. The 'Bella totalmente brutta' shares with her sixteenth-century predecessors similar repulsive physical features ('negro sen,' 'torto naso,' 'occhio ineguale'), and yet she is made into a source of attraction because of her ugliness. The ugly woman is used as a defective object whose imperfections allow the poet to display his bravura, to exercise his skills, in finding beauty where beauty is absent.

Adimari, like many seventeenth-century poets, also touches upon women's aging in the sonnets for the 'bella antica' and 'bella vecchia.' At first sight, this theme appears to effect a reversal of the loathing and moral contempt for older women expressed in medieval *vituperationes vetularum*. However, the motif of the old and beautiful woman, 'bella vecchia,' so pervasive in baroque poetry, appears in numerous variations and nuances.

Some baroque poets, deeply susceptible to the transience of everything earthly and to the devastating effect of time, claim to be attracted to or sympathetic with beauty in decline. They express their sorrow for the loss of feminine beauty due to aging. Despite the lack of invectives and the more positive treatment of female ugliness/imperfection in baroque poetry, as Marisa Trubiano notes, 'the woman is frozen in time and space, objectified like a precious jewel or decorative art piece affording the poet the opportunity to scrutinize his own feelings, which become completely divorced from the "object" admired. The description of the woman is, therefore, simply a poetic exercise' (179). The emphasis on one specific detail of the woman's body, eulogized and fantasized to the point of exasperation, leads to a fetishistic obsession with women's hair, mouth, birthmarks, or other body parts.[8]

The thematic richness and repetitiveness of baroque poetry in praise of women's physical aspect cannot here be accounted for in its entirety. My focus is instead on the most significant subcategories of the unconventional: the dark lady, the aging woman, and the woman with bodily infestation. These types are relevant for their pervasiveness and because, in their reversal of the medieval and Renaissance canons, they provide a meaningful yet provisional point of closure to this study.[9]

The Dark Lady

In a high literary tradition completely dominated until the sixteenth century by classical models of blonde beauty ('bellezza biondeggiante') and women with complexions as white as snow, the dark lady makes her appearance in lyric, high-style poetry only in the late cinquecento and thrives during the seventeenth century. It might seem somewhat confusing to the modern reader to talk about the dark lady of baroque poetry, for two groups can be distinguished in the motif: the dark-haired and the dark-skinned (or black) woman.[10]

The literary canon sanctioned by Petrarch and Petrarchism contributed to the affirmation of blonde hair as emblem of female beauty. Chapter 3 has shown how, after Petrarch, in the verbal homage to the beloved the lady's golden hair had become the primary symbol of female beauty; Berni and Doni, in their pursuit of anti-Petrarchism, composed sonnets deliberately subverting the most common metaphor used for the lady's hair, switching from gold to silver. Baroque poetry, in its attempt at innovation, draws on Berni and Doni's transgression of the convention but opposes black hair to the canonical blonde, thereby disrupting the pattern of blondeness as a universal symbol of beauty. By paying homage to beautiful women whose hair colour is other than blonde, seventeenth-century poets wittily distance themselves from the Petrarchan model and explore the gamut of possible hues. Giovanni Leone Sempronio and Pier Francesco Paoli praised red hair, and many others focus on dark hair, such as Marcello Giovanetti, Ciro di Pers, and Pietro Casaburi Urries.[11]

A brief examination of the situation before the baroque will serve to establish a possible tradition and dependency. The Bible presents the archetype of all dark beauties: the dark bride in the *Song of Songs*, who praises her own dark beauty: 'nigra sum, sed formosa' (I am dark but beautiful). However, by defining herself as dark *but* comely, the biblical bride stands in opposition to the canon, as a reminder that real beauty lies in its opposite.

Brightness and colour seem to be the two main elements that define female beauty across cultures. The emphasis on light and brightness comes from the medieval belief that beauty is whatever brings light as opposed to darkness, the latter considered a source of ugliness and a symbol of evil. And yet blondness as a symbol of beauty goes as far back as ancient Greek and Roman literature. Ovid stresses the motif in both *Ars amatoria* and the *Epistles*. Rudolf Bähr notes that blonde hair in medieval literature symbolizes high social status, and dark hair is reserved for women of lower rank or servants (145). Moreover, the hair of morally contemptible, dangerous, and evil female characters is often dark. Renier notes that one of the physical characteristics that appears most frequently in medieval European literature is the colour of women's hair, which is predominantly blonde (124). More specifically, Petrarch's Laura is blonde; her blondness is one of the dominant motifs of the *Canzoniere*, and blondness is one feature that has persisted over the centuries as emblem of female beauty both in literature and in life. Other famous literary heroines whose physical beauty has been described in detail share the same hair colour: Boccaccio's six beautiful girls in *Ameto* and Emilia in *Teseida* have blonde hair. In comic-realistic poetry 'grinze e nere' (wrinkled and dark) are negative attributes of old women criticized and ridiculed in medieval invectives. The non-mimetic nature of blonde women in literature is noted by most critics, who see in the colour of the woman's hair the primary element of the literary canon and the prerequisite of beauty.[12] After Petrarch the lyrical tradition is subjected to a strict canon prescribing both the parts of the female body and the way in which they should be described to be considered beautiful.[13] Since golden hair is the ever-present feature of the beautiful woman in literature, most poetry that sets out to deliberately deviate from the canon primarily targets hair colour. Very often, though, the dark beauty only reinforces the stereotype. In literature, being dark-haired and beautiful seems a rare event, already signalled in the *Song of Songs* by the presence of the adversative 'nigra *sed* formosa.' For Pozzi, to declare one's love for a dark lady in poetry was so unconventional before the late Renaissance that it would be perceived as unnatural or even indecent ('Temi,' 431).[14] Pozzi notes that dark beauty does not assert itself until the late cinquecento with Torquato Tasso and Celio Magno.

Tasso, the most authoritative example of infringement upon the canon, included in his *Rime* a mini-cycle of poems in praise of the dark lady. As Getto observes, Tasso's *Rime* represent 'la più vasta e autorevole ricapitolazione della lirica precedente, e insieme ... il punto di partenza della lirica successiva' ('the widest and most authoritative summary of previous lyric and at the same time ... the starting point for the poetry to follow'; *Interpretazione del Tasso*, 257). Tasso's poems on the dark woman do not target specifically the colour of her hair, but rather the entire person's complexion. Book 3 of Tasso's *Rime*, the one that contains 'liriche per varia occasione' (Occasional rhymes), includes canzone 369, 'O con le Grazie eletta,' in praise of the maid of Leonora Thiene Sanvitale, countess of Scandiano. In this canzone, composed in June 1576, the poet, who does not dare turn his gaze to the beautiful countess, diverts his attention to her chambermaid and praises her instead:

Bruna sei tu, ma bella
qual vergine viola; e del tuo vago
sembiante io sì m'appago
che non disdegno signoria d'ancella (434)[15]

(You are dark but beautiful like a virgin violet; and I get so much contentment from your graceful appearance that I do not disdain the sovereignty of a maid.)

The poem juxtaposes the two types of beauty, the conventional one of the countess and the extravagant one of the 'ancella.' The poet who declares his servitude to the beautiful dark maid is a theme that will reappear in Marino's sonnet for the dark slave. In Tasso, as in the biblical source, the adversative 'ma' in 'bruna ... ma bella' indicates an exceptional situation. Tasso's experience marks the early stages in the discovery of a different type of beauty. The praise of the chambermaid is also a stratagem to obtain the favour of the lady through her close servant. Tasso expands on the theme of the dark woman in two madrigals that immediately follow the canzone. Madrigal 372 opens with the same adversative 'Bruna sei tu ma bella,' which is repeated inverted in line 4, 'bella sei tu, ma bruna.'

Bruna sei tu ma bella,
ed ogni ben candore
perde col bruno tuo, giudice Amore.

Bella sei tu, ma bruna;
pur se ne cade incolto
bianco ligustro e negro fiore è colto.
Chi coglie ad una ad una
le tue lodi più elette?
chi te ne tesse in rime ghirlandette? (438–9)

(You are dark but beautiful, and each candour is overcome by your darkness, as Love can testify. Beautiful you are, but dark; and the candid privet falls untouched while the black flower is picked. Who collects, one by one, your special praises? Who weaves in rhymes your garlands?)

The metaphor of the dark flower judged more attractive than the white one indicates that a dark woman can be more desirable than a fair one. Neither poem specifies if the woman is dark-skinned or simply dark-haired. Madrigal 373, 'Bella e vaga brunetta' (Beautiful and graceful brunette), praises the woman's bright eyes; here it is not clear if the 'brunetta' has dark skin or hair or both.

Celio Magno also thematically explored the homage to the dark lady. This Venetian poet and diplomat, active in the second half of the cinquecento, is placed by critics in the trend of late Petrarchism and Mannerism. His collection of *Rime* (Muschi, Venezia: 1600, 54) includes the sonnet 'Nero e crespo ha 'l bel crin madonna' (Dark and curly is my lady's hair), which shows a definite departure from the classic Petrarchan model of feminine beauty. The opening verse reveals the novelty. The focus is on the lady's hair, without an adversative 'ma' as in Tasso, and the praised woman is not a chambermaid, nor is she of the lower social strata; rather, she is the traditional 'madonna' of Petrarchan poetry. Moreover, Magno specifically targets the lady's hair colour rather than generically describing, like Tasso, the darkness of the woman. Edoardo Taddeo notes the contrast generated by the juxtaposition between the dark hair and white face, which creates a charming and seductive effect (165).[16] As will be shown below, the contrast between darkness and brightness (chiaroscuro) is one of the founding elements of the baroque concept of female literary beauty.[17]

The emphasis on innovation, change, and thematic experimentation typical of seventeenth-century poetry is expressed by Giambattista Marino, whose goal was to break with the strict rules of Renaissance classicism.[18] Breaking the rules becomes an experimental exercise for Marino and the Marinisti. They attempt to combine in a new and unusual fashion elements of the previous culture, which has become a mere depository of themes and materials. The index of female beauty expands to include the different, the surprising, and the unconventional.

Marino's role as absolute innovator and initiator of the new school and style of *Marinismo* (according to Benedetto Croce, *Saggi*) has been revised by critics like Ottavio Besomi, who in his study on *La lira* has indicated the importance and influence of Tasso's *Rime* and of the late cinquecento lyric poetry on Marino's new style: Marino is not sole inventor of the new style, but is certainly its best representative (*Ricerche*, 98). For Besomi evidence of a new style, themes, and witty metaphors can be found already in some late sixteenth-century lyricists, who had a crucial impact on Marino. Particular relevance is attributed to Cesare Rinaldi, Guido Casoni, Tommaso Stigliani, and the Academy of the Gelati. This literary circle, founded in Bologna in 1588, whose primary focus was love poetry, is credited with the promotion of new themes different from those of the Petrarchan lyric. Besomi locates the motif of the dark lady in the collection *Ricreationi amorose* published by the Academy in 1590 (before Marino's *La lira*). The anonymous madrigal 22 is about the dark lady:

> Bruna è l'amata mia,
> e più bel m'è il suo brun d'ogni candore,
> e più m'alletta così bruna il core
> che se fosse di neve.
> Amor, son bruno anch'io
> però l'amo e desio,
> unisci Bruna e Brun, ch'a te fia leve,
> ond'io non sol sarò felice amante
> ma tanti bruni e tanti. (Besomi, *Ricerche*, 103)

(Dark is my beloved, and to me her darkness is more beautiful than any whiteness, and so dark she pleases my heart more than if she were of snow. I am dark too but I love and desire her, Love do join Bruna and Bruno, that should be easy for you, and then not only I shall be a happy lover but many, many other dark ones.)

The adjective 'bruna' reveals its indebtedness to Tasso's mini-cycle on the dark lady, while the paronomasia generated by the use of 'bruno/a' as adjective and proper name reveals the poem's wittiness, which makes this lyric closer to baroque poetry than to Tasso. Contrary to Tasso, here there is no adversative 'ma' as a reminder of the exceptionality of dark beauty; rather, the poet asserts the superiority of this beauty to the white one, and the woman is indeed the 'amata' and not a chambermaid.

The explosion of poems on dark ladies in baroque poetry is also attested to by the presence of the brunette in Gabriello Chiabrera (1552–1638), the initiator of the melic trend. Although Chiabrera's main poetic focus was on classical metre and musicality, in his canzonette descriptive elements of the beloved alternate canonical blonde beauty with the dark-haired variety, as in canzonetta 9: 'Del mio sol son ricciutelli i capelli, / non biondetti, ma brunetti' (202) (The hair of my sun is curly, not blonde, but brunette).[19] Chiabrera's popularity as the most celebrated seventeenth-century lyricist after Marino played a significant role in the affirmation in Italy and abroad of the non-canonical type of beauty.[20]

In Praise of Dark Hair

The theme of the dark-haired lady in Italian baroque poetry had considerable impact in its frequency and wide circulation. Following a chronological order, I will provide a representative sample of the motif in the Italian peninsula. Marcello Giovanetti (1598–1631), born in Ascoli Piceno and active in Rome at the papal court in the first decades of the seventeenth century, followed Marino's lead, praising him in a eulogistic sonnet that sparked an enthusiastic reply by the aging laureate, thereby consecrating the young poet's literary career.[21] As well as imbued with the distinctive traits of the baroque lyric, Giovanetti's poetry, William Crelly finds, 'is polite and correct and never betrays the slightest hint of controversy, vulgarity or even satire. Though bright and inventive it is resolutely discreet and high-minded' (9). Giovanetti's poem on dark hair belongs to the collection *Poesie* published in Bologna in 1620. The sonnet 'Loda una chioma nera' was highlighted by Getto as 'una delle liriche più ricche di valori tattili e visivi' ('Introduzione,' 16) (One of the richest in tactile and visual elements). Ferrero deems it the most 'ardito e schietto' (740) among the many on the theme of the beloved's dark hair.

> Chiome, qualor disciolte in foschi errori
> da la fronte vi miro in giù cadenti
> e velate al mio Sol gli aurei splendori,
> siete nubi importune, ombre nocenti.

Ma s'in groppo accogliete i vostri orrori,
nera cote sembrate, ove pungenti
rende Amor le saette; e l'ambre e gli ori
vincete d'ogni crin, chiome lucenti.

Escon da' vostri torbidi volumi,
come lampo talor da nube impura,
verso il mio cor d'accese fiamme i fiumi;

ch'arte fu, non error, se diè natura,
quasi pittor che mesce l'ombre ai lumi,
de la fronte al candor la chioma oscura. (Getto, *I marinisti*, 201–2)

(Hair, when I admire you in dark errors loosely falling down from the forehead, and you veil the golden splendour of my Sun, you are irksome clouds, bothersome shadows. But if you tie in a knot your horrors, you look like black whetstone, where Love sharpens his arrows; and your shiny mane wins the amber and gold of every hair. From your turbid volumes, like sometimes lightning from impure cloud, the rivers of lit flames come towards my heart; it is art, not error, if nature, almost a painter mixing shadow with light, gave to the candid forehead a dark mane.)

The sonnet centres on the juxtaposition of darkness and brightness and marks a clear rift with the medieval/Petrarchan model of female beauty based on colour-light. Here the shift is from classic to baroque aesthetics. Beauty is valued for its pictorial quality of chiaroscuro. Getto ('Introduzione, 17) proclaims this sonnet to be a positive antidote to the rigid stylization of traditional feminine models. The brightness of the dark hair surpasses that of blonde hair, which is devalued. The last stanza affirms the natural and pictorial quality of the contrast between dark hair and a white face. It is not error but art, a form of beauty that draws its worth from the chiaroscuro effect. The legitimation of the dark-haired beauty is effected through the authority of art and nature.

In Venice by the third decade of the seventeenth century, the homage to dark hair in beautiful ladies was the latest fashion in literary circles. At the Academy of the Incogniti Pietro Michiele was lecturing on this topic during its daily sessions. This academy was one of the numerous literary congregations that flourished in Italian cities between the mid-sixteenth and the early seventeenth centuries.[22] According to Giorgio Spini the academy is notable, if not for the quality of its writings, for including among its members the most famous literary figures of the time from Venice and abroad, including Leonardo Quirini, Pace Pasini, Paolo Zazzaroni, Marino, and Achillini, among many others.

In 1632 Pietro Michiele introduced a sonnet by Friulan friar Ciro di Pers to discuss the topic of dark hair at the academy. As indicated in a letter of January 1632, Michiele had invited his friend di Pers to compose the sonnet on 'Chiome nere' for a lecture at the Incogniti.[23] The discussion of dark hair precisely within the academy reveals the topicality of the theme; moreover, given the wide regional representation among the academy's membership, lecturing there about dark-haired female beauty must have contributed to an affirmation and circulation of the model of unconventional beauty outside the circle of Venetian intellectuals. Pietro Michiele, Venetian *literato* and author of *La benda di Cupido* (1634), composed 'versi marinisti' with many thematic parallels to Ciro di Pers. His collection, too, includes a sonnet on 'Chioma nera,' probably a reply to di Pers's 'Chiome nere.'

Di Pers's sonnet places the dark-maned lady at the source of a new type of beauty:

> Chiome etiope, che da' raggi ardenti
> de' duo soli vicini il fosco avete,
> voi di mia vita i neri stami sete
> onde mi fila Cloto ore dolenti.
>
> O del foco d'Amor carboni spenti,
> ma che, spenti, non meno i cori ardete,
> pietre di [Patto] che mostrar solete
> falsi d'ogn'altro crin gli ori lucenti.
>
> O di celeste notte ombre divine,
> in due emisperi è 'l ciel d'Amor diviso
> e voi del giorno suo sete il confine.
>
> Venga chi veder vuole entro un bel viso
> con una bianca fronte e un nero crine
> dipinto a chiaro scuro il paradiso. (22)[24]

(Ethiopian mane, you which from the ardent rays of two suns nearby get your darkness, you are the black threads of my life whereby Clotho spins my painful hours. Oh extinguished cinders of Love's fire, you, though extinguished, do not burn less the heart, you stones of Batto which reveal the falseness of shiny gold in all other hair. Oh celestial shadows of divine night, the heaven of love is divided in two hemispheres and you are the border of its day. Whoever wants to see a beautiful face with white forehead and black hair, come and see paradise painted in chiaroscuro.)

The beloved's hair is described with rich metaphors that reveal di Pers's baroque vein. The parallel with pictorial representation in the final verses, as in Giovanetti, aims at highlighting the effect of chiaroscuro inherent in the contrast between 'bianca fronte' and 'nero crine,' a motif found also in Celio Magno. With a mythological simile di Pers establishes a link between dark hair and the Stone of Batto, a rock believed to unveil false gold: golden hair, then, is no longer the paragon of beauty, since the hair of this lady, dark like the Stone of Batto, can unveil blonde hair as a false symbol of perfection and pulchritude.

Pietro Casaburi Urries, a representative of the 'barocco meridionale,' also dealt with the theme of the beloved's dark hair. Little is known about Casaburi except that he was born in Naples and was active in the second half of the seventeenth century. In the collection *Le sirene*, published between 1676 and 1685, are two sonnets on 'chiome nere.' Critics consider Casaburi's poetry the most eloquent example of the extreme metaphoric use reached by the baroque lyric.[25] Also famous is Casaburi's short tract on metaphor, published as the introduction to *Le sirene*, where he states that the task of poetry is to create 'traslati arditissimi,' as they were used by illustrious poets such as Petrarch and Tasso. Casaburi wrote his poems much later than Giovanetti or di Pers. His homage to dark hair gains authority from more remote mythological stories. The first sonnet on dark hair, 'Bella chioma nera,' is in the 'Concerto Primo' of *Le sirene*.

Tenebroso Meandro, entro il cui giro
naufragato m'avvolgo in dolci errori,
ombra ch'oscuri l'ombra e vinci gli ori,
mentre le tue caligini rimiro,

scorni agl'inchiostri tuoi gli ostri di Tiro,
onde sui petti altrui descrivi ardori,
e dagli ebeni tuoi vinti gli avori,
la tua leggiadra oscurità sospiro.

Notte filata, alle tue chiare luci,
che sul ciel d'una fronte hanno il chiarore,
nel bel regno d'Amor l'alme conduci.

Ma, se notte rassembri al vago orrore,
meraviglia non è s'amor produci,
poiché sol dalla notte è nato Amore. (27)

(Dark Meander, in whose swirl I wrap myself as shipwrecked in your sweet errors, shadow, you obscure the shadow and win over gold, while I admire your soot; you scorn with your ink the purple of Tyre, hence you cause ardour in other bosoms, and since ivory is won by your ebony, I sigh for your graceful obscurity. Nightly threads to your bright lights, which in the sky have the glow of your forehead, you lead the souls in the beautiful reign of Love. But, if you resemble the night in your graceful horror, it is no wonder if you produce love, since Love was born only from the night.)

Like Giovanetti and di Pers, Casaburi places black hair in contrast to the traditional blonde and affirms its superiority. Here the conventional concept of beauty (as colour and light) is reduced to light alone and is rejected. This dark hair not only exceeds in beauty the golden curls of Petrarchan ladies, but also surpasses the 'ostri' and 'avori,' metaphors traditionally used to describe colour (red and white), although here they are meant to refer to brightness overcome by blackness. Casaburi exploits a lesser-known version of the myth of Amore, generated by the union of Night and Erebus, so it is no wonder that this dark beauty produces love.

Casaburi's other sonnet on 'Chiome nere' is in 'Concerto Quarto,' a section subsequently added to the original collection. Casaburi's duplication of the topic, in an attempt to reach the highest level of invention in metaphoric language, reveals his ability in practising *variatio*. The sonnet displays a masterly use of metaphors to designate the beloved's dark hair. Tropes accumulate in a crescendo that climaxes in the first line of the last stanza, where all the metaphors are explicated as witty figures for the 'nero crine.'

Poems on dark hair do not always openly state the beauty of the woman; they also depart from the adversative 'ma' of Tasso, and the darkness is limited to one detail of the woman's body, her hair. By mid-seventeenth century the dark-haired woman is no longer an exception, as she was for Tasso. Now the focus is on the use and quantity of witty and sophisticated metaphors to describe dark hair.

The praise of the beloved's black mane, commending metonymically a part of the female body for the whole, reduces the woman to an object of minute observation and a vehicle for metaphoric invention. We have come to the point of dissolution of the descriptive praise that includes the various body parts. Choosing a single part of the woman's body to symbolize her beauty pushes to the extreme the process of objectification and fragmentation that inevitably mars verbal female portraits. As Nancy Vickers noted for French anatomic blazons, in their restriction of the depiction of the woman to a member of her body these poems are 'the exaggeration to the point of violation of the descriptive mode itself' ('Members Only,' 4). Needless to say, the dark hair of the woman is a mere pretext adopted by the baroque poets to display their prowess; female body parts become matter for poetic aggrandizement.

It is hard to mention a single, precise cause for the vast popularity of the dark-haired beauty in seventeenth-century poetry. The reversal of the Petrarchan model and the espousal of the motif by Tasso are some obvious reasons; however, some other less defined, non-literary influences may have played a role in the enthusiastic embracing of the new literary type, which marked a true revolution in depictions of female beauty. In the seventeenth century dark ladies were becoming more and more attractive to lyric poets across Europe. Shakespeare's cycle of *Sonnets* (1609) in praise of the Dark Lady is perhaps the most eminent example. Shakespeare opens his sequence on the Dark Lady (sonnet 127) by stating the change in the concept of female beauty from fair to black:

> In the old age black was not counted fair,
> or if it were, it bore not beauty's name,
> but now is black beauty's successive heir (96)[26]

Although Shakespeare's example provides the great literary theme for a new tradition of baroque poetry, critics have stressed that, because of her betrayal, the Dark Lady's beauty is tainted by her negativity; she does not serve as a positive model, and confirms the cliché that dark ladies are morally reprehensible or evil.[27]

One possible source of influence on baroque poetry about the dark ladies may be post-Reformation religious iconography, particularly of the Virgin Mary, who at this time begins to be depicted with dark hair. Medieval and Renaissance painting always presents the Virgin Mary as blonde and light-skinned; one need only mention the famous Madonnas of Raphael, Lippi, and Vasari. However, after the Reformation pictorial representations of the Virgin begin to show her, when not veiled, with dark hair, as in some of the famous paintings by Caravaggio. Literature and painting appear to be leading in the same direction, towards female representations that are more realistic.[28]

In Praise of Dark Skin: The Exotic Other

In baroque poetry the dark lady often appears as a woman with black skin. Unlike the colour of hair, which simply marks the difference between a blonde and a brunette, when the entire body colour is concerned there is a shift into a whole different realm of female representation, since issues of race and ethnicity are at stake. The choice of women from racial and ethnic minorities as the subject in these poems requires careful consideration. The main feature that characterizes the poems on dark-skinned women is the use, for rhetorical purposes, of individuals on the margins of the social and ethnic spectrum as poetic subject matter. The racially distinct Other is exploited by the male imagination to produce poetic texts, where the effect of 'meraviglia' derives from emphasis on the exotic and the outlandish. As Francette Pacteau points out, in Western discourse the black woman is doubly Other for being both woman and black. In the aesthetic of the woman she generally embodies ugliness as opposed to beauty (124). Baroque poets strive to conjoin the unattractiveness they inherently associate with blackness with the beauty of the feminine, all in an effort to challenge their poetic virtuosity. By depicting their beloved as black, baroque poets exploit metaphoric potential and the conceited coupling of opposites, to glorify their own art and achieve the utmost 'meraviglia' at the expense of the black woman, who is completely objectified, racially discriminated against, and oppressed. The less canonical and more unattractive the object of representation (woman) is perceived to be, the more challenging the task for the poet. Although praising dark hair required skill and wit, it was still a rhetorical exercise that displayed some renowned precedents, notably Tasso or even Cino da Pistoia. The disruption of the canon was bound to expand beyond dark hair; to be extremely daring poets could apply darkness to the woman's entire body and venture into praise of the black woman. Therefore, praise of black female beauty in baroque poetry is highly ambiguous; it should be evaluated in the context of what critics have viewed as male narcissism.[29] As a convenient occasion for self-aggrandizing, the baroque poet scours all possible variations of female marginality and exploits them as amusing oddities. The slave, the gypsy, the Moor (or the Ethiopian), the shepherdess – as long as the colour of the woman's skin is darker than the conventional snow-white – all these incarnations of the exotic Other are viable sources of poetic exploitation.[30]

In Giambattista Marino's sonnet in praise of a beautiful black slave, the challenge of extolling the black woman is even more conceited, because the woman is not only racially Other, but also socially outcast. Slavery is the emblem of complete oppression and domination. His sonnet on the 'bella schiava' exploits the potential inherent in the darkness as traditional symbol of ugliness, and turns it into the utmost example of beauty. In his idyll on the 'Bruna pastorella' the exotic Other is a shepherdess from a fictional pastoral setting who is compared, for extra-estranging effect, to a gypsy.

Other clichés used in baroque poetry to depict woman's blackness are the Ethiopian and the Moor, two figures that appeared in the mid-sixteenth-century 'Stanze in lode della donna brutta,' in paradoxical praise of the ugly woman. Our informed eye today allows us to acknowledge how Western imagination has used people of colour for a discourse of discrimination, oppression, and exploitation.[31] In seventeenth-century Italy black women were primarily rare and treasured servants, or other eccentric figures, kept as rarities in the houses of the aristocracy. Female slaves from Russia, Asia, and North Africa were quite common in Italian households up to the fifteenth century.[32] Later, with the closure of slave markets to Italian trade and with the fall of Constantinople, slaves were few and far between; in the sixteenth and seventeenth century they were found only in the houses of the rich, who acquired them as curious ornaments or diverting toys. At the court of Isabella d'Este and of other great ladies, slaves adorned the house and were kept as half-pets and half-buffoons. Coloured maids were known to be favourites among the aristocracy precisely because they had become so scarce and difficult to find, and were exploited as symbols of elitist status.[33] Ladies of high rank would keep dark-coloured pages and slave girls, which served to highlight by contrast their light-skinned beauty.[34] Servants of colour, then, fulfilled the precise function of exotic objects that aristocrats collected as evidence of their status and power. Besides being monsters of beauty, black women in baroque poetry functioned as *monstra*, that is, *mirabilia*, rare objects for collection and display that, starting in the sixteenth-century, began to cram nobles' and amateur scientists' *Wunderkammern* and *studioli*.[35]

Marino's sonnet 'Negra, sì, ma se' bella' is precisely in praise of a slave girl, but one cannot consider his homage to a representative of the oppressed a cry for racial equality, nor should one expect that this poem refers to an existing woman. The colour of the woman's skin and her ambivalent position as dominated/dominating are exploited by Marino for best rhetorical effect of 'meraviglia' and witticism. The sonnet, also known as 'La bella schiava,' belongs to the 'Amori,' one section of Marino's collection *La lira* (1604).

> Nera, sì, ma se' bella, o di natura
> fra le belle d'amor leggiadro mostro;
> fosca è l'alba appo te, perde e s'oscura
> presso l'ebeno tuo l'avorio e l'ostro.
>
> Or quando, or dove il mondo antico o il nostro
> vide sì viva mai, sentì sì pura,
> o luce uscir di tenebroso inchiostro,
> o di spento carbon nascere arsura?
>
> Servo di chi m'è serva, ecco ch'avolto
> porto di bruno laccio il core intorno,
> che per candida man non fia mai sciolto.
>
> Là 've più ardi, o Sol, sol per tuo scorno
> un sole è nato; un sol, che nel bel volto
> porta la notte, ed ha negli occhi il giorno. (Ferrero, 374)

(You are black but beautiful, oh comely monster of nature among the beauties of love; dark is dawn compared to you, beside your ebony ivory and purple dwindle and darken. When or where the ancient world or ours ever saw alive, or felt such pure light come out of gloomy ink or heat be born from burnt out cinders? I am the servant of my slave, here I carry the dark noose wrapped around my heart, that no white hand could ever untie. Oh Sun, where you burn the most, for your scorn only was born a sun, which in her beautiful face carries the night, and has in her eyes the daylight.)

This sonnet's *incipit* clearly echoes Tasso, where beauty is stated despite darkness, and therefore constitutes an exception that reaffirms the stereotype of the blonde. Dark female beauty is an exotic and rare event, marked by the adversative 'ma' that confirms the unconventionality of this type of feminine beauty. Marino opts for 'nera' instead of Tasso's 'bruna,' an adjective that defines more precisely the woman's racial difference. The blackness is reinforced when the poet states that 'nel bel volto porta la notte.' The sonnet about the 'bella schiava' is also a reminder that this beautiful woman, rather than being a member of an inferior social class, is a complete outcast from society, since as a slave she is the property of someone else. Servant and slave provide Marino with a suitable pretext for a pun on the traditional role of the poet as servant of love and of the beloved. In a reversal of traditional clichés, the poet becomes slave not to the lady/domina, but to a slave/dominated woman. Style and language are high, in the manner of the Petrarchan lyric, but the thematic juxtaposition of light and darkness produces bold effects in the metaphors, a typical strategy of baroque poetry. The dark woman is praised for her beauty and is also called 'leggiadro mostro' (lovely monster), an epithet that synthesizes the oxymoronic structure of the entire sonnet. The word 'monster' in its ambivalence gives way to the witticism. 'Monster' defines a deformed/monstrous human being, but in its Latin root ('monstrum') it indicates an exceptional, peculiar, marvellous phenomenon for admiration and display ('monstrare'), a *mirabilia* for everyone to admire. As in the case of the dark slaves at Renaissance courts, or the object in the *Wunderkammer*, the woman of colour becomes an object of display. The poet, as the aristocratic collector of the *Wunderkammer*, can show off the marvelous, precious object, which increases his prestige. For Marino the dark lady here is like the *mirabilia*, a source of marvel, 'meraviglia,' that can give him more luster and importance by enabling him to display a 'leggiadro mostro' and his poetic virtuosity. 'Alba,' 'avorio,' and 'ostro,' classic tropes used by Petrarch and the *Petrarchisti* to praise woman's luminosity, are obscured by the 'ebano' and 'inchiostro'of the beautiful dark woman, or, rather, light itself is said to arise from the 'tenebroso inchiostro' of the black woman. The metaphors in the last stanza sum up the conflation of opposites, of light and darkness. The woman's face contains both the night (darkness) in her skin and the shining sun (light) in her eyes.[36]

The image of the dark lady is revisited by Marino in the idyll *Bruna pastorella* from *La sampogna*, a collection dated 1620, chronologically subsequent to *La lira*. This poem, one of Marino's most famous pieces, is in Ferrero's view a remarkable document of self-description (509).

Through the words of the shepherds Lilla and Lidio, Marino takes the opportunity to talk about himself and to mention some of the poems that marked his success, among them the sonnet for the 'Bella schiava.' In this 'idillio pastorale' Marino explores another aspect of the exotic Other. His homage to dark beauty is addressed to the shepherdess Lilla, a woman with dark skin. This poem strives to make the dark woman an assertive model of female beauty. Marino establishes a parallel with figurative art and rediscovers Neoplatonic influences to legitimize the new beauty. Dark beauty is a perfect model, a true idea.

> Ninfa del ciel, quando il tuo bel sembiante
> prese a formar Natura,
> fe' qual pittor ben saggio,
> che con rozzo carbone abbozza in prima,
> quasi vil macchia oscura,
> ombreggiata figura, onde poi tragge
> colorite e distinte
> meravigliose imagini dipinte;
> perché la tua bellezza,
> disegnata di negro, è l'idea vera,
> il perfetto modello,
> dal cui solo essemplare
> prende ogni altra beltà quanto ha di bello. (Ferrero, 516)

(Nymph of heaven, when Nature began to shape your beautiful appearance, she acted like a wise painter, who first sketches with rough charcoal, almost a vile dark blotch, a shady figure, and then draws colourful and neat marvellous painted images; hence your beauty, drawn in black, is the true idea, the perfect model, the only example from which every other beauty takes what is beautiful in itself.)

Here Marino daringly states that dark beauty actually precedes and therefore is the foundation of any other form of female beauty. However, the dark woman is neither noble nor of high rank; rather, she is a shepherdess in the fictional bucolic world. Furthermore, the genre explored by Marino is the pastoral, not lyric poetry. The dark beautiful woman is compared to a gypsy, another type of the exotic so popular in the seventeenth century. Praise of the gypsy was common in baroque poetry, and it reflects an attraction to the exotic, usually identified with Africa, Egypt, Ethiopia, or other geographical places perceived as foreign and distantly appealing.³⁷ The exotic is also implicit in the words 'egizia vagante' used for the 'pastorella.' The passage from the sonnet for the 'bella schiava' to the *idillio* would seem to indicate an evolution, the espousal of the new style of 'poesia moderna,' in opposition to the Petrarchan canon; where the dark woman before was the exception to the conventional model of beauty (marked by the adversative 'nera, ma bella'), here the dark woman is at the origin of every beauty, as a Platonic idea, a model of modern style for other poets to follow.

Marino returns to celebrate the dark woman in *Adone*, but this time he limits the darkness to Venus's hair. Again the inspiration is provided by the exotic Other. In canto 15, where the reunion of long-separated Venus and Adone takes place, Venus appears disguised as a dark-haired gypsy. Octave 29 describes the 'donzella' as 'brunetta sì, ma sovr'ogn'altra bella' (brunette, but more beautiful than any other).³⁸ Marino experiments with the motif of the dark lady in different literary genres: the lyric sonnet, the pastoral eclogue, and the heroic poem. By reiterating the motif in different literary genres, he contributed to the consolidation and affirmation of a model that will influence many baroque poets inside and outside Italy.³⁹

The pair 'bruna ma bella' appears also in Girolamo Fontanella, a Neapolitan (1612~1643/44), considered by critics one of the best representatives of the 'barocco meridionale.'⁴⁰ His poem 'La bella bruna' begins with some rhetorical questions that attempt to investigate the origin of darkness in the beautiful lady. The opening, 'Zingaretta d'amore, / come bruna tu sei?' (Little gypsy of my love, / how come you are dark?'), follows the lines of 'Bruna pastorella,' where the exotic Other appears as a gypsy; and the 'zingaretta leggiadra' (comely little gypsy) evokes Venus disguised as a gypsy in Marino's *Adone*.⁴¹ The first three stanzas of Fontanella's poem are rhetorical questions on what causes the beloved to be dark. The second-last stanza revisits Marino's concept of Nature, setting an example of excellence where, for Fontanella, ultimate beauty draws its power from the contrast between darkness and light:

Nel bruno ch'in te accolse
la maestra Natura
altro mostrar non volse
ch'è più bella tra l'ombre alma pittura,
e dinotar che ne gli aerei campi
da la nuvola bruna escono i lampi. (187)

(In the darkness which Nature welcomed in you, as a master she just wanted to show that excellent painting is more beautiful in the shadows; and she wanted to highlight that in airy fields from a dark cloud comes lightning.)

The last stanza consecrates dark beauty through a mythological simile and identifies the dark beautiful woman with 'Notte,' the night, as the moment of death and as the time of erotic pleasure: 'Ma se Notte sei tu, prima ch'io mora, / fammi goder del tuo bel corso un'ora' (But if you are Night, before I die, let me enjoy one hour of your beautiful presence).

Leonardo Quirini, a Venetian noble who belonged to the Academy of the Incogniti, published his verse collection *Vezzi d'Erato* in 1649. His madrigal 'La bella bruna' opens with a line that presents a witty variation on the scheme initiated by Tasso and consolidated by Marino:

Bruna sei tu, ma 'l bruno
in guisa tal col bello tuo si mesce
che beltà non ti toglie, anzi t'accresce;
e di quel brun s'appaga
mia vista sì che di mirarti è vaga;
come agli occhi è più grato
cinto di nube il sol, che disvelato. (Getto, *I marinisti*, 495)

(You are dark, but darkness in you mingles so well with beauty that it does not take away, rather it increases, beauty; and my sight is so satisfied with that darkness that it longs to admire you; the sun is more pleasing to the eyes when wrapped in the clouds, than unveiled.)

This poem does not specify what feature of the woman is dark; we presume the entire face is dark. The poem, as in the case of many others, links beauty with sunlight and plays a witty game with the contrast between light and darkness; dark beauty is compared to the sun covered by clouds, which is more agreeable to the lover's eyes.

Giuseppe D'Alessando (1656–1715), who was from the Naples area, composed a madrigal with the title 'Per donna mora,' where the exotic Other appears in another of its variations, the Moor. 'Moro/a,' as both noun and adjective, in Italian lends itself to a double meaning. It defines the ethnicity of a person from North Africa (Ethiopia, Mauritania), a member of mixed Arab and Berber descent, but it also more generally indicates a person with darker complexion and dark hair. The opening line 'Moro per donna mora' (I'm dying for a dark woman), with its use of paronomasia, plays on the polysemy of the word 'mora' as both dark and Moor, and on the double grammatical function of 'moro,' which can act both as first person of the verb 'morire' ('to die,' a verb used in love lyric to define erotic passion) and as adjective/noun:

> Moro per donna mora:
> ella per me non more,
> anzi torva mi mira
> sprezzando il mio dolore;
> spesso fra morte e vita mi raggira:
> mio cor, tu che credevi
> dal ritratto d'inferno
> se non fiero tormento e cruccio interno?
> Ah no, che pur l'eban del caro viso
> languendo ammiro e mi ravviso anciso. (Getto, *I marinisti*, 466)

(I am dying for a dark woman: she does not die for me, rather she looks at me gloomily, despising my sorrow; often she keeps me between life and death: my heart, what did you think you could get from that portrait of hell other than fierce torment and inner trouble? Oh no, and yet the ebony of her dear face I admire languishing and I find myself dead.)

The ambiguity of the beloved called 'mora' allows for the exploitation of another incarnation of the exotic Other: the African, Moorish woman praised for her dark beauty. The metaphors 'eban' for the face and the 'ritratto d'inferno' betray the true perception of female darkness as the horror of infernal darkness produced by the lady's surly look at the poet ('torva mi mira'). The unresponsive woman breaks the poet's heart by not reciprocating his love, so that she kills him slowly. Again, the dark lady as 'mora' provides an occasion for a pun on the verb 'moro,' as well as the adjective qualifying her darkness, 'mora.' The exotic Other is a mere pretext used by the baroque poet to exploit the polysemy of language and to display his technical skills.

This mania for the dark lady during the seventeenth century is remarkable; it is a true exploitation of a racial female type for the sake of 'meraviglia' and metaphoric invention.[42] Clear evidence of the far-reaching impact of this motif is the appearance of burlesque imitation and parodies in the seicento. The dark lady becomes the object of satire and parody in Pier Salvetti's poem in praise of a 'Bella donna mora.'

Salvetti (1609–52), a Florentine priest, displays in this poem the antibaroque tendency of Florence. He uses the burlesque *capitolo*, the meter preferred by Berni, and parodies baroque poetry in the same way that Berni did Petrarchism in his famous paradoxical love poems.[43]

Female Old Age Revisited

Concern with the transience of everything earthly is a constant and obsessive theme in seicento poetry. Female ugliness as physical decay fits within the framework of human life's instability and constant mutability, which leads to aging, decline, and death. Even the most perfect beauty is doomed to change, and baroque poets lament the loss of woman's beauty due to the passing of time. However, to them woman's aging does not necessarily lead to ugliness and is not a symbol of evil. Feminine old age is perceived as beauty in decline. Descriptions of female ugliness due to aging are no longer a source of invective or scorn, but are couched in ambiguity, ranging from genuine sympathy to mild reprimand for woman's unresponsiveness, to witty humour. Woman is portrayed in the stages of aging. If the ugly and old were previously limited to the comic-realistic and in general confined to misogynist attacks in low genre, the baroque reveals a contamination of comic and aulic themes all mingled in high-style poetry. The relish of the 'Lirici marinisti' for descriptions of physical decay finds in the aging female body a fertile ground for representations of daring, conceited poetry, whose true purpose again is the glorification of the poet's skills rather than genuine interest in the fate of mature women. The motif of the aging beloved and her loss of beauty was inaugurated in high lyrical style by Petrarch, soon followed by Boccaccio, both of whom composed poems for the 'amata incanutita,' or grey-haired beloved. Petrarch and Boccaccio react differently to the evidence of female physical decline. Boccaccio, in line with the secular urgency of the *carpe diem*, deprecates the lady's cruelty and detachment and warns her to reciprocate his love before it is too late. There is some degree of pleasure taken by the poet who describes the devastating effect of time on the beloved's body ('le chiome d'oro, / vegga d'argento,' 'crespo farsi il viso di costei / e cispi gli occhi bei,' 'donna ... pallid'e vizza,' xliv; I see the golden hair made silver, her face becomes wrinkled and rheumy her beautiful eyes, woman ... pale and withered). According to Nella Giannetto, Boccaccio displays a vindictive attitude in reminding the lady of the horrible transformation that time will effect on her body, as if he wanted to stir regret for her rejection of him (29). In an attempt to control anxieties about his own aging, the poet takes aim at the beloved's beauty, supporting Dubrow's claim, of English early-modern poetry (234), that the *carpe diem* tradition often encodes poets' fear of their own mortality.

Petrarch touches on the theme of the aging Laura in sonnet 12 of his *Canzoniere*. Laura's perfect beauty is not attacked, even when she is described in a perspective of caducity ('De' be' vostr'occhi il lume spento,' 'e i cape' d'oro fin farsi d'argento'; The light of your beautiful eyes is extinguished; and the hair of fine gold becomes silvery). For Giannetto the transience of Laura's beauty in the context of aging is no longer feared but almost desired. Boccaccio's vindictiveness for unrequited love in Petrarch turns into elegy.

Torquato Tasso revisits in celebratory poetry the theme of the aging woman, and actually moves away from both vindication and elegy, electing instead to extol mature beauty. In his sonnet 'Ne li acerbi anni tuoi purpurea rosa,' addressed to Lucrezia D'Este, Tasso treats the problem of fleeting female beauty, but solves it in positive terms by declaring the survival of beauty confronted with the effects of time on the woman's body. Woman's beauty is not univocal. It is not just the splendour of the rising sun (youth), but also that of the sun at noon (maturity). Tasso, unlike Berni or Doni, deals with female aging seriously. For Tasso the charm of female beauty can persist and resist the passing of time. The medieval equation of old age and ugliness is finally dissolved.

Baroque lyrics on the aging woman reflect the modes that have been briefly sketched above. Some poets favour Petrarch's elegiac tones and sympathetically lament the beloved's loss of beauty. Some, like Tasso, extol the beauty of maturity, and others, like Boccaccio, insist on woman's haughtiness and proud rejection, revealing a sort of pleasure in lingering on the woman's physical decay.

Purely elegiac are Ciro di Pers's sonnets on 'Ama la sua donna ancorché men bella' (He loves his lady despite her diminished beauty) devoted to Nicea (Taddea di Collaredo), where the traditional Neoplatonic formula of love-beauty is reworked in the declaration of love's independence from external beauty. In the sonnet sequence for Nicea, di Pers proposes a concept of love no longer bound to perfection and immutability; rather, he opts for a personal and sentimental view of love and beauty, wherein love immortal triumphs over external beauty's transient fragility. ('Sempre per me tu sarai bella / ed io sempre amante per te,' 24; To me you will always be beautiful, and I shall always be your lover). Di Pers's other sonnet about Nicea's declining beauty ('Veggio veggio,

Nicea, le tue vezzose') has a more elegiac and lamenting tone, as the poet observes the effects of time on the woman's body: colour, luminosity, freshness of face are disappearing and yet the poet's love hasn't diminished: 'Scema in te la bellezza ... // ma non scema però l'affetto mio' (23; Beauty is diminishing in you ... but my love for you has not decreased).[44]

The Veronese Paolo Zazzaroni also mourns the loss of beauty in his beloved's body in the sonnet 'Non lascia d'amare la sua donna bench'ella invecchi' (He does not stop loving his beloved, despite her aging). The descriptive technique is the traditional one of Petrarchan lyric, yet the hair has turned silver, the eyes are compared to the setting sun, and the forehead is full of wrinkles. The poet in elegiac tone affirms the persistence of his love for her. Female beauty is no longer assumed to be eternal and unchangeable, as the Petrarchan model had presented it; beauty is unstable, precarious, and subject to the effects of time.

Like Boccaccio, other baroque poets pair the lament for beauty's fugacity with disapproval of the beloved's distance. Bernardo Morando (Genoa, 1589–1656) composed a sonnet on 'Bellezza fugace' where the lover Lidia is accused of being excessively proud of her beauty and is reminded of the transience of her looks. Female old age looms, and the poet describes it with those classic descriptive elements of bodily decay.

> A fior di gioventù fede non serba
> aspro giel di vecchiezza: or or vedrai
> cader neve sul capo, ombra sui rai,
> matura infradiciar l'etade acerba.
>
> Dannoso cambio, o Bella: ahi quelle brine
> avrai tosto nel crin, ch'or hai nel seno,
> e le crespe nel sen, ch'or hai nel crine. (Getto, *I marinisti*, 24)

(The harsh frost of old age does not keep faith with the flowers of youth; soon you'll see snow fall on your head, shadow on your rays, early green age rot in maturity. Harmful change, you Beautiful: alas that frost soon shall be in your hair, that now is in your breast, and the creases in your breast, that are now in your hair.)

The vindictive tone Morando takes against the beloved is also noticeable in Giuseppe Salomoni's sonnet 'Bellezza caduca e crudele.' The macabre decay brought about by death will turn even the graceful body of the obstinate and hard-hearted woman into 'limo deforme e terra oscura' (deformed mud and dark earth). Following Tasso's approach, Fabio Leonida is among the proclaimers of intensified female beauty in the aging woman. In the sonnet 'La bellezza al tramonto,' he states that time has allowed the beloved's beauty to grow more intense: 'anzi col tempo avien che 'l volto sia / cresciuto in maestà, l'alma in valore' (rather with time your face has gained more majesty and your soul more value) (Croce, *Lirici marinisti*, 204).

The loss of female beauty causes either melancholy and sadness, or vengefulness in the male poet who intends to punish the beloved's obstinate rejection. These two themes are so common in baroque poetry that the following are but a few representative examples: Giambattista Pucci penned a sonnet 'Oimé quel viso, amore, oimé quel petto' (Alas your face, my love, alas your breast) where he shares the sadness over his beloved's decaying beauty; Giovanni Canale has one sonnet on 'Beltà fugace' (Fleeting beauty), Pietro Michiele composed 'Ricorda alla sua donna che invecchierà' (He reminds his Lady that she will get old); Giuseppe Battista in 'La donna invecchiata nel giardino' (The aged woman in the garden) employs some clichés of medieval vituperative descriptions to depict the aging envious woman ('di solchi annosi il volto arata,' the face plowed by old furrows; 'col volto rugoso,' with wrinkled face [Croce, *Lirici marinisti*, 425]). The woman's envy, the usual feeling of old women towards younger ones in medieval poetry, is directed here to the *locus amoenus*, whose flowering beauty contrasts with her wrinkled body. The garden becomes the metaphorical site of juxtaposition between woman's bodily decay and the luxuriant beauty of the vegetation, whose specimens are traditional objects for comparison with female beauty. The myth of Platonic immutable beauty promoted by Petrarchism is revised and reduced, in light of a new concept of life shadowed by impending decay and death.[45]

An emblematic use of traditional Petrarchan language and style in combination with the subversive motif of praised feminine old age is found in the canzone 'La bella vecchia' by Giuseppe Salomoni. Included by Asor Rosa among the 'Marinisti di più stretta osservanza' (*La lirica*, 73), Salomoni displays in the canzone 'La bella vecchia' ironic awareness of his conceited style. The poem about the beautiful old woman artfully crosses the fine line between the serious and the comic; the parodistic undertone is concealed so effectively that we are left uncertain whether this poem should be read seriously or not. The deliberate ambiguity remains throughout, but the allegedly sympathetic eye of the poet towards the aging woman cannot be taken at face value, nor is it clear whether or not the poem is really about an aging woman at all; the closing stanza reveals the complexity and ironic ambivalence of the poem. This canzone belongs to Salomoni's *Rime* published in Udine in 1615. After the parodies of *Antipetrarchisti* such as Berni or Doni, Tasso's sincere homage to mature female beauty, and countless baroque conceited exaltations of old deformed women, Salomoni's treatment of the aging woman motif is quite original. In Berni the woman's old age was only deducible from the grey hair of the beloved, and in Doni it was slightly more prominent through details of the wrinkled face; in general, though, anti-Petrarchan poetry did not elect female old age as the main thematic impetus for poetic composition, as occurs in baroque lyric. Salomoni subtitles his canzone a 'palinode,' a subtle hint at the text's ambiguity. His homage to aging beauty is a retraction of another canzone, 'La brutta vecchia,' in which, in line with medieval misogynistic tradition, the poet reproached the old woman for uselessly attempting to revive her aging body with make-up and props. In 'La bella vecchia' Salomoni intends to effect a reversal of the tradition by changing style and content.

> Già menzognero e stolto
> biasmai, vecchia gentile,
> il tuo sen, la tua chioma, e 'l tuo bel volto;
> or, cangiando pensier, vo' cangiar stile,
> e farti udir d'ogni menzogna mia
> una palinodia: (285)

(Liar and fool, oh gentle lady, I previously scorned your breast, your hair, and your beautiful face. Now, since I changed my mind, I shall change my style and I want to let you hear of all those lies a palinode.)

Is this a paradoxical praise or not? It would seem to be, except that paradoxical praises usually state a supposed fact that is then refuted by the evidence presented throughout the text. Here the poet admits the lack of beauty in the female aging body, but continues to extol the attractiveness of the old woman. The whole canzone is based on concessive syntactic structures with 'ma' and 'sebbene.' As prescribed by rhetoric, the old woman's portrait is complete and follows the descending order from head to toe. The light of her eyes is fading and languishing, and yet it ignites in the poet the ardour of love. The wrinkles in her neck, cheeks, and breasts, thanks to passionate love, are still 'trofei di leggiadria, non di difetto' (trophies of comeliness, not defects). Bàrberi Squarotti finds the poem's orginality not so much in its praise of the most difficult type – of the beautiful and old woman – but in the 'audacia descrittiva' which 'coniuga sensualità estrema e insistenza sulla vecchiezza delle forme' (descriptive audacity, [which] conjugates extreme sensuality and insistence on the aging body forms) ('Introduzione,' xiii). The female body's physical decay becomes a challenging site for the poet's display of witticism, in a virtuoso performance that climaxes in the finale:

Sì, sì, bella mia vecchia,
vecchia sei, ma leggiadra,
e nel tuo bel la gioventù si specchia; (287–8)[46]

(Yes, yes, my beautiful old lady, you are old but comely, and in your beauty youth is mirrored;)

The reference to the beauty of the old lady reflected in youth ('nel tuo bel la gioventù si specchia') is particularly ambiguous if read in relation to the final stanza (envoi), where a direct connection between the canzone and the aging woman is established: 'Canzon, sen vola il tempo, / ma non temer però le sue quadrella, / ché diverrai ne l'invecchiar più bella' (288) (Canzone, time flies, but do not worry about its arrows, since, in getting older, you will become more beautiful). The courtly homage to the aging woman finally appears for what it really is, a hymn to the canzone, or to poetry itself, which should not be concerned about the passing of time, since poetry gains in beauty through aging. For Asor Rosa this poem is different from other baroque lyrics in praise of deformed or ugly women because it reveals the irony of the poet, whose intention right from the start is to showcase his witty ingenuity (*La lirica del seicento*, 73). Salomoni is not really interested in the tragedy of the loss of woman's beauty, since he effects a substitution of the old woman for old poetry; what matters here is the ability of poetry to resist the effects of time and retain its charm. If the aging woman is a metaphor for the canzone and poetry in general, the line 'nel tuo bel la gioventù si specchia' (in your beauty youth is mirrored) may be read as a hint to modern/new poetry, baroque poetry (as old and new at once), which is reflected in the aging woman's alleged beauty.[47] The wit is quite subtle here, and it masks an implicit ironical criticism of baroque poetry itself inherent in the connection between young/modern poetry and the aging, decaying lady. The witty game on old woman/new poetry allows the poet to produce 'meraviglia' and self-aggrandizement and at the same time to look ironically at it. Bàrberi Squarotti emphasizes the reversal of the poetical canon of beauty: irony and subtle game are employed to achieve utmost inventiveness (xii). This procedure is used over and over again throughout Salomoni's collection; he commends in other canzoni the beautiful woman with freckles ('le lentigini'), the beautiful mute woman ('la bella muta'), and even the woman with a limp ('la bella zoppa'). Salomoni uses his canzoni to pursue his poetic agenda. In Bàrberi Squarotti's words:

> L'ironia e il piacere non sono più nel capovolgimento delle regole canoniche di raffigurazione poetica o in prosa della bellezza femminile e della giovinezza, ma nella dimostrazione dell'abilità compositiva e sinonimica e di accostamento di suoni e immagini che il poeta esibisce fino al vistuosismo. ('Introduzione,' vii)

> (Irony and pleasure no longer lie in the reversal of the canonic rules of poetic or prose representation of female beauty and youth, but in the demonstration of the ability of the composition and of the use of synonyms, and in the coupling of sounds and images that the poet exhibits to the point of virtuosity.)

In such male display of virtuosity and poetic self-glorification Bàrberi Squarotti, however, fails to point out the objectifying results for women. Although Salomoni appears to reverse the traditional scheme of aging woman/ugliness and negativity, the ironic use of the decaying female body as a metaphor for young poetry is a masterly twist that implies a covert critique of the baroque poet on the deformities of 'poesia marinista'; in this sense, feminine old age and bodily decay remain vehicles for negativity. In a culture where women exist only in virtue of their physical attractiveness, old age and loss of beauty can hardly inspire genuine sympathy. While in the previous three centuries the male poetic imagination viewed female old age as an abhorrence and inveighed against it, baroque lyricists do include aging women in their agenda of poetic novelty and self-glorification but, as Salomoni's poem proves, they do not free aging female bodies from negativity and reification.

Lice and Fleas: Beauty and Vermin between Witticism and Parody

Unconventional beauty meets ugliness and the vestiges of the disgusting Other in some seicento lyrics where homage is paid to contaminated pulchritude. This poetry, classified by critics as baroque grotesque, reveals seventeenth-century poets' extreme delight in creating excessive, disgusting images for the sake of the utmost astonishment, exaggeration, and conceit, still incognizant of the modern appeal to ugliness, which inspired Romantic poets to sympathetically unveil the tragic aspect of human deformity, bodily infestation, and decay.[48]

Witticism, conceit, and metaphorical invention led to the most shocking and incongruous predications of female beauty, such as one that inflects physical attractiveness with disfigurement caused by bodily contamination or parasitic disease. The presence of fleas, lice, mites, and even mange/scabies on the beloved's body was exploited in baroque lyric with striking effects.

For Paolo Zazzaroni and Giuseppe Artale a flea on the beloved's breast allows for wider exposure of the body part, with piquant effect.[49] Zazzaroni's 'Ad un pulice per cagion del quale vide scoperto il seno a bella donna' (1641) and Artale's 'Pulce sulle poppe di bella donna' (1658) are epitaphs on the fleas killed by the 'amata.' Both sonnets exploit the combination of erotic and voyeuristic pleasure in looking at the woman's breasts and the astonishment, even disgust, at the presence of the bodily parasite. It is hard to determine whether seventeenth-century readers would have shared our instinctive sense of repulsion at the idea of a parasitic insect associated with uncleanliness on the beautiful female body. After all, as Georges Vigarello has argued, up to the eighteenth century bodily vermin was a fact of everyday life for everyone and transcended class distinctions.[50] Seventeenth-century readers may not have directly connected fleas with uncleanliness, but lyric poetry describing the presence of such an insect on the beloved's body was bound to produce 'meraviglia,' erotic titillation, combined with a sense of distaste. Both Artale's and Zazzaroni's sonnets, which focus on the privileged position of the little insect capable of direct access to the woman's breast, are hyperbolic hymns to the heroic fate of the flea killed by the lady.

Poems in praise of the flea reflect a vast tradition of eulogies of mosquitos, mites, flies, and other animals that live in close proximity to the desired woman. Marcel Françon, in an extensive study of the *topos* in love poetry, singles out as the source for all poems about the flea on the beloved's breast the pseudo-Ovidian Latin *Carmen de Pulice*, a poem where the flea is praised as accomplice of a gallant occasion (326).[51] Eulogies of animals enjoyed wide popularity in the Renaissance. Ortensio Lando composed a series of facetious animal eulogies in his *Sermoni funebri nella morte di diversi animali* (1548), and Lodovico Dolce exploits the motif in his salacious 'Capitolo del Pulice' (published in 1555); the interest in the flea pervades all of Europe, in England with John Donne's 'The Flea' (1633), in France with Ronsard's 'Folastrie VI' (1553), and climaxing with the publication in 1582 of the collection *La Puce de Madame Des Roches*.[52]

If praise of fleas is a tolerable occasion for witty homage to female beauty, particularly for the titillation created by the fantasy of the beloved's exposed breast, the shift from fleas to lice diminishes the eroticism and increases the disgust, since lice are more obviously linked with uncleanliness. However, this shift allows some baroque poets to up the ante in the search for daring metaphors and astonishing effects via which they paid homage to any aspect of the beloved's body, even when that body houses unclean insects.[53] The praise of lice or other vermin on the female body or hair amounts to a true subgenre of baroque lyric, where disgust prevails over gallantry and sensuality. Besomi (*Esplorazioni*, 82) believes this genre was inaugurated by Giambattista Mamiani, who penned the sonnet 'La bella pidocchiosa' (*Rime*, 1620) and continued with Anton Maria Narducci's infamous pair of sonnets, one on mites under the beloved's skin ('Cava un pedicello alla sua donna') and another about lice in her hair ('Bella pidocchiosa').[54] These poems are unanimously deemed by critics the most disgusting expression of *Marinismo*. In fact, Salvator Rosa may have had in mind verses from Narducci's 'Bella pidocchiosa' when he launched his fierce attack on contemporary poetry in his satire 'La poesia.'[55]

Narducci's sonnet is more widely known because of its inclusion in Croce's, Ferrero's, and Getto's anthologies. However, Mamiani's poem, since it was published three years earlier and most likely served as the model for Narducci's, deserves greater consideration:

> Ne la selva gentil d'aurato crine
> vidi fere vagar leggiadre e snelle
> e in varie torme unitamente belle
> far del candido sen dolci rapine;
>
> altre liete scherzar sovra il confine
> del bianco collo e con gemmata pelle
> sembrar quasi nel ciel lucide stelle
> o perle dentro il mar candide e fine.

Quivi, qual cacciatore, il dito audace
con lo strale de l'ugna ogn'or procura
a le belve d'amor turbar la pace.

Ma che? quasi idre poi l'alma natura,
ad onta de la morte empia e rapace,
di novo avviva con pietosa cura. (Belloni, 66)[56]

(In the gentle forest of your golden hair I saw lovely and slender animals wandering and in various herds handsomely grouped they were making sweet plunder of the white breasts; others were gaily playing on the line between the white neck and the begemmed skin, they almost seem like shiny stars in the sky or candid and fine pearls in the sea. Here, like a hunter, the bold finger with the pointed nail constantly stirs the peace of the beasts of love. But what? Almost like hydras, then, despite evil and rapacious death, nurturing nature again revives them with pitiful care.)

The similarities between Mamiani's and Narducci's sonnet are extensive, particularly in the use of conceited metaphors to define the lice, which, for both authors, are similar to wild beasts in the golden forest of the lady's hair. (For Narducci: 'Fere d'avorio in bosco d'oro,' Ivory beasts in a golden forest).

Female beauty marred by bodily vermin and uncleanliness carves its own niches within *Marinismo* and continues to feed male poetic imagination, as is confirmed by Alessandro Adimari's variation on the genre of bodily parasites. Adimari's *Tersicore* includes a sonnet on the 'bella rognosa' (beautiful woman with scabies), where the disfiguring rash caused by skin mites is deemed a supreme sign of attraction.

Chi potria rimirar cosa più grata
ne' campi di cristallo alabastrini?
in tal guisa se' tu, beltà macchiata
di coralli sanguigni, e di rubini. (39)[57]

(Who could admire a more pleasant thing in the crystal fields of alabaster? Likewise you are, beauty tainted by sanguine corals and rubies).

One should note here the ultimate shift in the use of the traditional figurants for woman's beauty. Crystal, coral, and rubies in Petrarchan poetry designate the beautiful parts of the woman's body (lips, forehead), whereas here they have become the signs of a skin disease caused by parasitic mites.

As discussed in chapter 3, in late Renaissance poetry the woman with lousy hair and with scabies or mange was praised in mock encomia targeting persons of lower social strata and from peripheral regions. Dirt, insects, and bodily parasites were emblems of the female disgusting Other. As Mauro had proclaimed in his 'Capitolo delle donne di montagna,' and as was stated in the 'Stanze in lode della donna brutta,' mountain women and ugly women on the geographical margins, with their bodily dirt and lice-ridden hair, not only extinguished any erotic desire but also served as the most effective antidote to male sexual arousal. Baroque poets revive the lice-ridden, bodily infested woman of mock encomia and, by freeing her from any class and elitist discourse, astonishingly attempt to turn her from symbol of disgust into a symbol of attraction, of tainted beauty. This type of poetry, which accounts for the worst form of *Marinismo*, reveals how, for the sake of conceit and wit, disgust, dirt, and disease come close to attraction, in a manner similar to Romantic and Decadent poetry.

The pervasiveness of the motif of the 'bella pidocchiosa' is confirmed by the flourishing of satirical and parodistic poems on the same topic. According to Besomi (*Esplorazioni*, 82), in 'L'amante stoltisavio,' a poem from the *Amori giocosi*, Tommaso Stigliani as early as 1623 parodies the theme of the lice-infested beloved praised in many baroque sonnets. Stigliani describes the woman cleaning her golden hair with an ivory comb: 'D'animate immondizie il crin purgava' (She was purging from her hair live rubbish). The astonishing spectacle of dirt falling off the woman's hair is described as follows:

E scendea mescolata
con un nuvol volante
d'altro bel sudiciume,
ch'a biondi atomi d'or s'assomigliava. (*Esplorazioni*, 82)

(And it was falling together with a flying cloud of other beautiful filth, which looked like blonde golden atoms).

Stigliani's parody of baroque literary fashion reaches its peak in the metaphors used for the most 'honourable/horrible' insects, the lice here called 'immondizie animate' and 'biondi atomi' (live rubbish, blonde atoms).

The same parodistic vein also appears in neo-bernesque poetry in Neapolitan dialect. The filthy women of Neapolitan urban poor quarters are described with revolting details of beauty and dirt in the collection *Tiorba a taccone*. This *canzoniere* in ten books by Felippo Sgruttendio de Scafato, most likely an alias for Neapolitan dialect poet Giulio Cesare Cortese (born 1575?), targets with satirical bite the most abused themes of baroque lyric poets. Chapter 4 presents a series of parodistic sonnets praising women said to be beautiful in their imperfection (beautiful hunchback, stutterer, crooked eyed, etc.) and in their uncleanliness. Sgruttendio magnifies and reworks in comic terms the theme of female beauty and dirt, as it was presented in poets like Mamiani, Narducci, and Adimari. Narducci's infamous sonnet about the 'bella pidocchiosa' finds its parodistic reprise in 'A la bella pedocchiosa,' and the catalogue of disgusting beauties includes the woman with scabies ('A la bella rognosa') – perhaps an echo of Admiari's sonnet – and the beautiful woman covered in dirt ('A la bella zazzarosa'), possibly the extreme example of the conjunction of beauty and dirt.

Baroque poetry presents female ugliness as unconventional beauty and appears highly ambiguous. While it seems to liberate the ugly woman from the prejudice, discrimination, and negativity of medieval and Renaissance poetry, it exploits the entire thematic roster of previous comic poetry – the old and aging woman, the disfigured and filthy woman – to gratify the poets' search for self-aggrandizement and virtuosity. In seventeenth-century poetry there is a trend towards hybridization of the motifs of the Petrarchan and anti-Petrarchan/comic traditions. Women's undesirable physical attributes are extolled and presented as attractive simply because they allow baroque poets to display their ingenuity and mastery in pairing beauty and deformity. Remarkably, baroque lyric poets completely ignore the hegemonic discourse of class, gender, and aesthetics that appears in mock encomia about peasants. No one among the numerous women praised by *Marinisti* carries the marks of the 'villana' or 'contadina.' Baroque poetry extends its praises to commoners, servants, and even slaves, but the format of the verbal homage is the conventional one of the Petrarchan tradition; rather than paradoxical, the commendation becomes witty and conceited, and yet it does not free the commended woman from the author's poetic agenda. Despite baroque authors' interest in deformed, exotic, old, black women and even slave women as subjects for their poetry, the unconventional women honoured and praised continue to serve merely as objects. Disfigured, contaminated, dark femininity is a pretext for displaying wit and virtuosity, for achieving 'meraviglia,' and for pursuing a male agenda of narcissistic aggrandizement.

Conclusion

As philosopher and feminist Rosi Braidotti observes "'I, woman" am affected directly and in my everyday life by what has been made of the subject of "Woman"; I have paid in my very body for all the metaphors and images that our culture has deemed fit to produce of "Woman."' (187). Some of the images and metaphors used in medieval and early modern Italian poetry to describe the ugly woman still haunt us today, in our effort to make sense of clichés about female evil, deviancy, marginality, and non-conformity constructed as physical repulsion and filthy materiality. We as women must come to terms with the onus to comply and conform with existing rules of bodily proportion, youth, blondness, and perfection or otherwise be called ugly old hags. The general perception of female ugliness in literature as mere rhetorical game, *lusus*, and parody, fails to account for this serious matter, which subtends a cultural discourse permeated by prejudice and misogyny. Non-conformity to standards of beauty reveals male anxiety about possible spaces for women's dangerous power and male preoccupation with moral, aesthetic, social, and racial transgression.

In Italian literature from the Middle Ages onward, female beauty has been celebrated in unsurpassed universal models such as Dante's Beatrice and Petrarch's Laura and in many other beautiful women such as Boccaccio's Emilia and Poliziano's Simonetta or Ariosto's Angelica and Alcina; these paragons of beauty have been revered, imitated, and extensively studied in critical work. By contrast, female ugliness in Italian literature, and particularly in poetry, has been completely neglected, swept aside, as a brief parenthesis in a long tradition of glorification of female beauty. As this study shows, the ugly woman in Italian literature not only appears frequently, but is the subject or rather the

166   The Ugly Woman

object of a genre, that produces female types marked by transgression and deviancy. But since female ugliness appears primarily in comic and parodistic poetry, mainstream criticism tends to dismiss it as right-hearted game, *lusus*, a joyful pastime for entertainment and escape from the serious matters of love and beauty, which dominate the Italian lyric tradition.

This diachronic survey of female ugliness in Italian poetry suggests that the representation of the ugly woman is constructed as deviancy from norms and standards accepted in dominant culture regarding age, morality, class, aesthetics, and race/ethnicity. Studying the modes of poetic representation of female ugliness has led inevitably to an examination of the traditional referents of literary beauty: the hegemonic discourse, which ugliness evokes by opposition, and the aesthetic foundations that give rise to a new literary convention.

This book attempts to illuminate some crucial aspects of the way male imagination has generated concepts of female ugliness in opposition to culturally normative beauty in literature. Misogyny, transgression, and parody have been traced throughout this study as the cues in representations of female ugliness. In the medieval mind, female ugliness is rendered most notably as old age, occasionally as bad smell, and often as moral deviancy and inappropriate conduct, ranging from lust and immoderate sexuality to infringement of the rules on speaking and looking. Although in Italian comic poetry the ugly old woman is at times depicted in an authoritative position, as a guardian, her power does not lead to the subversive 'woman on top,' but is promptly vanquished by male poetic dominance through rhetoric and fierce verbal attack on a female body incapable of providing male visual pleasure. Some categories of women have appeared as the most likely candidates for ugliness in medieval poetry: guardians, witches, and prostitutes, women who transgress the codes of behaviour and appropriate conduct in a patriarchal society.

In the Renaissance there is a shift of focus from ugliness as moral deviancy to ugliness as social marginality and transgression of the aesthetic canon dictated by the elite. In sixteenth-century poetry the ugly woman is typically the subject of mock encomia in burlesque style, rather than invectives, and she is a young peasant or a type on the social and geographical margins. Here the ugly woman is a female Other, which stirs ambivalent feelings of both attraction and repulsion. Her physical features (disproportion, large size, abundance, youth) are not completely rejected; rather, they are described in a way that betrays male attraction towards female plenitude and sensuality, confirming Stallybrass and White's contention that 'disgust always bears the imprint of desire' (191). Scorn for the peasant and her non-canonical beauty allows the elite to reaffirm their aesthetic and cultural supremacy. The discourse of beauty and ugliness in the Renaissance targets primarily social difference. The more marginal the socio-geographical group of the woman represented, the more disgusting her physical body. Female ugliness is not only aesthetic deviancy from the canon, but also social inferiority, incivility, bodily dirt, and contamination.

Renaissance depiction of female ugliness also takes the shape of a pointed infringement on the literary canon sanctioned by Petrarchism. In poems that depict the ugly woman as the anti-Laura, the disfigured shadow of perfect beauty is used to stir an ideological polemic against literary stereotypes in lyrical poetry, rather than to address the issue of objectification and the inadequacy of literary female representation.

In the baroque lyric, male poetic imagination shapes a type of unconventional beauty rather than ugliness, in which women are no longer attractive in their perfection, blondness, youth, and light skin. Beautiful dark slaves, dark-haired ladies, older women, and countless examples of women marred by bodily parasites provide suitable female material for witty literary creation. Irregular female body types are essentially a medium for male self-glorification through poetic virtuosity in exalting arduous concepts of beauty. Much remains to be to explored in baroque poetry, which is still not fully accessible to general consultation. The trends sketched constitute only a sample of the richness of motifs one could explore. The focus here is on those themes which allowed the establishment of some connection with previously surveyed material. Other favourite baroque themes, such as female physical beauty/ugliness in relation with disease, decay, and death, would undoubtably bring interesting results.

This study throughout did not aim at completeness, but rather at unveiling significant trends in a poetic genre that in the sixteenth century became a distinctive literary convention. With the exception of few male-filtered poems, no women's voices have been heard, perhaps not surprisingly given women's limited literacy and access to literature in medieval and early modern times. But perhaps, and more importantly, women do not speak of female ugliness because this is the domain of misogyny, a sentiment that springs from male insecurity about and fear of the female ugly body.

In writing this book, I granted preference to poetry with the greatest abundance of textual sources, but the motif of the ugly woman appears in other genres such as epic romance and narrative, which could be investigated to either confirm or refute the findings of this study. One should, of course, mention Boccaccio's *Corbaccio*, the misogynist narrative par excellence, where female ugliness figures prominently. In Luigi Pulci's comic epic *Morgante* the physical ugliness of Creonta, as Orvieto points out, draws from medieval depictions of old hags and of devils (*Pulci medievale*, 125). Chivalric romance appears to favour the motif of the beautiful-woman-turned-hag, as embodied in Ariosto's Alcina, whereas the figure of Gabrina echoes Cavalcanti's 'scrignutuzza,' an old woman mocked for masquerading as a young and courtly damsel. Letter writing seems conducive to grotesque descriptions of femininity; in addition to Machiavelli's encounter with the disgusting Veronese prostitute, Luigi Pulci uses the rhetorical clichés of female negative *descriptio* in the grotesque portrait of Zoe Paleologa. In the sixteenth century vituperative verses against courtesans appear in schemes and *topoi* that confirm the trends set in medieval texts. Poems describing the ugly appearance and depravity of courtesans were written by authors such as Francesco Beccuti ('Capitolo' against the courtesan Ortensia) and Quinto Gherardo ('Capitolo contro una cortegiana').

Another avenue for further investigation is the way in which gender affects the treatment of ugliness if man is the object of poetic expression in either comic or serious literature. Male ugliness has been used in the early modern period by authors such as Burchiello and Francesco Berni, who actually paint a negative literary self-portrait. Aside from the fact that depictions of female ugliness never seem to be the result of self-representation, as Silvia Longhi points out, depiction of physical deformity in burlesque male self-portraits such as Berni's is a conscious choice, where external ugliness is selected to emphasize by contrast the positive inner qualities underlying the unattractive surface. Conforming to the sixteenth-century Platonic myth of Socrates Silenus, burlesque poets emphasize the discrepancy between the exterior and the interior, deformed physical appearance hiding the inner qualities of the virtuous man (*Lusus*, 122–3). Approaches to female ugliness/non-conventionality/grotesque in modern and contemporary literature and culture seem to lead in different directions than medieval, Renaissance, and baroque Italian poetry. In the works considered in this study female ugliness is purely and unequivocally an expression of negativity, male fear, and misogyny.

Romantic and Decadent sensibility have effected a revision of female ugliness from unambiguously negative to more problematic and ambivalent; a new appeal for the Ugly as aesthetic category leads Romantic authors, under the influence of Victor Hugo, to search for the allure of tainted beauty, deformity, and disease. Unlike baroque poets, whose interest in female ugliness is merely as source of witticism and 'concettismo,' Romantic and post-Romantic authors have explored the tragedy of ugliness and the decadent appeal of deformity and contamination of the female body, as did Baudelaire in *Fleurs du mal* (one can think of 'Les petites Vieilles') or the ugly woman as *femme fatale* in Iginio Ugo Tarchetti's novel *Fosca*.

Mary Russo's study of the female grotesque has shown how prevalent is the association between gender and the grotesque in modern and contemporary Western culture. Russo proposes a new understanding of the female grotesque, and attempts to find literary and cultural instances of the excessive female body (in Angela Carter's character Fevvers in *Nights at the Circus*, for example) that can suggest a liberatory, positive prospect for what she calls the 'aerial sublime,' far from the negativity and misogyny that characterize the types of the ugly woman that emerge from this study. Charlotte Wright (*Plain and Ugly Janes*), who studied ugly women as a new character type in twentieth-century American literature, has shown that female heroines who are ugly and undesirable are freed from the emotional and physical burdens of family and society and can pursue their own fates with unprecedented freedom. In modern Italian fiction, Carmen Covito's *La bruttina stagionata* (1990) makes female unattractiveness empowering; with irony Covito demystifies the clichés of physical beauty and youth, traditional assets for literary heroines, and casts a plain and mature woman in a positive and assertive role. In other contemporary forms of cultural expression, American photographer Cindy Sherman has produced pictures of the female grotesque where the distortion and degradation of woman's beauty functions as a critique of conventions and codes of behaviour for women; inverting and parodying the types of voluptuous, seductive female figures, Sherman mocks the conventions of artistic, literary, and popular culture.

As revealed in the preceding pages, with respect to female ugliness, medieval and early modern Italian poetry finds itself in a misogynistic morass that is hardly unique to this celebrated literary tradition. Only a broader and more effective participation of women in the literary and cultural arena can successfully challenge this bias against unattractive women so pervasive in the Western canon. As works by Covito, Sherman, and Carter show, the specifically female imagination can disassociate female ugliness or the female grotesque from negativity, and construct images and metaphors that can provide an empowering force and suggest what Russo sees as a 'redeployment or counterproduction of culture, knowledge, and pleasure (62).

Appendix

Anonymous Texts on the Ugly Woman from Codex Magliabechiano VII 1078, Quoted in Tommaso Casini's *Studi di Poesia antica*

I

Do, mala vechia, lo mal fuogo l'arda,
lo mal nimigo te possa portare!

Tu teni la mia dona sì celata
che a poco a poco me fa' consumare:
fa bona varda si tu la sa' fare,
che al to dispeto te la vo' involare;
fa bona varda si tu la sa' fare
che per amor ela convien basare. (217–18)

II

Laida vecchia stomegosa,
maladeta se' tu ogni ora,
che in del mondo ní de fora
non fo mai sí mala cosa.

Quanto tu sei brutta e ria
dir non posso a parte a parte,
de bruteze tu sei dia,
d'ogni vicio tu sai l'arte;
mo volgendo pur lodarte
como posso e tu sei degna,

comenzando da la tegna
dico che tu sei tignosa.

De la copa vien la marza,
che te colla zo del capo,
la codegna te se squarza
sí che 'l fa parer un napo;
e non voglio dir un napo,
ma el se inpliría le sechie
con quel che e[sce] da l'orechie,
che te fa tutta lodosa.

A chi piase aver sonalgi
verdi, zali, grandi e grosi,
sí recolgia quii scarcasi
che tu spudi quando tosi;
par[e] che senpri [tu] fosi
o pregara o beroldiera,
tanto è quella to gorziera
de fastiedio copiossa.

Tu à' la mufa d'una alloca,
i ochi tuo' par do scalogne,
et te puza più la bocha
che non fa mile carogne;
una porca quando grogne
tu me soni a la favela;
brutta vecchia, laida, fela,
Dio te dia vita penosa.

Tu à' la golla como sponga
da trincar vin e vinaza;
grisa barba, folta e longa,
la più laida petegaza
non se truova né arzoalda;
morta sei' da pietra salda,
como cagna rabiosa.

Chi guarda el to bel volto
cun le galte adorn' e vage,
tu me pari un omo in volto

cun la barba a quatro page;
chi volese aver lumage
tu n'à senpre pien lo naso;
ch' el te posa dar un baso
una serpe velenosa.

Non se truova in villa vallo
che tegnise el to letame,
non è stala de cavallo
in che sia tanto letame,
non à canpo tanto strame
che netase el to canale,
ché più puzi da nadale
che non ol de mazo rosa.

Tu à' pelose più le lache
cun le cosse e le zenochie
che non à né buo' né vache;
le s'è piene de pedochie,
como grani de fenochie:
un migliaro ie bagorda
ne la to quintana lorda,
che vorìa mai far posa.

E' te manderò un barbiero
cum rasori e forfesete,
che non faza altro mestiero
che tosar quele to tete,
e la barba che ne mete
a le to masele granze,
ch'ha color de meleranze:
melio è dir d'una leprosa.

Non è lengua in taverna
più canina e più mordaze,
se la fose in vita eterna
el conturberìa la pace;
mo, perché ne la fornaze
de l'inferno se renchiude
le mal vechie e le svanzude,
tu te serìa nascosa.

Nel mal dir tu te nutrichi,
como salamandra in foco;
tuti i vicii son to amici.
la virtù in ti non à loco:
a ti piace ogni mal zuoco,
a ti piace ogni custume,
par che invidia te consume
più che ogni altra invidiosa.

El to volto è de naranze,
tuto pieno de magagne;
porti quel de driè da nanze
dalle spalle a le calcague:
mo, s'el vien che tu me incagne,
io te farò cum nimico,
pezo assai che non dico,
grama, trista e dolorosa.

Lasa star le done honeste
con la to lengua perversa;
e' non credo al mon[do] peste
sì feroze e sì diversa:
che Dio te dia tal fersa
che tu perdi ogni lenguazo,
sì che tu non faci oltrazo
a nisuna vertuosa.

Ballatina mia lizarda,
vàne cun tuo' voce ardita;
fa che quela vechia ladra
de mal dir sia [dis]gradita:
de cantar non far finita
le malici' e sue bruteze;
fin a tanto che se sveze
quela lingua scandolosa. (218–21)

III

La vecchia d'amor m'à biasemata:
non pasar per la mia contrata.

La vechiarda rinalda, scarfalda
m'aguarda quando [tu] m'adochi;
mal fugarda, rutarda, bifarda,
musarda, che volto e che ochi!
Perché m'ài così incolpata,
crudel vechia rinigata?

Con ardore, furore, fiammore,
tremore, sopra [de] mi stride;
sì ch'ognore vanore, temore,
dolore, ben par che m'ocide:
et à me tanto lagniata
ch' i' son tucta sfigurata.

Biastemando, lagnando, saltando,
giostrando, d'intorno travasa;
[e] butando, minando, runpando,
spezando per tuta la casa;
et dice che m' à trovata
con uom stare a la celata.

S'io t'apelo, fratelo mio belo,
per quelo ella mi rinpogna;
à el cuor felo, miselo, rubelo,
or ve' lo pien d'ogni menzogna:
dice che so' svergognata,
poi ch'i' ebi sua brigata.

Ogni male avale mortale
sia tale sopra a la sua testa!
et [or] vale, non vale, ché l'ale
ti cale tanto se' molesta:
taci e c' or fostù abrusciata,
soza vechia scortigata.

[O] gotosa, malosa, noiosa,
gri[n]tosa, ogne male ti vegna;
invidiosa, gavosa, gri[n]tosa,
noiosa, di mal dir sei pregna.
Ancor non se' gastigata
di chiamarme innamorata?

Com morsechia l'orechia, una vechia
stortechia si mette per gioia;
la bertechia ingordechia smordechia;
scannechia e la par una troia:
crudel vechia rinigata,
tu sarai la mal trovata.

È gran briga, fatiga far liga
co' striga e sbirfa indovina;
no' è miga l'antiga mia amiga,
ch'è ispiga di bona vicina:
ma tu, vecchia, se' sempre stata
patarina in esta contrata.

O sannuta, dentuta, grabuta,
spaluta, gran noia mi fai;
[o] barbuta, berruta, grognuta,
gozuta, tu mal ci starai:
io so' sí amaistrata
che tu rimarrai scornata. (211–12)

IV

Canzonetta Adespota, quoted in Vittorio Cian, 'Un codice ignoto di rime volgari appartenuto a B. Castiglione'

(D')una vechia ch'è zilosa,
la qual m'à sì tolto a peto,
la me crede far dispeto
per tenir mia dona ascosa.

Questa bruta vechionaza
che m'à tolto sì in graveza,
de[h] g[h]e vegna el strangoione!
La me vuol pur dar tristeza,
dio g[h]e dia (la) mala grameza
a questa vechia maledeta.
La me va senza bereta,
che la par una piègora raxa.

L'è tuta toxà per i pulexi,
come i can su per la schena;
la me par de queste anedre
che se speluca la matina.
La me va senza capelina
ed è tuta toxà a scalete,
l'à le buganze a le garete
questa vechia sgargaiosa.

Questa vechia [è] cu[s]ì bruna
che la me par un scaravazo,
le suo rechie par la luna
e sì à fato molto oltrazo.
L'à si stranio visazo
che la me fa pur paura,
el non n'è al mondo sozura
che sia tanto tribolosa.

El par una piva da vilà
propriamente quel suo naso,
el zeruelo i xè semà,
e sì à tuto 'l muso raxo.
La me par un omo quaso,
perch'è la femena barbuda;
ma chi la vedes[s]e nuda
a mo' d'un orso l'è pelosa.

Ma l'è ben quel suo muxone
che par un beco de botone;
l'è sbalorda a mo' d'un moltone,
e sì à un ochio scarpelino.
Ma chi la sente lo matino
g[h]e puza el fiato da can vechio,
la se va a mirar in spechio
e si se tien tropo ponposa.

L'à quel suo viso afaldato
che par proprio una gonela,
l'à quel volto regrignato,

li par li denti e ogni masela,
quando el vien che la favela
l'apre quela sua bocaza,
l'à più d'un palmo de lenguaza
che li sta sempre boaxa.

La me par de cuoro cotto,
tanto è 'la seca e dolorosa;
la slovigna a muo' d'un porco,
e si è tuta a muo' rognosa,
la xé storta e gropolosa
e sì me par da Nadal cavedone,
la me sta in ribaltone
di continio senpre onbrosa.
... co do tetaze
... ai da calefado,
... [so]nando le nacare
... su per le cale.
[qu]ando vien che i puti zase,
[la] vien zó per le cadene,
[sì] g[h]e zuza le suo vene
[que]sta vechia rabiosa.

[Questa] vechia me botoniza
[qua]ndo pas[s]o de la via
[s]enpre mai la me deliza
[e m]e dixe vilania
... der cazar via
[no vor]ave che v'amas[s]e.
[Se] questa vechia crepas[s]e,
[sareste?] la mia morosa. (80–82)

V

Pierantonio Legacci dello Stricca (?), 'Capitolo rusticale contando le bellezze de la sua inamorata,' Biblioteca Trivulziana H 193/1

All'in che disamorato e senza dama
vengha a veder la mia manza bellona
ch'un migliaio al lunge a sé li amanti chiama.

L'ha una sperticata sua persona
che piace sì che in piaza tra fachini
di nulla, altro che lei non si ragiona.

Ell'è proprio un boccon da cittadini
se un messer sol a mie dimin havesse
paghare' com i' gl'ho duo bolognini.

Che le belle[zz]e sue contar volesse
a una a una ci fare' facenda
e po' non credo anchor che si potesse.

Pur prego ognun che 'l mio cantar attenda
perché le gran beltà di questa dea
vo' che dal capo al fin ciascun l' entenda.

Bianchi e' cape' com'una ciminea,
succidi, lendinosi, arroncicati
come son gli oncini d'una statea.

La fronte ha tonda come pan fichati,
bianca lustrente come son carboni
pare un cuperchio d'un prival da frati.

L'ha nelle tempie sì begli orechini
che chi le mira quando le va intorno
dice che paian proprio dui targoni.

Le celle l'uno e l'altro n'ha tanto atorno
ch' asimigliarle in me facto ho pensiero
né puì né manco ho due volte di forno.

Un occhio all'a stravisa biancho et nero
che quando adosso fissi a un li pone
paion pur que' d'un gatto forestiero.

El naso ha proprio come un stangone
e' buchi ha larghi come duo bertesche
gli è torto, aguzo come un bel picchone.

Ell'ha duo gottinelle bianche et fresche
da baciuchiarle ognun mal volentieri
ch'ha posto paiono duo stiacciate ovesche.

E' denti ha radi et pochi ve n' enteri
e non vaglion tra tutti un bolognino
tanto son rotti barbeggiati et neri.

Com'una bufolaccia ell'ha el linguino
la boca è larga et torta et ha un fiato
che sona el corno com' un paladino.

El mento l'ha pinzuto et raguagliato
com'una fossa che cupa una spanna
et lustra sì che pare insavonato.

La gola è larga com'una ciscranna
sì ve dico bugie non mel crediate
che spesso advien che 'l poco amor inganna.

Le spalle l'ha ossute et smisurate
rognoso lorde che son tanto belle,
un miglio allonga chiamon le granate.

Ell'ha nel petto un pa' di bocciarelle
nizo et sconfita e che dicon pur vienne
el resto è ossa in sur un po' di pelle.

Le braze ha sperticate come antenne,
le mane ha moze: et più oltre v'assegno
che le son gialle che paion codenne.

Ell'ha un busto sì pullito et degno
che ohi quando la va mente li pone
dice che la par proprio un hom di legno.

Ell'ha un corpo ritratto a saione
vizo grinzoso; o che dolce conforto,
com'un canicio apunto ell'ha gropone.

Nulla dirò della ficaia e l'orto
perché son parte un po' vituperose
l'hanno un odor da far fugir un morto.

Ruvide ell'ha le cose et mollicose
et sempre ha un po' di lazarina,
le gambe com'un orso ell'ha pilose.

Chi mirassi e suo' pie' quando camina
certo dira resuscitato el zolla,
la cenna de gir in sala et va in cucina.

Sì che di torl' a se nisun favella
che prima aspettarei duo spadacciate
ch'en terra me gittasen le budella.

Perché queste beltà ch' i' vo' contare,
m'hano in tal mo' trasformato el cuore
che'l dì, la notte, el verno con la state
vo' sempremai come gatti in amore.

VI

'Stanze in lode della donna brutta,' Firenze: Stamperia del Doni, 1547

I

Donna, il cui viso rincagnato e piatto
e di varii color vecchia pittura:
che perché 'l naso il ciel lungo v'ha fatto,
et le poppe di sotto a la cintura,
et le man da fachin gli occhi di gatto,
troppo altiera ven' gite e troppo dura:
udite le dolcissime parole
del vostro Amante, che lodar vi vole.

II

Ben volse dar materia a noi di riso,
e empir d'alto stupore il secol nostro

Natura, quando vi compose e il viso,
vie più sereno e candido ch'inchiostro.
Non vi fece ella in Ciel, né in paradiso;
ma nel inferno; e dal più brutto Mostro,
che nel inferno sia, tolse il modello,
quando ella fece il vostro viso bello.

III

Che né Aletto, Tisiphone, e Megera,
né Atropo anchor, né Lachesi, né Cloto
o se altra furia v'è più scura e fiera,
o mostro per horror più chiaro e noto,
certo non ha di voi più brutta ciera.
Non venne di paese aspro e remoto
Mora giamai con così horribil faccia,
che la vostra assai più non ne dispiaccia.

IV

Che non è faccia al mondo sì villana,
sì ridicola e sozza e mostruosa,
che la vostra non sia di lei più strana,
più spiacevole, e scura, e minacciosa.
Chi la fame o l'invidia, o la Quartana
ritrar volesse od altra brutta cosa
a mirar voi gli occhi e la mente volga;
da voi la forma, e 'l bel dissegno tolga.

V

Chi potria dir a pien de bei vostri occhi,
che l'un sempre vi cola e l'altro è losco:
o 'n quanto dispiacer per che trabocchi
chi mira il guardo lor crudel e fosco.
Chi mira i crin, dirà son de' pidocchi
questi e di tinga pur certo un bel bosco.
Stupirà poi veggendo i rari denti,
vie più ch' ebeno fin chiari e lucenti.

VI

Quando talhor la bocca larga aprite
smaltata ogn'ora di biacca, e di verzino,
et così ben la ragion vostra dite
con un parlar spiacevole e fachino,
restan le genti attonite e smarrite.
Et e sentono un odor di quel bocchino,
che par che s'apra un puzzolente vaso,
che a tutti quanti fa turare il naso.

VII

Il pie', ch'ogni altro di grandezza eccede,
che tra le dita tien muschio nascosto,
è sì vago e gentil, che chi lo vede
brama d'haverlo alla stagion del mosto.
Et seco dice: o che perfetto piede
da premer l'uva mezza al fin d'agosto.
Sdruscite sempre ha le scarpette sotto,
sempre le calcie co 'l calcagno rotto.

VIII

Da sì stupendo e smisurato sesso
di larga bocca, e dal pie lungo e greve
ben può pensar chi vi contempla spesso,
qual ogni parte del corpo esser deve.
In fin sete di fuor verzino e gesso:
havete solo i crin gli occhi di neve,
d'ebeno il resto delle membra belle
et sotto panni sol sete ossa e pelle.

IX

Voi sete contra Amor, contra li suoi
stimoli acuti una ottima ricetta:
non è lusuria dove sete voi.
Non adopra Amor face né saeta:

fosse ogni donna tal, beati noi.
Questa vostra beltà sia benedetta,
ch'almen non è cagion che si sospiri,
et che l' huom' viva in lagrime e 'n martiri.

X

Potrete ben al Ciel erger le mani
e lodar Dio con le ginocchia chine,
che tra noi specchio di costumi humani,
v' ha fatto, e di beltà rare e divine.
Mertate ben che tutti i ceratani
sonando le tiorbe e le sordine
cantin di voi; e che risuscitasse
Cinotto e 'l Casio, che v'immortalasse.

XI

Potete nuda gir dove vi piace,
et senza compagnia la notte e 'l giorno:
che sì lussurioso e sì salace
giovin non è, che vi facesse scorno.
Tutti vi lasciariano andare in pace,
fuggirian tutti da quel viso adorno.
Non vi darà mai penitenza frate,
perché tentation mossa n' habbiate:

XII

Certo se foste in un gran bosco sola
tra lupi e tra leon, ch' havesser fame
harian shiffezza d' ungersi la gola
di così brutto e fracido carname.
Né ogni altro augel ch'alle carogne vola
ardiria di gustar cibo sì infame.
Potete ben sicura il dì e la notte
il tralli monti, e tralle scure grotte.

XIII

Et se di notte per la via per sorte
qualchun solo soletto vi incontrasse,

sia pur quanto esser puote ardito e forte,
che seria forza che di voi tremasse:
che pensaria che ci fosse la morte,
che da quella hora vagabonda andasse,
o 'l Diavol dall'inferno empio e atroce,
et si farebbe il segno de la croce.

XIV

Se voi nella stagion che nel vago horto
ogni arbore, ogni pianta si rinverde
ve ne andate talhor così a diporto
per la campagna dilettosa e verde,
tosto ogni fior ch'è da voi tocco, morto
giace, e 'l color e la vaghezza perde.
Muoion l'herbette, così sono offese
da non so che, ch'a voi vien ogni mese.

XV

Se nel mezo del campo il buon villano
mettesse voi, non è si fiero ucello,
che molestasse i suoi fagioli o 'l grano,
che voi sareste un spaventacchio bello.
Non è Priapo con la falce in mano,
col naso adunco e con il suo capello,
né può formarsi in mezo a campi mostro
spaventacchio più bel del viso vostro.

XVI

Come quando s'uccella alla civetta
presso la siepe e la frondosa macchia,
tratti dal odio naturale in fretta
vien la passera il tordo e la cornacchia
e ogni altro uccello, e contra lei si getta,
chi di qua, chi di là la punge e gracchia,
così al vostro apparir la turba corre
et stupisce, v'odia e v'aborre.

XVII

Quando vi vidi senza cuffia in testa
torcer quel dì con tanta gratia il fuso,

col grembiul unto sopra della vesta,
con lo sputo una spanna alto su 'l muso,
O dio, che buona robba essere dee questa,
o beltà ch'io non son di veder uso.
Ché volse, ohíbo, Natura quando
mandolla qui tra noi, dissi sputando!

XVIII

Per far razza di voi bella e altera
nascer al mondo, ben sarebbe d' huopo
a dar sì bella donna per mogliera
a un bel marito, a un Nano a un Ethiopo.
O, se egli è ver che così horribil era,
perché non viene a questi tempi Esopo,
che vi togliesse? e così giunti insieme
feste una razza del ben vostro seme.

XIX

Forse che voi non state in sul contegno,
et fate il viso a noi sempre dal'arme,
et se talhor per parlar vosco vegno
degnar non vi volete di ascoltarme.
Non ho donna, non ho sì poco ingegno,
che con tanta beltà voglia impacciarme.
Vorrei, più tosto ch'esser mai sì matto,
di Cibele esser sacerdote fatto.

XX

In questo tempo pregherò Natura
ch' in ciò almen mi contenti e sodisfaccia,
che come vi fe' brutta oltra misura,
così infelice e misera vi faccia;
che sempre così brutta creatura
al Cielo, al mondo e allo inferno spiaccia.
(Hor qui men taccia) e la rogna e i pidocchi
al fin dentro un spedal vi chiudan gli occhi.

Notes

Introduction

1 This type of woman still pervades popular culture in the media and fashion industry today. Throughout the different eras in Western culture blondness has been a near-universal feature of female beauty, but Petrarch's Laura remains the canonical and most recognized model of such beauty. As Verina Jones has observed, 'In Medieval and Renaissance literature blonde hair is always a prerogative of beauty at least in women. If we take a random list of famous women in European literature, we find that the color of their hair is either not specified or else blonde' (38). The impact of blondness on feminine beauty is still dominant. Cathy Newman's article 'The Enigma of Beauty' specifically addresses the issue of blondness in women: 'Statistics show that 40% of women who color their hair choose blond, a choice women also made in ancient Greece' (108–9).

2 'Comic-realistic poetry' is the label used by critics like Mario Marti and, recently, Paolo Orvieto to identify a corpus of medieval poetry that in its realistic themes and low style is viewed as the opposite of the *Stilnovismo*. I delve into the issue of comic-realistic poetry in chapter 1.

Writing on the topic of misogyny in medieval and early modern Italian literature, and in comic-realistic poetry specifically, is astonishingly sparse. From August Wulff's dated essay on antifeminism in medieval Romance literature, which includes a short chapter devoted to Italian poetry (considered much less harsh than French) and C. Pascal's early-twentieth-century article on 'Misoginia medievale,' limited to medieval Latin poetry, we have to turn to Paolo Orvieto's and Lucia Brestolini's recent *La poesia comico-realistica. Dalle origini al cinquecento* to find any treatment of misogyny in comic poetry. Orvieto and Brestolini take a first step in revealing the rich tradition of misogynist texts in Italian vernacular.

188   Notes to pages 4–6

3 Marina Zancan's introduction to *Il doppio itinerario della scrittura* identifies the problem of a literary tradition marked by the absence of feminine voices. Throughout the history of Italian culture women's writings are numerous, but they are external to the literary tradition (ix–x). Recent works such as Panizza and Wood's *History of Women's Writing in Italy* are attempting to fill the void, going beyond conventional genres classed as literature. However, the medieval and early modern periods are the areas of least output.

4 The first and ever-so-rare case of an ugly heroine in an Italian novel is in Iginio Ugo Tarchetti's mid-nineteenth-century *Fosca* (1869 [1988]), roughly as that theme was becoming more popular in other European narratives, such as Charlotte Brontë's *Jane Eyre* (1847), Adalbert Stifter's *Brigitta* (1847), and Theodor Fontane's *Schach von Wutenow* (1882).

5 With some notable exceptions that we will mention below, silence is the most common situation for women in medieval Italian poetry. In whichever form men construct female identity in these poems, we can learn a great deal about the taboos and preconceived opinions that men in positions of power could disseminate and consequently about the clichés that pertained to the ugly woman.

6 Mary Russo's (1995) study of the female grotesque in modern culture explores this concept in literature (Angela Carter, Georges du Maurier), film (David Cronenberg, Ulrike Ottinger), and other cultural expressions (pilot Amelia Earhart, freaks, midgets, Siamese twins). In her categorization of the female grotesque, which includes the abject, the uncanny, and the aerial sublime, Russo suggests some liberatory prospects for the female grotesque; in Angela Carter's novel *Nights at the Circus*, for example, Russo locates the aerial sublime in the grotesque heroine Fevvers, where the female grotesque 'may suggest new political aggregates – provisional, uncomfortable, even conflictual, coalitions of bodies which both respect the concept of "situated knowledges" and refuse to keep every body in its place' (179). Kristeva draws on Mary Douglas's categories of purity and defilement to formulate the concept of the abject, which she finds fully expressed in Céline's misogynist and antisemitic writing. In Céline the ultimate abjection is in the category of the maternal and in the maternal body during childbirth, a site of liminality and defilement: 'the scene of scenes is here not the so-called primal scene but the one of giving birth, incest turned inside-out, flayed identity' (*Powers of Horror*, 155).

7 Lois Banner, who has written a history of feminine old age from a feminist perspective, attempts to find some space for positive representation of feminine old age in Western culture and identifies wisdom and power as two aspects that made old women less negative figures. In Italian poetry from

medieval times to the baroque, however, there is not much space for validating the figure of the old woman.

8 Nancy Vickers ('Diana Described,' in reference to Petrarch's *Rerum vulgarium fragmenta*) and Patricia Parker have explored the problem of fragmentation of the female body in descriptive praise in medieval and Renaissance poetry and prose.

Chapter 1. Female Ugliness in the Middle Ages: The Old Hag

1 This is not to suggest that hostility was the only sentiment directed towards women in medieval culture. Early Christian discourse reveals a bivalent attitude towards the feminine. In Christianity woman is simultaneously viewed as inferior to man but also his equal; as the source of all evil woman is follower of the first sinner, Eve, but as follower of the Virgin Mary she is the redeemer. As long as woman renounces the temptations of the flesh and practises asceticism, she can become the 'bride of Christ' and be granted equal status with man. Bloch shows the liberating potential of the Christian egalitarian message; by practising asceticism and joining religious orders, Christian women could escape patriarchal subjugation and achieve relative independence and freedom to travel and educate themselves. Yet mystic women, bound to the pact of virginity and renunciation of the flesh, de facto passed from subjugation within the patriarchal family to the tutelage of the new family of the religious orders (*Medieval Misogyny*, 91). Blamires, who compiled an anthology in English translation of mainly misogynist classical and medieval texts (*Woman Defamed*), later in *The Case for Women in Medieval Culture* shows in medieval discourse on women the existence of a lesser known corpus of ideas that champions pro-feminine stances and retaliates against misogyny.

2 For misogyny in patristic tradition see, for example, Rogers (*The Troublesome Helpmate*, 14–22) and Bloch (*Medieval Misogyny*, 29–35). Among the church fathers, Tertullian (160–230) seems to be the harshest and most hostile to women. I take a more detailed look below at his work, particularly his condemnation of women's propensity for ornamentation.

3 Juvenal's satire is a punctilious and detailed analysis of women's faults and evil. This text became a traditional source of misogynist accusations. The long tirade against women's vices was influential as late as the Renaissance.

4 The subject is amply documented, and therefore I shall rely on general observations easily found in numerous studies. See Blamires (*Woman Defamed*), Bloch (*Medieval Misogyny*), and Rogers (*The Troublesome Helpmate*).

5 See also how Bloch in chapters 1 and 3 of *Medieval Misogyny* attempts to find

sources for Christian and biblical misogyny in the pagan classical tradition. The association of woman with the material and the senses, for example, has its roots in Platonic tradition; as well, the definition of woman as matter and her subjugation to man is found in Aristotle's work.

6 Blamires's *Woman Defamed* is a useful anthology of mainly misogynist classical and medieval texts.

7 Eco also focuses on the contrast between external and internal beauty, a common theme in medieval thought, particularly that of mystics, who lamented the transience of earthly beauty and found comfort in interior beauty (9).

8 Bloch identifies such *topoi* of misogyny first in his article 'Medieval Misogyny' and later in *Medieval Misogyny*.

9 This is the title of chapter 2 of *Medieval Misogyny*, where Bloch shows that the 'idea of woman is allied with the supervenient and the contingent, with the realm of the senses, with the decorative or cosmetics and with symbolic activity in general' (65).

10 Bloch calls this treatise the 'first expression of "cosmetic theology"' (71) in the sense of early Christian obsession with the esthetics of femininity.

11 'Cultum dicimus quem mundum muliebrem uocant, ornatum quem immundum muliebrem conuenit dici. Ille in auro et argento et gemmis et uestibus deputatur, iste in cura capilli et cutis et earum partium corporis quae oculos trahunt. Alteri ambitionis crimen intendimus, alteri prostitutionis' (26).

12 I draw this quote from the bilingual Latin-Italian edition by Maria Tasinato, *Gli ornamenti delle donne* (II, 5, 2), pp. 44–6. The English translation is by Edwin A. Quain, pp. 135–6.

13 Feminist social historians have recently contested the association of the private space of the house with woman and public space with man, and have emphasized the need to distinguish between prescriptive rules of conduct and real-life situations. In medieval and early modern times some women gained more freedom and control in their lives and occasionally became public agents participating in the public sphere; see Kuehn and Jacobson Schutte. Nevertheless, hortatory, omiletic, and conduct literature specifically targeted the issue of woman's space, strongly advising women to remain confined within the protected sphere of domestic and family life.

14 One notices first of all the absence of a systematic study, or of any anthological selections, on misogyny in Italian literature. Alcuin Blamires's *Woman Defamed* offers in English translation and chronological order excerpts from misogynist texts ranging from ancient Greek and Latin philosophers, to early Christian theologians, to medieval vernacular texts. In Blamires's

anthology Italian misogynist tradition is represented by Boccaccio's *Corbaccio*. In August Wulff's 1914 study on misogynist poetry in medieval Romance literature, chapter 4 is devoted to antifeminist poetry in Italian early medieval literature. Wulff notes the limited corpus and yet completely excludes comic-realistic poetry; he mentions instead Gerardo Patecchio and proverbs, one of Jacopone da Todi's *laude*, a tirade on women's ornaments, and the anonymous *Proverbia quae dicuntur super natura feminarum*. With the notable exception of Boccaccio's *Corbaccio*, probably the most studied misogynist work in medieval Italian literature, scholars of Italian literature have simply mentioned the existence of misogynist themes and of an antifeminist tradition, also with reference to medieval comic-realistic poetry, but have never really focused on this subject.

15 In chapter 2 Orvieto establishes a connection between misogyny and medieval comic poetry and finds antifeminist *topoi* in Dante's *Fiore*, and the work of Faitinelli, Nicolo de' Rossi, Cecco Angiolieri, Franco Sacchetti, and Antonio Pucci. In chapter 13 Brestolini examines the misogynist motifs in early modern literature and cinquecento burlesque poetry. Although Orvieto's and Brestolini's study constitutes perhaps the best treatment of misogyny in Italian comic poetry so far, their work does not offer much insight into the motivations behind the male imagination and the patriarchal culture that produced them.

16 The text is in vol. 2 of Contini's *Poeti del duecento*, pp. 520–55.

17 *Proverbia quae dicuntur super natura feminarum* is an Italian version of the French *Chastiemusart* in monorhyme quatrains. It includes historic and literary anecdotes, as well as similes from bestiaries. It dates to approximately 1152–60. Contini, who believes this text originated in the Veneto or Emilia regions, considers it lacking in artistic quality. The other texts in the codex containing the *Proverbia* (Saibante codex at Oeffentliche Wissenschaftliche Staatsbibliothek in Berlin) bear traces of Franciscan and Mendicante traditions. Authoritative sources for this text, mentioned in the opening verses, are Ovid, Cato, Cicero, and the medieval Latin comedy *Pamphilus*, the latter also included in the Saibante codex. Critics have agreed that the 756 verses are an incomplete text.

18 Unless otherwise stated, from here on translations are my own. They do not aim at any poetic or stylistic rendering of the originals; rather they intend to provide clear prose translations of the texts.

19 Sienese thirteenth-century poet Bindo Bonichi laments in proverbial tones women who claim their virginity after having married four times (sonnet 'Fra l'altre cose non lievi a portare'), and Pieraccio Tedaldi composes sonnets against getting married and against his wife.

20 Attempting to define how old an old woman is and to attach a number to women's age in the Middle Ages is quite problematic. Joan Cadden notes that Albert the Great believed women lived longer than men because they were less taxed by intercourse and purified through menstruation (176). In Boccaccio's *Corbaccio* the widow, who is described as decrepit and disgusting, was in her late thirties, hardly old by today's standards. Only one poem by Cammelli, in chapter 2, gives a precise age for an old widow: forty-seven years.

21 On feminine old age in the Middle Ages, see Shahar, 'The Old Body in Medieval Culture,' and Banner, *In Full Flower*. Neoplatonic doctrine does not confirm the negative perception of feminine old age. Women's wisdom is celebrated in the figures of Diotima and Ismedora, aging women who guide and inspire. Boethius in his *De consolatione philosophiae* (sixth century) portrays Lady Philosophy as a mature dignified matron, who guides one to a spiritualized understanding of reality. Philosophia represents Boethius's conciliation between Christian mysticism and Platonic idealism. Boethius's influence can be found as late as Dante's *Commedia*: Philosophia was a model for Dante's Beatrice, but Beatrice never reached maturity in her mortal life.

22 According to Helen Rodnite Lemay this text, no longer believed to be Albert the Great's, is part of the tradition of Albert and was central in spreading condemnation of menses. Rodnite Lemay also discusses *De secretis* in connection with the *Malleus maleficarum*, the fifteenth-century treatise on witches, and argues that the author of *Malleus* used medieval tracts as an ideological basis for concluding that women are prone to witchcraft. As we shall see in chapter 2, witches were often accused of killing young children. For discussion of the negative effects of menses, see Cadden (175).

23 In 'Senso e funzione del termine *joven*' Köhler primarily uses, as his reference for 'youth,' the young men who frequented the feudal courts. However, 'youth' is explained as a code of social behaviour, and in this sense it also involves the women of the court, who take part in the rituals of the *fin'amor*. So, for example, Peire Vidal is mentioned for a poem where old women are deprecated for their vicious behaviour and for living against the precepts of love and *joven*. Orvieto also refers to the term *joven* of courtly poetry and stresses the fact that 'youth' entails morality and courtly behaviour (*La poesia*, 67). Vittorio Cian locates the origin of medieval hostility towards old women both in classical tradition (Ovid, Horace, Martial) and in chivalric tradition, troubadour poetry, and medieval Latin literature (311). For old women in medieval French torbadour poetry, see Gouiran.

24 Translation by Parr, p. 43.

25 See Salmon (528). According to Bähr the systematic portrait in the Middle

Ages was first used in French literature in the twelfth century and then spread to other Romance literatures. Bähr distinguishes between the non-signaletic portrait, with no physical description, and the signaletic one, which contains an orderly systematic enumeration of physical traits from head to toe. The first example of the new method is to be found in *Roman de Thèbes*'s portrait of Adraste's daughters.

26 In the medieval comedy *Pamphilus* the protagonist is an old go-between whose physical appearance is repulsive.

27 I quote Beroe's complete portrait from Faral: 'Est Beroe rerum scabies, faex livida, vultu/Horrida, Naturae desipientis opus, / Altera Tesiphone, confusio publica, larvae/Consona, conspectu sordida, tabe gravis, / Corpore terribilis, contactu foeda, quietas/Cervicis scabies non sinit esse manus. / Dum latitat scabies rigido servata galero, / Debita deesse sibi pabula musca dolet. / Pelle, pilis caput est nudum, ferrugo rigescit / Fronte minax, turpis, lurida, sorde fluens. / Silva supercilii protenditur hispida, sordem / Castigat, fruticis obice claudit iter. / Triste supercilium tabes retinere laborat / Cervicis, nares progrediendo tegit. / Auris sorde fluit, non orbiculata redundat / Vermibus, hunc illuc pendet obesa madens. / Livescunt oculi, sanies decurrit, inundat / Fluxus, lippa regit lumina, faece replet. / Dum volitant avidae circum sua pascua muscae, / Palpebra fiscatas muscipulare solet. / Naris sima jacet, foetens, obliqua meatu / Distorto, flamen exitiale vomit. / Proxima labra madent, fluxus distillat et aegrum / Naris ad hospitium pendula spuma redit. / In rugas crispata riget gena foeda, lituris / Obsita, quas oculus tabe fluente notat. / Pendula pallescunt et marcida labra, saliva / Cerberei rictus stercorat aegra sinus. / In dentes rubigo furit, quos spiritus aeger / Et tineae duplici perditione premunt. / Non parcit scabies collo vicina, quod horret / Nodis, quod sordet ulcere, tabe natat. / Venis distrahitur pectus simulatque mamillas / Consona vesicae panniculosa cutis. / Livida costarum macies exire videtur; / Pellis conqueritur carnis egere latus. / Turgescit stomachus scabie, quam proxima Lethe / Suscitat, inferni janua, triste Chaos. / Gibbi pernicies staturam contrahit, ergo / Inscriptus breviter terga tumere facit. Emeritis hirsuta pilis hiat olla lacunae / Consona, sulphurei gurgitis unda rubet. / Sentibus horrescit descensus ad ilia, latrat / Cerberus, exundat faece lacuna patens. / Est genuum compago rigens, imbuta fluenti / Diluvio, spargi se Flegetonte dolet. / Tibia vermescit scabie, cogitque ciragra Reciprocos digitos esse podagra pedes.' (130–2).

Vendôme follows the prescribed descending order and gives a complete physical description of the old woman accompanied by moral depravity. Beroe is a public disorder, second Tisiphone (one of the mythological Furies that inhabit the infernal regions), whose belly roils with lust.

28 Virtually every history of Italian literature or anthology of medieval poetry defines a part of medieval poetry as 'Poesia comico-realistica.' From Cecchi Sapegno to the more recent Enrico Malato, and from Contini's anthology *Poeti del duecento* to Piero Cudini's anthology *Poesia italiana del duecento*, this categorization of the medieval lyric is firmly established.
29 Alfie takes this position about comic authors like Angiolieri: 'Deconstructionists overturn the hierarchies so as to revalourize the normally disdained end of the spectrum ... In contrast, comic authors embrace the negative valences associated with the downtrodden ... by demonstrating the negativity associated with the body, sin, and rural people. Angiolieri may depict the material world, but he also demonstrates its insufficiency without the spiritual realm' (27).
30 Translation of Cavalcanti's poems is by Lowry Nelson, Jr., p. 3.
31 The genre of *lauda* was of course established in vernacular religious poetry. Devotional religious practice originating in the liturgical celebration included the *laude* or psalms in praise of God. The most famous are Saint Francis of Assisi's *Laudes creaturarum* and Jacopone Todi's laude. For praise of the lady love in the *Stilnovisti*, the thematic repertory compiled by Savona (*Repertorio tematico del Dolce Stil Nuovo*) provides an exhaustive list of quotations.
32 Marti's *Cultura e stile nei poeti giocosi del tempo di Dante* marked the moment of re-evaluation of comic-realistic poetry. Marti also talks about Filippi's 'bifrontismo stilistico.'
33 Translation by Nelson, p. 3.
34 For the tradition of the invective and *vituperatio* in early Italian literature, see Suitner and Ricci.
35 'Quid enim Rusticus et alii quidam, laudis ex vituperiis per eos impintis contra dominas reportarunt' (*Documenti d'amore* I, 90–1).
36 Giuseppe Marrani's recent edition (1999) of Rustico's sonnets includes an appendix with 'Vogliendo contentarmi di composte,' a sonnet that some critics do not include in Rustico's corpus because of its crudity, but that confirms his penchant for associating the woman with disgusting corporeal waste, typical also of the poem for the old hag. The sonnet describes the revolting ingredients used by the poet's 'donna' to prepare him some compote, which includes rheum from her eyes ('cispa d'ochi'), mites and lice ('zimizi e pidochi'), and urine ('piscio puzolente'), (Marrani, 186).
37 Epode 12, 'namque sagacius unus odoror, / polypus an gravis hirsutis cubet hircus in alis / quam canis acer, ubi lateat sus' (440).
38 'Cum tibi trecenti consules, Vetustilla, / et tres capilli quattuorque sint dentes, / pectus cicadae, crus coloroque formicae; / rugosiorem cum geras stola frontem/ ... /et illud oleas quod viri capellarum' (220–2).

39 'Buggeressa' derives from the verb 'buggerare,' which means to deceive or cheat. Yet in the old vernacular the verb is also used in relation to sodomy. Mengaldo and Marrani, unlike other commentators, believe that the 'buggeressa' is a prostitute.
40 Giulia Sissa in *Greek Virginity* notes that in ancient tradition the various orifices of the female body were considered interchangeable. The upper and lower portions of the female body were believed to be symmetrical in Hippocratic medicine; hence 'the mouth (*stoma*) through which food is ingested and from which speech emanates corresponds to the "mouth" (*stoma*) of the uterus ... the latter is nevertheless equipped with lips that close, just as the lips of the upper mouth are sealed in silence' (53). Thomas Laqueur in *Making Sex: Body and Gender from Greeks to Freud* shows that the link between feminine genitalia and the mouth was also known in the Middle Ages.
41 In Rustico bad smell is associated with women and sexuality. In the sonnet 'Volete udir vendetta' Acerbuzzo is comically depicted as the victim of stinky women. He refuses to make love with his wife because of her bad smell ('così gran puzzo!') and turns for sexual satisfaction to his sister-in-law, only to discover that she stinks even more than his wife. Franco Suitner in *La poesia satirica e giocosa nell'età dei comuni*, writing about bad smell in medieval realistic poetry, notes that the foul smell of the 'buggeressa' is closely connected to that of the prostitute, as it is described in the troubadour poetry of Marcabru, who composed poetry against a smelly whore (163).
42 In various books of *De vitis patrum* (quoted in Cervigni, 148), for example, stench is associated with the temptation of lust. In Jacopone da Todi's *Laudi* we find the same theme.
43 Hans Randisbacher studies European literature from the rise of the middle class to modern times and establishes the link between smell and sexuality. Perfume and scent are two rhetorical devices to express both open and repressed sexual attraction in literary texts, whereas foul smell is associated with decay and death in the literature of the Shoah.
44 In *The Invention of Sodomy in Christian Theology* Mark Jordan notes that sodomy, as it was intended by the Latin doctors of the church, was a particular type of *luxuria*, a sexual sin, the perverse desire originating from the stench of the flesh (38). Considered as fleshy sin, *luxuria* was described as staining, polluting, stinking; when *luxuria* was practised with another man it was considered worse even than sinning with a beast.
45 The line 'Perché non ti spolpe' is dubious in the manuscript. Some commentators have opted for 'scolpe,' asking the woman to clear her name of Rustico's base accusations. However, I agree with Marrani's most recent

comment, which finds 'spolpe' more appropriate to the strong invective. 'Spolpare,' literally 'to remove the flesh,' makes this attack violent but also more consistent with Guinizzelli's sonnet to the old woman that we will examine next. The old hag is invited to actual dismemberment; the attack on the old body is similar to the treatment of witches. Old women were often considered witches, but in Italian poetry this connection becomes more prominent in the fifteenth century.

46 *The Divine Comedy*, translation by Charles Singleton.
47 Cervigni in *Dante's Poetry of Dreams* offers the most interesting interpretation of this allegorical episode (chapter 4, pp. 123–52) by connecting the physically deformed hag-turned-siren with the seven purgatorial sins that Dante can defeat only through the help of the holy lady.
48 Also in Cecco we find the aversion to old women as typical of medieval poetry as the love of female youth. In the final stanza of Cecco's most famous sonnet 'S'io fosse foco, ardere', il mondo,' we read 'S' i' fosse Cecco, com' i' sono e fui /torrei le donne giovani e leggiadre:/le vecchie e laide lasserei altrui' (163).
49 Lanza includes this sonnet in Cecco Angiolieri's *Rime* in the section of poems of uncertain attribution.
50 Angela Giallongo (*Il galateo e la donna nel Medioevo*, 136) notes that in his *Reggimento* Francesco da Barberino follows the generally accepted opinion in the Middle Ages that women's use of make-up is not only immoral but also harmful to the body.
51 For misogyny and filogyny in Boccaccio, see these two items in Bragantini's and Forni's *Lessico critico decameroniano*. For a recent contribution on misogyny as men's fear in the *Corbaccio* and *Decameron*, see Psaki.
52 The *Corbaccio*, which has been extensively studied, is in this work considered only tangentially. It is indeed an important text in the portrayal of feminine ugliness but deserves a separate investigation. For research, English translation, and bibliographical literature, I have followed Anthony Cassell's *The Corbaccio*.
53 Nicolò de' Rossi's *Canzoniere* was the first collection in vernacular to be personally edited by the author. Nicolò, who studied law in Bologna a few years after Cino da Pistoia, was a notable of Treviso and the copyist of codex Vaticano Barberiniano 3953, one of the most important documents of early Italian poetry; he was therefore very familiar with the poets of the Sicilian School, with the *Stilnovisti* as well as Tuscan comic-realistic poetry. He may have personally known Pietro de' Faitinelli, who spent some time in exile in Treviso.

54 For the different uses of 'femmina' and 'donna' in medieval literature, see Bonfante, and for a more recent perspective, Passera.
55 On parody in general see Genette, *Palimpsests: Literature in the Second Degree*. On parody in the Italian literary context see Gorni and Longhi, p. 460, and Bàrberi Squarotti's *Lo specchio che deforma*. In relation to the limited parodistic production in the Middle Ages and on Cavalcanti's sonnet, see Baldissone's 'Il canto della distanza,' the opening article in *Lo specchio che deforma*.
56 See Usher's chapter on Cavalcanti in *The Cambridge History of Italian Literature*; the quotation is from p. 23.
57 Cassata in his commentary to this sonnet identifies some parodistic elements (236). Giusi Baldissone goes further and states that this poem is important precisely because it is perhaps the earliest example of self-parody: 'Guido Cavalcanti, con il sonetto "Guata Manetto, quella scrignutuzza," si sdoppia parodiandosi' (16).
58 Translation by Nelson, Jr., 85.
59 Stylistically, this sonnet uses the rhyme in '-zz-,' which Dante in his *De vulgari eloquentia* categorically banned for lyric courtly style. This same stylistic choice is found in Guinizzelli's comic sonnet 'Chi vedesse a Lucia un var capuzzo.'
60 See, for example, Ciccuto ('Una figura'), Agamben, Gorni, and Giunta.
61 Giunta's interpretation is charming because it brings a fresh approach, but it remains unconvincing. Giunta has explicitly excluded the possibility that the 'scrignutuzza' is an old woman so as to reject affiliations with the *vituperatio vetuale* tradition. Yet he writes that in the episode of Zeuxis, death by laughter is caused by the sight of an old woman. Furthermore, Giunta connects this sonnet to 'Deh, guata, Ciampol,' a text we will examine in detail below, and again a piece where the ugly woman is an old 'vecchiuzza.'
62 The seminal text for love phenomenology is, of course, Andreas's *De amore*, which posits the crucial role of looking at the beautiful woman as the origin of the passion of love.
63 Gorni claims that the 'scrignutuzza' is not old at all, since in fact she is a disfigured Beatrice, whose deformity should be a warning of the powerful effect of her beauty, beauty destined to fade quickly (33). Giunta too claims (316) that the 'scrignutuzza' is not old.
64 Lanza (note to Angiolieri's *Rime*, p. 258) and Cassata (234) see the connection between Rustico, Guinizzelli, and this sonnet.
65 Dantean connections are in the verse 'e quel che pare quand'ella s'aggruzza,' which reworks 'quel ch'ella par quando un poco sorride' (verse 12) in the sonnet of *Vita nuova*, 'Ne li occhi porta la mia donna Amore' (chapter 21).

To Beatrice's smile in the *Vita nuova* Cavalcanti opposes the angry frown of the 'scrignutuzza.' Contini noted that Cavalcanti's closing verse 'o tu morresti, o fuggiresti via' follows the same scheme of the verse 'diverria nobil cosa, o si morria' in the canzone 'Donne ch'avete intelletto d'amore' (chapter 19).
66 Text and translation are from the bilingual edition by Cervigni, p. 49.
67 Cavalcanti's choice as companion in amusement of Manetto, possibly the Portinari brother of Beatrice, adds to the theory of a precise and pointed attack on the lady of Dante's *Vita nuova*. Cavalcanti is inviting Manetto and perhaps Dante to establish a very close oppositional connection between the hunchback and the courtly lady of *Stilnovismo*, embodied by Beatrice in the *Vita nuova*.
68 The Stilnovistic lady is typically depicted as coy, measured, and adorned with the natural beauty of her youth. In Savona's *Repertorio tematico del Dolce Stil Nuovo* only one instance is found, at the entry 'moda,' and it refers to Cavalcanti's canzone of the Mandetta, where the poet describes the woman of Toulouse 'accordellata stretta,' a detail about the corset.
69 De Robertis's comments are taken from Letterio Cassata's critical edition of Cavalcanti's *Rime*, p. 234. A famous episode of an old hag masquerading as young and attractive is *Orlando Furioso*'s canto 20, where the old hag Gabrina ridiculously dons beautiful young Doralice's clothes. For masquerade and the Gabrina episode, see Finucci's article 'The Female Masquerade: Ariosto and the Game of Desire' in Finucci and Schwarz.
70 Antonio Lanza in his edition on Cecco Angiolieri's *Rime*, places this sonnet among those falsely attributed to Cecco. Lanza firmly states that the sonnet is by Niccola Muscia of Siena.
71 Contini includes this sonnet among Angiolieri's, and Thomas Caldecot Chubb translated it in his book on Angiolieri's poetry, p. 71.
72 Anna Bruni Bettarini finds this sonnet more repetitive than Cavalcanti's (90).
73 Massimo Ciavolella conducts an important study of the love illness in its philosophical and medical aspects and connects the Arab tradition with the Greek and medieval one. Ciavolella informs us that in the epitome of medicine called *Canon* the Arab doctor Avicenna (980–1037) enlists old women to act as wise counsellors who, by disparaging the beloved woman, convince the lover to forget her. Western tradition seems to deny old women even this dubious instance of assertiveness.
74 In Boccaccio's *Corbaccio* similar themes reappear, and the entire book can be read as a *Remedium amoris* in the Ovidian tradition. The widow is described in the *Corbaccio* in terms of her physical disgust and decay to provide shock

therapy to the seriously ill protagonist, who is on the verge of suicide. The age of the widow would not qualify her as old in modern times, since she is in her late thirties.

75 Giorgio Agamben uses Gordon's text as a source for his interpretation of Cavalcanti's sonnet of the 'scrignutuzza.' Paolo Cherchi ('Per la femmina balba') quotes this medical text as a possible source for Dante's 'femmina balba.' In that episode, as in Gordon's medical handbook, the disgusting reeking woman appears after the discussion of love's phenomenology and etiology.

Chapter 2. Transgression in the *Trecento* and *Quattrocento*: Guardian, Witch, Prostitute

1 For the relations between the *Roman* and *Il fiore*, as well as for the attribution of the latter to Dante, see Baransky and Boyde.
2 For more on old women in comic literature, see Bailbé.
3 The figure of the old bawd as guardian and servant in the *De vetula* was influential on Boccaccio's novella (VIII, 4) of monna Piccarda and her ugly old maid Ciutazza. For the influences of *De vetula* on Boccaccio, see Francesco Bruni.
4 In *Reggimento* this point is reiterated numerous times, with special emphasis for women of higher social ranks. In part 1, concerning the conduct of the young girl, we read: 'quando sta fra gente / gli occhi suoi lievi poco' (10). In part 2, prescribing the appropriate behaviour of girls soon to be married, we read: 'E quando pur le vien guardato alcuno, ... non sia ridendo quel cotal guardare, né fermo tenga a uno riguardo gli occhi' (19). In part 3 the woman who is past the age of marriage is advised to stay away from the window and the entrance: 'Lasci l'usar a finestra e ad uscio' (30). According to Giallongo the visual continence and self-discipline advocated for women derives from the ascetic model, which advised the rejection of the senses (*L'avventura dello sguardo*, 214).
5 For a recent study on the love passion and optics in Giacomo da Lentini, see Musacchio, who notes that the medieval theorization of love and falling in love, with its focus on vision, the eye, and the sight of the beloved, recycles a theme already present in classical Greek philosophy, in Aristotle (*Nicomachean Ethics*) and Plato (*Cratilus*) (339).
6 Quoted in Pagani. See Pagani for a complete list of entries on sight and looking in courtly love phenomenology.
7 *Repertorio tematico del Dolce Stil Nuovo*, p. 9.

8 Despite the general sense of passivity and absence of the woman in lyric poetry, the male poet in courtly and *Stilnovista* poetry attributes to the woman's eye the power to enchant and wound him with the complicity of Cupid's arrows. In fact, the role of the eye in courtly love dynamics is dual. The poet's eye is both the object of love's darts, originating from the woman's beauty, and the seeker of love. For the aggressive eye *topos* in lyric poetry, see Donaldson-Evans.
9 Stanbury also talks about the line of the female gaze in 'Feminist Masterplots.'
10 The essential source here is to Laura Mulvey's famous essay 'Visual Pleasure and Narrative Cinema,' later discussed by Ann Kaplan in 'Is the Gaze Male?' Kaplan stresses the great difficulty of the female viewer's taking up an active position as subject of the gaze. On the screen woman is reduced to an object of the male gaze.
11 Linda Williams examines the negative consequences of female appropriation of the gaze in horror films. The woman who looks is punished for her curiosity, for transgressing the rules of a cultural code whose literary origin dates back to medieval times.
12 That the evil eye can threaten masculinity and virility is demonstrated by the apotropaic use of phallic symbols or gestures to counteract its action; see Lobanov-Rostovsky.
13 See the *Dizionario etimologico della lingua italiana*, vol. 2.
14 Massera in his *Sonetti burleschi e realistici dei primi due secoli* quotes this *tenzone* from Chigiano L.VIII. 305. Although he does not find that these two sonnets fit with Angiolieri's main style, Massera attributes at least one of the sonnets to Angiolieri. However, in a more recent edition of Angiolieri's *Rime*, Antonio Lanza excludes these sonnets even from the section of 'rime dubbie.'
15 Emphasis in text is my own. 'Santa Tecchia' may be a variation on Santa Tecla constructed in order to create another word rhyming in '-ecchia.'
16 Sara Esposito, who recently edited *La battaglia*, points out that the poem reflects the late Gothic motif of the 'donna-sole' ('woman-sun'), whose luminosity strongly contrasts with the gloominess/darkness of the old women (10). A key point in the poem is indeed the old hag's *vituperium*, which includes various descriptive elements: 'la buccia crespa' (cantare 1, 63, 6–7) and 'co' denti neri e colle carni bolse' (cantare 1, 65, 6).
17 The text is integrated by Ageno with another version of the Codex Laurenziano. The brackets in quotes on Sacchetti's poems indicate the parts integrated in Ageno's edition. The devilish nature of old women is reiterated, for example, in the ballad 'Di diavol vecchia femmina ha natura,'

where evil, arrogance, and anger are the defects attributed to all old women, who are said to be envious of young women's beauty. Sacchetti takes up another classic misogynist motif in the 'Canzone contro la portatura delle donne fiorentine,' a satire against Florentine women's excessive use of dress and make-up.

18 Emphasis in text is mine.
19 The *pastourelle* promotes an ambivalent concept of love. On the one hand is the physical love worthy of a shepherdess, on the other hand are the lofty ideals of the courtly poet. Most *pastorelle* in Italian vernacular are in form of *contrasto* ('contrasto d'amore') between a suitor (usually of higher social status) and a young peasant, the opposite of the sublimated form of love found in the *fin'amor* and in Italian *Stilnovo*. In *Stilnovo* love is always spiritual and unrequited; in the *pastorelle* and in the *contrasto* the poem ends in consummation. In fact, some critics have defined the *pastorelle* as 'sublimated rape' (quoted in Orvieto and Brestolini, 103).
20 The old woman/guardian caught in the act of mumbling ('borbottare') will appear in quattrocento Tuscan poetry in Burchiello's sonnet ('Col borbottar mi parti lagrimando') and in the madrigal 'Andandomi l'altrier pur solazzando' by Filippo Scarlatti ('Una vecchia m'apparve borbottando' in Lanza's *Lirici toscani del quattrocento*, 498). The envy of the guardian is explicit in Donato da Cascia's madrigal 'Una smaniosa e insensata vecchia' (Corsi, 1047), in the anonymous ballads of minstrel repertoire, and in Giambullari's ballad 'Queste vecchie grinze e nere,' examined below. The old guardian is said to be jealous in Alesso di Guido Donati's madrigal 'In pena vivo qui sola soletta' (Corsi, 541) and in the anonymous *canzonetta* 'D'una vechia ch'è zilosa,' examined below.
21 For more on the power of the female gaze and the legendary animal basilisk, see Lobanov-Rostovsky.
22 This same rage against the old woman's body is found in two anonymous sonnets in a miscellaneous manuscript (Fondo principale ms. 10) at the Biblioteca Comunale of Udine: 'Veder ti possa vechia scarpelata' and 'Veder ti possa vechia rabiosa,' possibly from the beginning of the fifteenth century. Both sonnets wish for the old woman's bodily dismemberment, and the second one more precisely invokes birds of prey and other animals to feed on her stomach and entrails.
23 See Orvieto and Brestolini's observations about love between a knight and a peasant girl as discussed in Andreas's *De amore* (101–2).
24 Saffioti recognizes that the first difficulty is defining the 'giullare,' a term used for artists ranging from the street performer to the charlatan and the vagrant, and including the troubadour and the court jester (chapter 1).

Saffioti believes that one should distinguish the 'giullare' from the 'trovatore' since the former belongs to a lower social class.

25 Emilio Pasquini expresses similar views in 'La poesia popolare e giullaresca' (117).
26 For 'poesia per musica' see Lanza's 'Caratteri e forme della poesia per musica del secolo XIV.'
27 Emphasis in text is mine. Evidently the love sought by the poet here is not the fully spiritual and abstract one of which the angelic creature of *Stilnovo* is the object.
28 Casini assumes that Guinizzelli was harassed by an old woman 'colpevole di far troppo buona guardia alle figliuole' (207); likewise Cian (312).
29 It is ironic that the presumed male authorial voice in the poems, by resorting to the art of rhetoric and the power of speech, commits the same sin – excessive use of words – for which the old women are attacked in the poems. Bloch (*Medieval Misogyny* 56) notes the same paradox in misogynist authors, who, to support the case against women's excessive use of words and ornamentation, write essays in the most ornate and pompous style.
30 In *Rabelais and His World* Bakhtin discusses the grotesque in relation to the popular forms of art typical of medieval and Renaissance culture and in Rabelais's *Gargantua et Pantagruel*.
31 Zemon Davis's essay shows how in the comic environment of medieval and Renaissance festive celebrations the female grotesque occasionally serves a subversive purpose by allowing women to be on top and rule over men.
32 The Codex contains various metric types (canzoni, sonnets, ballads, strambotti) and themes, all meant for song and dance. The mini-series on the old women includes the ballad 'La vecchia d'amor m'à biasemata,' 'Do, mala vechia, lo mal fuogo l'arda,' and 'Laida vecchia stomegosa.' One should note, however, that these poems do not appear in Codex VII, 1070 in a sequence; rather, they are scattered throughout the manuscript. Due to their length and to the relative unavailability of such poems, the complete texts are provided in the appendix.
33 For clichés about women's loquacity in medieval canon law, exegesis, theology, and literature, see Casagrande. Clichés from centuries of misogynous literature were embedded in sermons, moral treatises for women, literature, and scriptures. The petulant, loquacious woman abused the supreme gift of words. Woman's loquacity, particularly if she dared speak in public, was also considered a threat to her chastity. Scorn directed towards garrulous women resulted in invectives against their evil tongues. For more on the sins of the tongue and the proverbial excess of women's tongues in relation to rhetoric, see Parker's 'On the Tongue.'

Notes to pages 57–62   203

34 The ballad 'La vecchia d'amor m'à biasemata' was also preserved in Codex Magliabechiano II, 61. The variations in the ballad confirm the problems of anonymous texts for oral performance, where differing versions exist. Casini proceeds to merge and organize the various stanzas to make the content more consistent. I shall use Casini's printed version here as a reference. The main differences between the version in Magliabechiano VII, 1070 and Magliabechiano II, 61 are as follows. In each version the ballad has the same *ripresa* and seven stanzas; another stanza (seventh in Codex VII, eighth in Codex II) is distinctive of that version. The stanzas in common follow a different order; hence Casini has proceeded to merge and reorder the stanzas, providing us with a whole poem. I am grateful to the personnel in the Sala Manoscritti at the Biblioteca Nazionale Centrale in Florence for allowing me to view the original version of the ballad in the Codex VII, 1070. Saffioti reprints Casini's version of the poem on pp. 404–5.

35 Despite the lack of women's voices in medieval literature, the female appears in medieval anonymous poetry and 'poesia giullaresca.' Particularly telling are the laments of married women ('malmaritate') or of widows, quite common in minstrel repertoires. Female voices often appear in *contrasti* or poetic dialogues between mother and daughter or between lover and beloved, and one should not forget the 'Compiuta donzella,' the first female voice in Italian literature. However, in most cases it is presumed that the authors of such poems were men. Saffioti shows that among the jongleurs it was not uncommon to find 'giullaresse,' who were either independent, or wives and artistic partners of 'giullari' (42–6).

36 The rule of silence for honest women affected the 'giullaresse,' who, for leading a vagabond life and appearing in public performance, were often accused of sinfulness and being prostitutes (Saffioti, 42–6)

37 Anne Jacobson Schutte discusses the problems of female speech in the case of confessions or 'commanded autobiographies,' where the female voice is filtered through male-authored reports; it is difficult to determine how much the female subject did contribute to such transcriptions (12).

38 In a sonnet by Adriano de' Rossi, 'Cara compagna del compagno mio' (in Giuseppe Corsi's *Rimatori*, 905), we find the invective of a younger woman against the old 'arrabbiata vecchia secca,' who is also given the epithet of 'bertuccia.'

39 Cadden points also to the ambiguity of hairy wild women, since occasionally they are found in stories or images of saints grown wild in isolation, or as unicorn tamers, a role usually reserved for virgins (182)

40 The anonymous *canzonetta* is quoted in Cian. The codex described by Cian as containing miscellaneous material, including Petrarch's lyrics, poems by

Giusto de' Conti, and verses by Veneto poets such as Antonio da Tempo and Leonardo Giustinian, includes a considerable amount of anonymous *canzonette* that echo Giustinian's style. Dislike of the old woman is a motif employed by Giustinian in the poem 'Chi se vol piacere dare/tutte vecchie lasse stare,' confirming that the anonymous *canzonetta* may have been influenced by Giustinian. Due to the length and relative inaccessibility of this poem, 'D'una vechia' is quoted in its entirety in the appendix.

41 For Hurwitz, Lilith is an archetypal figure of the dark feminine, who is highly relevant to the psychological understanding of today's evolving masculine and feminine identities. Hurwitz identifies a dual aspect of the Lilith figure: the most ancient (Lamashtû of the Babylonians, later in Greek mythology known as Lamia) and terrible mother-goddess, child-stealing and child-killing demon; and the later seductress who leads men astray (Ishtar). All the myths and legends have in common the theme of the dangerous female demon, who is vanquished by a male hero. See Hurwitz's *Lilith, The First Eve*.

42 The topic of the wild woman is quite vast and cannot be extensively studied here. My focus is on her physical aspect. All references to the witch's and wild woman's appearance are contained in Bernheimer's study. Bernheimer mentions the sculpture of Luxuria in the church of Moissac in France. The woman with drooping breasts so long as to be thrown over the shoulders is also in Boccaccio's *Corbaccio*. In the medieval Spanish *Libro de Buen Amor* by Juan Ruiz (thirteenth century), the wild woman is a *serrana*, a mountain woman notable for her huge size, extreme ugliness, and lechery. Here the wild woman's role reflects the ancient tradition of the dangerous liminal beings who guard the mountain passes and engage travellers in rites of passage. For more on wild women in Spanish literature, see Roger Bartra.

43 Zemon Davis notes several popular festivities of the Middle Ages in Germany and Austria where sexual inversion includes males disguised as grotesque females, or bear chases in France involving lustful bears and men dressed like women. Zemon Davis also establishes a connection between her study and Bernheimer's.

44 A wild man's hunt is described in Boccaccio's novella of Frate Alberto (*Decameron* IV, 2).

45 As Orvieto observes, the ugly old woman motif conflates several features of medieval chivalry romance of the tradition of *cantari* and is found in allegorical stories. Her features evoke the representation of devil, giant, and infidel in the character of Arabas ('Aveva i suoi capelli insino alle calcagna, neri et grossi come code di cavalli'), the hairy and ugly old mother of giant Marabus in Andrea da Barberino's *cantare Ugone d'Alvernia*. She is an old

sorcerer in the anonymous *Fabula del Pistello da l'Agliata* ('Una vecchia scapigliata et nuda./Sì strana et contrafacta era costei / Gobba, sciancata, guerza, et tanta nera, / Che al lume della luna io mi credei, / Che ella fusse Thesiphone o Megera'). In the view of Orvieto, from whom all these quotes are taken (*Pulci medievale*, 120–5), the features of these old hags influenced the negative *descriptio* of the sorceress Creonta in Luigi Pulci's comic epic *Morgante* ('Creonta, / ... / barbuta e guercia e maliziosa e pronta / ... / pilosa e nera, arricciata e crinuta, // ... e Satanasso n'arebbe paura, / e Tesifóne ed Aletto e Megera,' cantare XXI, stanzas 26–7). Both in the *Fabula* and in *Morgante* the old hag is compared to or associated with the Furies Alecto, Thisiphone, and Megaera, a detail that helps explain epithets in the anonymous 'Stanze in lode della donna brutta' that will be examined in chapter 3.

46 Ariosto's Latin poem 'In Lenam' attacks an old prostitute. Niccolò Franco describes in a sonnet a lascivious, disgusting old woman who wants to have sex with the poet. Aretino's interest in prostitutes is much more profound; in the *Sei giornate* he devotes an entire dialogue to prostitution as a viable profession for women.

47 In the Veneto the old woman is also under attack in the works of Leonardo Giustinian (1388–1446), a Venetian poet who chronologically precedes the Tuscan examples. In his *canzonetta* 'Chi se vol piacer dare, / tutte vecchie lasse stare' the poet warns all younger women to beware of old ones and enumerates all of the latter's defects and vices. The poem ends with the wish that all old women be burnt to death, like witches. Delcorno Branca also mentions the anonymous ballad 'Questa vecchia rimbambita' (note 116). In his repertoire of courtesan poetry Serafino Aquilano includes a *canzonetta* against an old woman.

48 The focus on the witch is limited to how she appears in literary texts. Witches and witchcraft have been the subject of extensive study. Romeo De Maio's *Donne e rinascimento* has a chapter on 'L'inquisizione e la donna' with extensive notes and bibliographical references. Also of note is Bernheimer's study on demonology, where the witch is associated with the wild woman and the popular rituals of Carnival and Epiphany. For an interesting iconographic study of the figure of the witch, Battisti's chapter 'La nascita della strega' (138–57) is particularly relevant. Battisti sees, towards the mid-fifteenth century, the rise of a new phase in the iconographical history of the witch as clearly identified with the devil; in medieval iconography, on the other hand, the figure of the witch was intertwined with the sorcerer, the magician, the popular figure of the 'Befana,' and the folklore figure of the country healer.

49 Although some of Bernardino's sermons seem to preach equality between men and women and advocate female rights, he is particularly harsh on witchcraft. His obsession with witches is discussed in Iris Origo's *The World of Saint Bernardino*. Giovanni Battista Bronzini's 'La predicazione di San Bernardino da Siena fra scrittura e oralità' explores the theme of witchcraft in sermon 35 and in the Sienese sermons of 1427.

50 Stephens maintains that theorists were not motivated by moral or ethical questions about women. Rather, they were interested in defending fundamental Christian principles at a time of crisis of confidence in the efficacy of Christian sacraments (*Demon Lovers*, 30).

51 One should also distinguish between the witch and the sorcerer who practised white magic. In medieval popular folklore the sorcerer was often equated with a healer who performed a mixture of magic and medicine and was frequently a respected figure in the countryside. See Camporesi, pp. 16–17.

52 This sonnet is now included in Zaccarello's recent critical edition of Burchiello's sonnets from the 'vulgata quattrocentesca.' It was previously only available in the so-called London edition (but most likely Lucca or Pisa, 1752) with some variations noted below.

53 The sonnet displays a rich texture of literary borrowings: the wrinkled face 'agrizzando il volticel vecchile' is one of the recurring elements in depictions of old women. This old woman is caught mumbling ('borbottar'), a common activity of old guardians, as noted above.

54 For Stephens the origin of the figure of the witch in the Western modern world lies in the inquisition of heresy and popular rural culture; see 'Il ruolo' and *Demon Lovers*, chapter 8).

55 For the London edition we have consulted the CD-ROM of *LIZ*

56 For more details on witches' transformations see the item 'Metamorphosis' in Robbins's *Encyclopedia of Witchcraft and Demonology*. Toads were considered innately evil and poisonous. Stephens also discusses the connection between toads and witches, reporting Kramer's episode of the Toad Witch, who confessed that her powders for working *maleficium* contained the body of a toad (*Demon Lovers*, 252–3)

57 Lanza finds the peculiarity of Giovan Matteo's corpus in a mixture of archaic and strongly innovative elements (*Freschi e minii*, 264, 266). He considers the *vituperia* the most original poems in Meglio's small corpus. Although he mentions Giovan Matteo's renewal of some misogynist motifs, he fails to take any position on Giovan Matteo's antifeminist virulence, treating the misogynist poems with indifferent matter-of-factness, simply as expressions of a literary style and genre.

58 In sixteenth-century literature many poems inveigh against prostitutes, or courtesans. Ariosto's 'In Lenam,' modelled on classical tradition, attacks an old prostitute, as does Niccolò Franco in the sonnet 'Una vecchiazza, ch'è tutta canuta.' Francesco Beccuti (il Coppetta) attacks the courtesan Ortensia, whom he had praised in a previous capitolo. Quinto Gherardo has a 'capitolo' against a courtesan. The figure of the procuress, retired prostitute, and expert in witchcraft has broad roots in European literature. Ferdinando Rojas's *Celestina* (1499) is perhaps the best example. See also Banner's chapter on the procuress and the witch.

59 In Giovan Matteo the invective is not limited to old women but extends to ugly women in general, regardless of age; lust and depravity are recurring themes. The sonnets 'O chalandorna' and 'O falsa ladra' are invectives that introduce particularly coarse language, until then unheard in such poetry; the woman is called 'bagascia' and 'vacca e troia.' In a total of five poems the lascivious prostitute is the subject of four.

60 The *Sonetti faceti* were published in 1511 after Cammelli's death. Upon Isabella's initiative, since she was always eager to discover literary novelties and pleasurable verse, Cammelli's verse was edited first by Nicolò da Correggio and later by Giovanfrancesco Gianniniello. Cammelli's descriptive technique includes conventional praise of beautiful women in which a somewhat parodistic tone occasionally surfaces; a group of sonnets (67–70) is famous for praising the women of different cities where Cammelli resided (Florence, Siena, Ferrara, Milan). The poet contaminates the traditional encomium by mentioning physical deformities.

61 For a full discussion of 'poesia rusticana-nenciale' see chapter 3. In the verb 'aguzza' can be found some resonance of Cavalcanti's and Muscia's old women.

62 For Bakhtin's interpretation of Carnival, see *Rabelais and His World*, chapter 3. For medieval laughter as relief from fear, see chapter 1, 'History of Laughter.'

63 Delcorno Branca considers both the ballad and the Latin ode samples of the stylistic category of *lusus* or playful exercise ('Il laboratorio,' 194). According to Tateo this ballad revives 'il gusto della divertita rappresentazione della donna disgustosa, che ritoviamo nella lirica latina' (183).

64 A negative physical description also appears in Poliziano's disgusting portrait of Febris in the Latin elegy 'In Albieram.'

65 Of course this episode does not have to be read as an actual experience. The description of the old woman's body and private parts imitates familiar literary clichés. The tradition is very rich. Yet the rhetorical choice to recount the unpleasant event in the first person to a sympathetic audience

lends itself to identification of author and poetic persona and to the realism of the situation. Fictional or not, the subject matter exploited in the ballad reveals the axieties of the male subject about a transgressive female type.

66 In her socio-historical study on prostitution in the Renaissance Lyndal Roper emphasizes the link between drinking and prostitutes.

67 See, among the examples quoted by Delcorno Branca (200), the proverbs 'La puttana fila: dicesi per scherno perché quando le puttane filano le sono ridotte al verde' or 'Va mal quando le puttane filano,' and in Ariosto's *Orlando furioso* (XII, 39) the words of Orlando to Sacripante: 'Che potria/ più dir costui, s'ambi ci avesse scorti/per le più vili e timide puttane/che da conocchie mai traesser lane?'

68 Poliziano revisits the motif of the witch in *Lamia*, the proemial lesson of his course on Aristotle's *Priora*. Here the slanderers gathered to deride Poliziano's philosophical activity are compared to a gathering of witches; although the witches are not portrayed in caricatural tone like the ballad, they are described as spinners.

69 Behind the ballad Delcorno Branca sees the contemporary production of *frottole*, particularly Leon Battista Alberti's 'Frottola degli innamorati,' which shares with Poliziano's vernacular poetry many thematic-lexical elements (195). Alberti's poem includes a parade of ugly women, which may have provided Poliziano with a picturesque gallery of grotesque feminine portraits: 'L'una ha un sopraosso / in sul naso, e gli occhi infiati; / l'altra ha gli oc[c]hi schiacciati / adentro un mezzo miglio; / l'altra ti porge un piglio / e par ch'ogni uom gli puta; / quale è scrignuta, / monca o sciancata, / cispa e sdentata, / o vizza o rognosa' (83). The grotesque aspect of Alberti's women evokes the traditional medieval examples from Cavalcanti to the wrinkled-faced hag, endless examples of which have been encountered so far.

70 Some of Poliziano's most famous ballads (*canzoni a ballo*) are a glorification of spring, as a symbol of youth and beauty of the woman. See, for example, 'I' mi trovai, fanciulle, un bel mattino' and 'I' mi trovai un dì, tutto soletto,' where the month of May and the blossoming spring setting hint at the youth of the woman during the season of new love. Concerning the codes of proper behaviour for a young woman in love, in the ballad 'Egli è ver ch'i porto amore' Poliziano also insists on the importance of preserving the beloved's honour.

71 In Franco's sonnet, anthologized in Muscetta and Ponchiroli, p. 994, the 'vecchiazza' with decaying body displays particularly obscene behaviour towards the poet, and bears a remarkable physical resemblance to Poliziano's 'vecchia.' In Ariosto's Latin ode 'In Lenam' the poet inveighs against an indecent,' white-haired old bawd – 'venditrix libidinum' (vendor

of lust) – who deceitfully lured him into sexual relations with prostitutes. She is compared to a baby-devouring witch and linked with hell.

72 Franco's sonnet, where the man eventually succumbs to the advances of the disgusting prostitute, presents a situation parallel to the one described by Niccolò Machiavelli in perhaps the most notorious literary encounter with a lustful prostitute in Renaissance Italian literature. Machiavelli recounted his sexual adventure with an old prostitute in a letter from Verona to Luigi Guicciardini in 1507. Here again an old prostitute is described in all her physical disgustingness and decay; Machiavelli cannot reject her with scorn because he is entirely possessed by lust ('foia') and is denied the ability to see her aging, repulsive body. Hence the revolting finale, where the author vomits after discovering the ugliness of the old prostitute. For an excellent feminist reading of this letter, see Schiesari. In the sixteenth century the target of the attack in many persons is the more refined and dignified type of the courtesan, instead of a generic prostitute. Quinto Gherardo ('Capitolo contro una cortegiana') and Coppetta wrote a *capitolo* against a courtesan. Rage against prostitutes was common at a time when the number of prostitutes active in major cities was extremely high and when some courtesans had achieved a privileged status. For more on prostitutes and courtesans in Renaissance Italy, see Graf and Rosenthal.

Chapter 3. The Portrait of the Ugly Woman in the Renaissance: The Peasant, the Anti-Laura

1 The terms 'Other' and 'hegemony' have taken on various meanings in critical theory. In such a vast and complex area of theory, my observations and bibliographical references here offer just a few inevitably limited suggestions. Michel Foucault's work on society and its forms of exclusion, and the incorporation of the Other into the same, have been a key theoretical reference in the development of the concept of the Other in postcolonial studies. Hegemony and the subaltern (as subordinate or underclass) are concepts first developed by Antonio Gramsci in *The Prison Notebooks* ('The Formation of the Intellectuals') and later fruitfully expanded in critical theory. Hegemony is viewed as the domination of a set of ruling beliefs and values through consent rather than through coercive power. Gramsci sees the role of intellectuals as key in the function of hegemony: 'The intellectuals are the dominant group's "deputies" exercising the subaltern functions of social hegemony and political government' (*Literary Theory: An Anthology*, 277). Spivak extends the category of the subaltern to women and gender issues. As Robert Young notes: 'In postcolonial studies generally, the sub-

altern has become synonym for any marginalized or disempowered minority group, particularly on the grounds of gender and ethnicity' (354). For the category of the Other and the subaltern, see Young's *Postcolonialism*, particularly part 5, 'Formations of Postcolonial Theory.'

2 The only full-size portraits I found in medieval Italian vernacular were in the anonymous ballads of 'poesia giullaresca,' and in Poliziano's 'Una vecchia mi vagheggia.' Thanks to the longer format of the ballad, these poems provide more detailed descriptions of female ugliness.

3 The descriptive convention of *effictio* or *descriptio extrinsica* does not appear in the poetry of Dante and in the *Stilnovo*, despite the fact that Brunetto Latini provided in his *Tresor* the most important and influential examples of *descriptio pulchritudinis* in his elaborate description of Iseult's beauty (Dempsey, 56).

4 Pozzi develops these concepts in two articles ('Codici, stereotipi' and 'Il ritratto della donna') that are summed up in 'Temi, *topoi*, stereotipi.' In *Arts and Beauty in the Middle Ages* Umberto Eco delineates precisely proportion, light, and colour as the founding elements in the medieval aesthetics.

5 The eleven stanzas containing Emilia's description are translated into English in Charles Dempsey (59–60). In *Ameto* feminine portraits of the six nymphs all focus on harmony, balance, and proportion. Many female literary portraits are so similar because of their adherence to rhetorical norms and their imitation of conventional models such as Boccaccio's; see, for example, Luigi Pulci's Antea, Poliziano's Simonetta, or Ariosto's Alcina. Dempsey detects this same aspect in the pictorial representation of the female goddesses in Sandro Botticelli's painting *Primavera* (60). For more on female descriptions of literary beauty in Italian vernacular, see Mario Martelli and Paolo Orvieto (*Pulci medievale*).

6 The numbers in brackets refer to the conventional numbering of poems in Petrarch's *Canzoniere*. Vickers ('Diana Described,' 96) underscores the fragmentary nature of Laura's portrait, which is impossible to find in one single poem, but rather is scattered throughout the entire *Canzoniere*. The quotations, concerning Laura's body parts are just a sample; for more quotations see Renier, pp. 103–5.

7 Female beauty is sanctioned in Bembo's *Asolani* (1505), where the woman's body is described as colour, perfection, and proportion in terms similar to those of Boccaccio. See, for example, how Gismondo describes female beauty in book 2, chapter 22. On female beauty and decorum in Castiglione's *Cortegiano*, see especially book 3, devoted to women. For the importance of beauty and for the role of feminine beauty in Renaissance culture, see Cropper's introduction to *Concepts of Beauty in Renaissance Art*.

8 The 'poesia rusticana' originates in the *strambotti* (one-stanza poems in hendecasyllables, usually an octave or sextet), one of the most ancient Italian popular verse forms, and *rispetti* (stanza of eight verses usually with the following rhymes *abababcc*.) Its flourishing in fourteenth- and sixteenth-century Italy, had in the past led critics such as Carducci to believe that *strambotto* might have exclusively Italian origin. Cirese has shown that *strambotto* is one of the most ancient poetic forms, found in Western Romance vernaculars as early as the twelfth century. For precursory evidence of the *Nencia* tradition in Boccaccio, one should refer to the novella of Belcolore (*Decameron* VIII, 2) and to *Ameto*; see Fido.

9 Giulio Ferrario (*Poesie pastorali e rusticali*) collects chronologically some of the most significant texts in the rustic tradition, among them Anton Francesco Doni's *Stanze dello Sparpaglia alla Silvana sua innamorata* and Francesco Baldovini's *Lamento di Cecco da Varlungo*. The adventures of Nencia became so popular that many anonymous spin-offs followed every aspect of Nencia's life; Ferrario published a *canzonetta rusticale* 'In morte della Nencia,' and Bernardo Giambullari also composed stanzas about the death of Nencia.

10 We have four versions of the *Nencia*: (V) = Vulgata in 50 octaves; (A) = Volpi in 20 octaves; (P) = Patetta in 39 octaves; (CN) = Messina in 12 octaves. Version (A) in 20 octaves is considered the original of which all the others would be remakes and further expansions. For the much-debated issue of *Nencia*'s authorship and various editions, see the *Nencia da Barberino* edited by Rossella Bessi, with a lengthy introduction and including all four versions.

11 Orvieto and Brestolini see in 'testi nenciali' the convergence of medieval comic ingredients of the *pastorelle* and the 'contrasti d'amore': rejection of courtly ideals, fulfilled sexuality, the male lover bragging and boasting, obscenity, and language degradation (109).

12 Other themes, which De Robertis traces back to Latin pastoral and bucolic literature, are the lament for unrequited love, the cruelty of the beloved, the prayer and invectives against the woman, the enumeration of the presents Vallera is willing to offer her, and the qualities that should make him attractive to the girl. Perhaps the most significant text to be added to the four versions of the *Nencia* is the *Stanze villanesche*, published by Domenico De Robertis, a series of 'rispetti nenciali' that constitute the largest nucleus (55 stanzas) of original material and show a distinctive Sienese influence; for De Robertis they mark the shift from the Nencian to the rustic genre, so popular in the sixteenth century. Longhi (*Poeti del cinquecento*, 724) believes that the *Stanze villanesche* are very close in time to Berni's two 'Capitoli' to his 'innamorata' and to Strascino's 'Capitoli' for his 'dama.'

13 For an engaging commentary on the version of *Nencia* attributed to Lorenzo de' Medici, see Orvieto and Brestolini (109–18), where the critics highlight the parodistic elements of the medieval courtly tradition and the degradation of courtly love codes and language in the peasant context.

14 The rustic genre, particularly the altercations and rivalries between peasants, was well suited to theatrical pieces that present the comical adventures of the 'villani.' Some of these rustic comedies, often stories of intrigue and love complications that culminate in marriage, include a verbal portrait of the contended rustic girl. This rudimentary plot was exploited by Francesco Berni in his early 'scherzo rusticale' *La Catrina* (before 1517?), in the anonymous *Il Mogliazzo*, and in other theatrical pieces classified under the name of 'mogliazzo' (in Tuscan regions) or 'mariazo' (in the Veneto region), marriage play. The best play in rustic theater is *La Tancia*, a comedy composed in 1611 by Michelangelo Buonarroti il Giovane.

15 Although there is no precise date of composition or publication for Campani's two 'Capitoli,' by following Valenti's hypothesis that they were part of Strascino's early repertoire, predating his theatrical pieces, we can assume that they were composed before 1511. Almost certainly they were first recited at public gatherings and only later made available in print. Longhi (*Lusus*, 257) finds them in the second Giuntina edition of *Opere burlesche di Francesco Berni, del Molza, di M. Bino, di M. Lodovico Martelli, di Mattio Franzesi, dell'Aretino, et di diversi Autori* (Florence: Giunti, 1555). Longhi considers Campani's two 'Capitoli' particularly important for their influence on Berni (*Poeti*, 938).

16 Longhi rightly points out that during the cinquecento the *capitolo* supplants the sonnet as the preferred metric format for jocose poetry (*Lusus*, 4).

17 Longhi's statement applies specifically to Campani's two capitoli on the 'dama' but also involves Berni's, Firenzuola's, and Mauro's negative verbal portraits of the woman.

18 The fragmentary description of the body appears in many Renaissance dialogues even in allegorical figurations. See, for example, Leone Ebreo's *Dialoghi d'amore* (I, 53), where the descripiton of Amore is effected through fragments, and similarly in Bembo's *Asolani* (1, 171) for the portrait of Cupido.

19 In Castiglione's *Cortegiano* Strascino is mentioned in book 2 (chapter 50) in the part devoted to discussion of 'moti e facezie' and in general to all those arts the courtier should possess to entertain the prince. To dress as a peasant is very suitable for a professional comedian like Strascino but not appropriate for a courtier. Here Castiglione shows that the hegemonic

groups are both attracted and repulsed by lower social class embodied by the peasant.

20 Although mainstream criticism (e.g., Ulysse) considers Strascino, along with figures like Legacci and Mescolino, to be among the pre-Rozzi, or precursor of the 'Congrega dei Rozzi,' established in Siena in 1531, Valenti rejects that label for artists like Campani, Stricca Legacci, or Mescolino. She prefers to define them as 'comici artigiani' since she believes that the 'comici' acted before but also simultaneously with the Rozzi. They were artists who fused in their comic artistry the mercantile mentality acquired as bell-makers, blacksmiths, candle-makers, and the like. For a complete discussion of the sociocultural scene that subtends the artistic activity of the pre-Rozzi, see Ulysse.

21 As Valenti informs us, Strascino spent some time entertaining the court of Mantua for Carnival celebrations of 1521. In fact, it was Isabella d'Este's son Federico Gonzaga who instructed Castiglione to obtain the pope's permission for Strascino's trip to Mantua (51). Valenti believes that the 'comici artigiani' entertained in an area including Siena, Rome, Ferrara, and other 'corti padane.'

22 Strascino is the author of some comic poetry, but is best known for his eclogues or 'farse villanesche,' a form of comedy where laughter originates from the clash of peasant characters with urban middle-class citizens or characters of the pastoral genre. His plays *Strascino*, *Magrino*, and *Coltellino*, composed between 1511 and 1520, each stage the contrast between the 'villano' and the city dweller or the shepherd of traditional pastoral drama. The 'Lamento,' a long poem about Strascino's battle with syphilis, is also very famous. Valenti notes that given Campani's success in performance, printed versions of his work often appeared several years after their original creation (65).

23 In *Rabelais and His World* (Introduction, pp. 26–9, and chapter 5) Bakhtin discusses the features of the grotesque body in opposition to the classical canons of antiquity. The grotesque body does not fit the framework of the 'aesthetics of the beautiful' as conceived in the Renaissance. The literary and artistic canon of antiquity, which provides the basis for Renaissance aesthetics, represents the classical body as a completed, finished product, totally enclosed, with no mention of inner parts or openings.

24 Spackman examines the grotesque description of the apothecary's wife in Tifi Odasi's *Macaronea* and finds that it is not the product of subversion, but belongs to the *topos* of the 'enchantress-turned-hag' as seen in Dante's 'femina balba,' in Ariosto's Alcina, and in Machiavelli's 'lavandaia' in the letter to Luigi Guicciardini. This female grotesque for Spackman 'stands as

hermeneutic figure par excellence, for it would reveal truth beneath falsehood, plain speech beneath cosmetic rhetoric, essence beneath appearance' (22). Spackman sees true subversion in the grotesque female body of the unruly 'woman on top' in Natalie Zemon Davis's essay 'Women on Top,' and in Peter Stallybrass's essay on Othello and the 'body enclosed' in 'Patriarchal Territories.'

25 Ulysse (223) notes that Ginzburg had already singled out millers as the most hated people in the Renaissance Italian countryside.

26 The logic of the world turned upside down typical of Carnival and folk festivities, which Bakhtin sees as a temporary suspension of all hierarchical rank, privileges, norms, as an occasion for subversion, does not lead to true subversion in Strascino, precisely because poems like Strascino's were not composed for folk entertainment but for divertissement of the elite.

27 Both Orvieto and Brestolini make this point in *La poesia comico-realistica*. See, for example, the extensive reference to gastronomic items in the paradoxical praises of sausage, boiled eggs, cardoon, broad beans, melons, and so on, in Berni, Molza, and Firenzuola, most often with homosexual connotations (216–17).

28 Some similes rework *Nencia*. 'E quel *nasin* tanto ben *bucherato*, / che pare un sampognin da far cristeri' echoes this feature in the *Nencia* (3 V; 21 P; 3 A): 'E in quel mezzo ha il *naso* tanto bello, / che par proprio *bucato* col succhiello' (emphasis is mine). Other diminutives are used for the mouth ('bocchin par quel d'un campanello') and the chin ('mentino auzzo e tondarello'). In Strascino the same comparative formula ('che par') is used for the nose, but the disgusting detail of 'cristeri' lowers the gracious tones of the *Nencia*. For more intertextual references, see Longhi's notes to the poems in *Poeti*, 938–43.

29 The metaphor of the earth/land and 'orto' for the woman's genitals and the activity of tilling or working the earth is common in popular literature and in 'poesia rusticana,' but is also found in Boccaccio's *Decameron* (II, 10; III, 1) and in Poliziano.

30 Many textual parallelisms exist between this *capitolo* and the *Nencia*. Strascino's 'dama' is introduced as an incomparable model of beauty similar to Diana and superior to Helen and Morgan le Fay: 'Tu mi pari oggi la deia Driana, / ... tu matti Elena e la fata Morgana.' In *Nencia* (M, stanza 6) the peasant is compared to Morgan and Diana as a star: 'I' t'ò aguagliata alla fata Morgana, / ... i' t'assomiglio alla stella diana.'

31 In terms of proportion, rustic poems ambiguously oscillate between the excessive (*accrescitivo*) and the diminutive. In the second *capitolo* the diminutive prevails. For the face of the 'dama' Stracino uses 'faccino,' which is

indebted more to Pulci's *Beca*: Strascino's 'bocchin' (little mouth) and 'bel mentin' (pretty little chin) appear in Beca, who is 'piccina' (petite) and has a 'bocchina.' Other textual parallels with *Beca* are in the language of agricultural tradition: 'pagliaio' and 'maio' are in *Beca*'s stanza 9 and in Strascino's verses 2 and 4. In stanza 12 are found 'fichi ... e mele,' which also appear in the 'Capitolo' in verse 24.

32 After his first years in Florence, Berni moved to Rome in 1517 during Medici's Leo X pontificate and worked for Cardinal Bernardo Dovizi; later he worked for the bishop of Verona, Giovan Matteo Giberti, the papal datary of Clement VII, another Medici pope.

33 In his collection of *Rime* Berni pays tribute to some of his masters. In one sonnet he honours Cammelli ('O spirito bizzarro del Pistoia') and in another one Burchiello ('S'i' avessi l'ingegno del Burchiello').

34 See Anthony Oldcorn's section 'Berni and Berneschi' in *The Cambridge History of Italian Literature*.

35 The academy was founded in Rome by Umberto Strozzi after the Sack of Rome and included many *literati* of the papal court such as Giovanni Mauro, Francesco Bini, Giovanni della Casa, Agnolo Firenzuola, and Francesco Maria Molza. The name 'Vignaiuoli' alludes to the fact that academy members used burlesque nicknames that referred to peasant life and agricultural products. The academy became the gathering point for Renaissance burlesque poets who pleased the papal court. See Maylender, vol. 5, 466–7.

36 Berni himself had experimented with the rustic genre in his early play *La Catrina* (circa 1517). This one-act piece is a rustic marriage play, a genre that was becoming popular in Tuscany and in other regions of the Italian peninsula. Particularly important are the 'mariazi' that developed in the northeastern regions, in the area of Padua. 'Mariazi' were composed in the local dialect, both anonymously and by Angelo Beolco, who is famous for his five-act play *La Betìa* (circa 1524). Berni's and Beolco's marriage plays include verbal homage to the 'villana.'

37 Longhi mentions Petrarch's *Canzoniere* 142, 'Non volsi al mio refugio ombra di poggi,/ma de la pianta più gradita in cielo' (11–12), echoed in Berni's 'e ch'io contemplo la cima e 'l pedone' (2), where 'cima' and 'pedone' refer to the extremities of a plant or tree. However, 'pedone' also works as the augmentative for 'piede' and reinforces the series of agumentatives that characterize the body of the peasant.

38 Firenzuola is best known for his *Ragionamenti* (1548), an unfinished collection of short stories bringing together the novella tradition of Boccaccio's *Decameron* and the dialogue tradition of Bembo's *Asolani*. Among his comic poems is the famous desecrating elegy 'In morte di una civetta' ('On the

death of the owl'), a parody of Bembo's famous tragic canzone on his brother's death. Expanding on Berni's repertoire of uncommendable objects with sexual double-entendre, Firenzuola praised peaches, the bagpipe, and the sausage, among others.

39 The use of descriptive praise of feminine beauty as an ambiguous means of fragmentation and domination of the body has been studied by Vickers ('Members Only'). For this theme in Firenzuola's *Celso* and in Trissino's *Ritratti*, see my 'Corpo di parti.'
40 *On the Beauty of Women*, trans. Eisenbichler and Murray, 47–8.
41 The treatise includes forehead, teeth, tongue, chin, leg, foot, and hand, elements that are ignored in the *capitolo.*
42 Firenzuola's personal circumstances, his early years spent in the elegant ambience of the papal Curia, soon ended because of his battle with syphilis. His dispensation from monastic vows led him to settle in the peripheral region of Prato. Here he could come in closer contact with the peasant lifestyle he describes in the *capitolo*. This might generate familiarity with but also stronger criticism of the lower classes.
43 For fragmentation as a technique to contain the erotic attraction to the female body in the *Dialogo delle bellezze*, see my 'Corpo di parti.'
44 Melanie Klein's study 'Some Theoretical Conclusions Regarding the Emotional Life of the Infant' (in Klein and Riviere) examines the way in which the infant perceives the breast. This study can provide an interesting clue to a psychoanalytical interpretation of Firenzuola's poem. For Klein the breast occupies a privileged place in the infant's relation to its internal and external world; it is perceived by the infant as both a 'good' breast and a 'bad' breast. The infant projects its feelings of tenderness and rage towards the good and the bad breast respectively. The aggression towards the bad breast engenders fantasies of destruction in which the infant bites and tears up the breast.
45 Valenti quotes six lines from the *capitolo* that coincide exactly with the verses from the anonymous poem ('Capitolo rusticale contando le bellezze de la sua inamorata') housed at the Biblioteca Trivulziana in Milan. Valenti's bibliographical information on the 'Capitolo' is from the Biblioteca Apostolica Vaticana, which owns Legacci's *Strambotti et Capitoli alla Villana*, published in Siena in 1546. I was not able to access the book at BAV to confirm that the two *capitoli* are the same; if they are not identical perhaps, as in the case of 'poesia giullaresca,' they indicate the existence of a repertoire of cliché verses used by various artists, which Legacci could have used for his poem. This little mystery can be solved with some diligent philological work. Even assuming that the two poems are the same and belong to

Legacci, I take the precaution of calling the author of the anonymous 'Capitolo' pseudo-Legacci. I am grateful to Marina Litrico of the Biblioteca Trivulziana for making available to me the complete text of the 'Capitolo.'
46 The entire 'Capitolo rusticale contando le bellezze de la sua inamorata' in the version of the Biblioteca Trivulziana (H 193/1) is quoted in the appendix.
47 Contempt for 'contadini' and 'villani' runs through Italian literature from the Middle Ages on; see, for example, the 'Alfabeto dei villani.' Merlini (120) notes how the 'facchini' were particularly hated by other workers who migrated to the city, since the former had an advantage in the competition for employment: they were willing to accept any type of manual labour. In his *Piazza Universale di tutte le professioni del mondo* (1585), an almost contemporary encyclopedia of customs and people, Tommaso Garzoni describes the porters as those people who came to Venice and other large cities from the mountain regions surrounding Bergamo, and who were the favourite target of everybody's jokes for their roughness and stupidity. From the type of the 'facchino' developed the character of the Arlecchino, or servant of the 'Commedia dell'Arte.'
48 Stallybrass and White use the term 'abjection' without any specific reference to Julia Kristeva's 'essay on abjection' (*Powers of Horror*). Although in Kristeva the abject is fully represented in the pregnant female body, the notion of 'abjection' also emerges in other areas such as the hierarchic caste system in India or in mythical and biblical abominations.
49 The expression 'manzotta' is found in the anonymous rustic marriage play *Mogliazzo*, which is close to Berni's rustic piece *Catrina*.
50 This insistence on filth bears traces of abjection as Kristeva analyzes it in her essay *Powers of Horror*. In Kristeva's survey of biblical tradition abjection is located in the unclean and improper body. In Leviticus impurity is located in leprosy, 'the disease [which] visibly affects the skin, the essential if not initial boundary of biological and psychic individuation' (101). For Kristeva, leprosy, like other physical defects and bodily impurity, is considered a threat to identity, as they all mark the non-symbolic body.
51 Longhi (*Poeti del cinquecento*, 904) believes this epistle was written in the summer of 1532 when Mauro was in the fortification Rocca Sinibalda in the region of Sabinia (in Latium), a property of the Cesarini family.
52 In chapter 4, I note how the themes of lice in the woman's hair and the flea on her breasts become a source of wit and conceit in baroque poetry, where dirt and uncleanliness do not undermine the sensual attractiveness of the woman.
53 Stallybrass and White note that in nineteenth-century England an emphasis

on filth and dirt pervades discourse about the poor and the emerging proletariat, who lived in slums. The division between cleanliness and dirt is articulated as a division between Christian and pagan, civilized and savage (131).

54 Longhi mentions Mauro's particular attraction to courtesans, noting that his first two *capitoli* in praise of the fava bean, as well as one in praise of Priapus, were addressed to the Roman courtesan Flaminia (*Lusus*, 37). In the Renaissance social purity and civility are obviously not diminished by immoral female behaviour, if courtesans can be elevated above the vulgar, thanks to their observance of correct techniques of the body and their refinement and propriety. In this poem wives of the mountain village are debased, whereas Roman prostitutes are elevated for their compliance to the new codes of bodily propriety.

55 In Berni's poetry Bàrberi Squarotti finds a 'netto distacco dai canoni cinquecenteschi del decoro e della convenienza, ... nel senso dell'essenzialità lirica (petrarchismo bembiano)' ('Introduzione' in Berni's *Rime* burlesche, 5). For Mario Marti (*Letteratura Italiana*, 1094) Berni possessed a realistic and burlesque disposition that was moulded during his first years at the Medicean court. The proclamation of anti-Petrarchism is well expressed in Berni's 'Capitolo a Fra Sebastiano del Piombo,' where Michelangelo's art is assumed as the model for a new poetic in opposition to Petrarchism: 'tacete unquanco, pallide viole/e liquidi cristalli e fere snelle:// e' [Michelangelo] dice cose, e voi [petrarchisti] dite parole' (245). Anti-Petrarchism and paradoxical praises of women were hardly limited to the Italian tradition; they were rapidly exported throughout Europe and adapted in distinctive ways to the settings of distinctive cultures. According to Dubrow (166), Berni's poetry was particularly relevant to a strain of little-known poetry in the 'ugly beauty' tradition, a genre that began to appear in Tudor and Stuart England. Paradoxical encomia of unattractive women, or of women who simply did not conform to the prevailing cultural norm, were composed by lesser poets like George Gascoigne and John Collop, but also by Philip Sidney and John Donne. For the 'ugly beauty' tradition in Tudor and Stuart England, see Dubrow, chap. 5.

56 Berni's 'Chiome d'argento' appropriates the style and the metric format of the sonnet and some vocabulary of Bembo's 'Crin d'oro crespo' and turns it into a paradoxical praise. Longhi ('*Le rime* di Francesco Berni,' 290–1) locates a clear textual derivation with Bembo's 'Crin d'oro crespo' and 'Moderati desiri, immenso ardore' and therefore dates Berni's sonnet around 1530, the year Bembo's *Rime* were published. For an in-depth analysis of the textual connections between Berni's and Bembo's sonnets,

also in relation to Doni, see also my 'Discourse of Resistance.' Here is Bembo's sonnet: 'Crin d'oro *crespo* e d'ambra tersa e pura, / ch'a l'aura su la neve ondeggi e vole, / occhi soavi e più chiari che 'l sole, / da far giorno seren la notte oscura, // riso, ch'acqueta ogni aspra pena e dura, / rubini e perle, ond'escono parole / sì dolci, ch'altro ben l'alma non vòle, / man d'avorio, che i cor distringe e fura // cantar, che sembra d'armonia divina, / senno maturo a la più verde etade, / leggiadria non veduta unqua fra noi, // giunta a somma beltà somma onestade, / fur l'esca del mio foco, e sono in voi/ grazie, ch'a poche il ciel largo destina.' (510–11).

57 Translation by Rebay, p. 83.
58 In Petrarch's *Canzoniere* 'argento' appears only in sonnet 12 to describe the hair of the aged Laura. Feminine old age appears in another poem of Berni's *Rime*, in the so-called 'Sonetto della Massara' where the comic description of the wrinkled old maid follows the *topos* of the medieval *vituperatio vetulae*.
59 As will be seen in chapter 4, baroque poetry challenged the perfection of the beloved. Seventeenth-century poetry extolled old women, physically flawed beauty, and dark ladies. Baroque portrayals of non-canonical beauty do not appear in burlesque but in witty, serious poetry, which appears to lend the dignity of high literature to unconventional feminine models. For reference to the anagram formula and its use in John Donne's elegy 'The Anagram,' see Dubrow (175, 236–7).
60 After working at courts in Piacenza, Milan, and Pavia, he started an independent career by opening his own press in Florence, without much success. His shop lasted only two years, and eventually he moved to Venice, the capital of printing in Europe, where he worked as a *poligrafo*. Notable is Doni's interest in political reform and ideal states. In 1548 he helped publish a vernacular translation of Thomas More's *Utopia* and envisioned his own version of an ideal state in *I mondi* (1552–3), where he describes a model of a city free of evil and based on social equality.
61 See Candela.
62 *La mula la chiave e madrigali satirici*, 35.
63 The talking statue was a common cultural phenomenon in sixteenth-century Italy, particularly in Rome, where the statue of Pasquino became the favourite site for anonymous satirical poems ('Pasquinate') that targeted notable contemporary personalities and even popes.
64 *I marmi*, 71–2.
65 Renaissance commentators on *Canzoniere* as well as *Antipetrarchisti* were well aware of Petrarch's blatant omission. As Quondam notes, skilful imitators of Petrarch were conscious of this absence. Stefano Guazzo in his dialogue

Civil conversazione (1574) devotes one part of the discussion to the problem of Laura's nose. The cultural code of Renaissance classicism and its refinement does not allow for mention of the nose, since it is the organ of bodily secretions that would hint at the grotesque body; therefore in hegemonic culture such a body part most often remains unremarked on. Graf mentions Ludovico Gandino, who 'compose una lezione sopra un dubbio come messer Francesco non lodasse espressamente Laura dal naso!' ('Petrarchismo,' 22).

66 Doni insists on this element in one of the *Madrigali satirici* where the mock encomium of Crezia describes her ugliness as cadaverous: 'Portate pinta la disgrazia in volto che sembra ... il ceffo d'un ebreo vecchio e sepolto,' and then 'puzzate tutta come una carogna' (35).

67 In Rustico's 'Dovunque vai con teco porti il cesso,' 'Li denti 'n le gengìe tue ménar gresso.'

68 In Doni the mock encomium of the beloved reappears in the madrigal 'Crezia, con verità posso ben dire' (*La mula*, 35). Here again high style and realistic vocabulary coexist.

69 Montanile sees the presence of long golden hair as a symbol of beauty, order, and pictorial harmony in poetic and figurative tracts like Paolo Pino's *Dialogo della pittura* (1548) and Lodovico Dolce's *Dialogo della pittura intitolato Aretino* (1557) as well as in Firenzuola's *Dialogo* (60).

70 For the French blazon and counterblazon, see Nancy Vickers's 'Members Only.' In restricting the depiction of the woman to a part of her body, these poems exaggerate 'to the point of violation ... the descriptive mode itself' (4). Other anti-Petrarchan themes such as the aging woman's hair appear in Du Bellay. Spanish burlesque poetry often chose the old woman as its subject matter: Diego Hurtado de Mendoza, Quevedo, and others wrote poems mocking the old woman. For anti-Petrarchan poetry in the 'siglo de oro,' see Martìn.

71 Paul Larivaille (chapter 5) sees in the *Dialogo* a penchant for an adaptation of early material rather than true parody. Aretino revives some unpublished anti-Petrarchan poems that date back to his early years. Despite the uncertain attribution of such early poems, Larivaille (note 81, p. 474) finds confirmation of Aretino's paternity in the *Codice Marciano It.* XI, 66.

72 Among the poems included in the second and third days of the *Dialogo* some are in burlesque style with obscene themes: 'Io ho, donne, una cosa,' 'Madonna, per ver dire,' 'Madonna, io 'l vo' pur dir che ognun m'intenda,' and 'La mia donna è divina.'

73 The result of Quinimina's inability to distinguish between Petrarchan praise

and its distortion is quite damaging. By accepting the poetaster's advances and yielding to him, Quinimina ends up badly beaten. For more European texts on anti-Petrarchism, see Hösle.

74 Shakespeare's *Sonnets* have been traditionally grouped in two sections: poems addressed to the Fair Friend, with Petrarchan tone, and poems for the Dark Lady, in anti-Petrarchan style (particularly sonnets 127 to 154). Although such rigid division has been recently contested as too limited, it is clear that the central attacks on Petrarchism occur in the sonnets between 127 and 154. Dubrow considers this group a virtual anthology of the counter-discourses of Petrarchism (132). Shakespeare's sonnet 130 mentions four body parts that are already in Aretino (hair, eyes, lips, mouth); both poets use the same metaphor of the sun for the shining eyes. The most distinctive detail in both texts is the reference to the foul smell from the mouth. I say more on Shakespeare's sonnets on the Dark Lady in chapter 4. Further bibliographical references are found in the Cambridge edition and commentary and in Stapleton.

75 It is not clear whether Shakespeare could have known Aretino's madrigal. Although there is no evidence of a direct influence, as noted by Hendrix (34), Aretino's *Ragionamenti* were published in London by John Wolfe in 1584, so Shakespeare could have accessed Aretino's work in London; but his knowledge of the Italian language casts doubt on his ability to read Aretino in the original.

76 In his *Rime burlesche* (Venice: Sessa, 1570) Giovanfrancesco Ferrari has a *capitolo* 'In lode delle donne brutte.' This poem, however, does not include physical description of the ugly female body. The whole mock encomium is based on classic misogynist themes such as concerns about women's infidelity and the rapid decline of their physical beauty, which may be viewed as advantageous.

77 The entire poem is quoted in the appendix. The 'Stanze,' preserved in the Biblioteca Nazionale di Firenze, are bound in a seven-page booklet without numbers. The date of publication, printed on the last page, is February 12, 1547, not coincidentally during the Carnival celebration, a time of year more suited to texts that could provoke laughter. My thanks go to the staff of the Sala manoscritti of the Nazionale for making this text available.

78 Some influence in the depiction of this ugly woman may come from Pulci's comic epic *Morgante*, specifically from the figure of the monstrous sorcerer Creonta, who, like this ugly woman, is associated with the Furies Alecto, Thesiphone, and Maegera. But Tesiphone was also used as a negative epithet for Beroe.

79 There is a whole series of rustic poems that are 'a la fachinesca,' or in the style of the 'facchini,' a social class, as noted above, possibly even lower and more scorned than the peasants. See Merlini.
80 Beliefs about the evil effects of menses on plants and persons has a long tradition dating back to Isidore of Seville. On this point see Cadden, p. 175.
81 Socio-historic studies reveal that women of colour appeared, particularly in the fifteenth century, as servants/slaves working in domestic settings in most of central and northern Italy. However, the presence of black or eastern slaves declined in the sixteenth century and became limited to noble and wealthy families. See Origo's 'The Domestic Enemy.'
82 Russo, who devotes chapter 3 of *The Female Grotesque* to 'freaks,' distinguishes between the grotesque body as described by Bakhtin and the grotesque spectacle of the freak. It is precisely the idea of spectacle that in the nineteenth century leads to the inclusion of the freak in the codified world of spectacle instead of the Carnivalesque space of festivity where 'audiences and performers were the interchangeable parts of an incomplete but imaginable wholeness' (79). Russo quotes Susan Stewart's study of culture and scale to point out that the freak is 'inextricably tied to the cultural other' (80).

Chapter 4. New Perspectives in Baroque Poetry: Unconventional Beauty

1 Marino enunciates the new poetic in his famous verses 'È del poeta il fin la meraviglia / (parlo de l'eccellente, non del goffo):/ chi non sa far stupir, vada a la striglia' (*Murtoleide*, fischiata XXXIII), quoted by Asor Rosa in the section on Giambattista Marino of the *Letteratura italiana*, Vol. 5: *Il seicento*, 406.
2 See, for example, Giovan Francesco Maia Materdona's sonnet for the 'bella libraia,' Claudio Achillini's poem for the 'bella mendicante,' the poems of Agostino Augustini for the 'bella pollarola' and 'bella sartora,' and Giuseppe Salomoni's homage to the 'bella fornaia,' 'bella metitrice,' and 'bella vendemmiatrice,' as well as the poems for servants examined below.
3 The list of women's deformities or blemishes in seicento poetry is quite lengthy; this limited sample includes some of the most common variations on the theme. Marcello Giovanetti praises the beautiful woman with red spots on her face ('bella donna con macchie rosse sul volto') and Salomoni the beautiful woman with freckles ('le lentigini'); Maia Materdona, Lorenzo Casaburi, Alessandro Adimari, and Salomoni celebrate the beautiful mute woman ('bella muta'). Antonio Bruni, Adimari, and Salomoni admire the beautiful blind woman ('bella cieca') and Adimari the beautiful bald woman

(bella calva). The index of female beauty expands to include the different, the surprising, and the traditionally undesirable.
4 Alessandro Adimari is mostly remembered for his encomiastic verses and for his famous translation of Pindar's *Odes* (Pisa, 1631). His output includes six collections of fifty sonnets, each named after one of the Muses: *Tersicore* (Florence, 1637), *Clio* (Florence, 1639), *Melpomene* (Florence, 1640), *Calliope* (Florence, 1641), *Urania* (Florence, 1642), and *Polinnia* (Florence, 1642). His poetry has been defined as 'Piuttosto versificazione di notizie erudite che manifestazione di vena poetica' and his style has been called 'ridondante' (D'Addario, 278).
5 Mario Praz mentions Adimari in the opening chapter of his classic *La carne, la morte e il diavolo nella letteratura romantica*, where he talks about 'bellezza medusea' (23– 48), that typically Romantic taste for beauty conjoined with deformity, disease, and suffering. Praz rightly excludes Adimari from the legitimate precursors of Romantic and Decadent beauty that defines poets like Baudelaire.
6 There is no limit to the absurd monstrosities this author puts forth as gems of ingenuity.
7 In the Table of Contents the women are indexed in alphabetical order according to their defects, but the sonnet sequence in the text is the following: 1. Pargoletta, 2. Piccola, 3. Con vaiolo, 4. Gobba, 5. Zoppa, 6. Sciatta, 7. Oppillata, 8. Guercia, 9. Sorda, 10. Muta, 11. Rognosa, 12. Sfregiata, 13. Adirata o sdegnosa, 14. Stracciata, 15. Calva, 16. Lunga, 17. Cieca, 18. Bugiarda, 19. Scilinguata, 20. Ridente, 21. Piangente, 22. Con un occhio, 23. Sdentata, 24. Negra, 25. Gozzuta, 26. Insensata, 27. Pazza, 28. Incostante, 29. Dispettosa, 30. Ferita, 31. Semplice, 32. Astuta, 33. Macchiata, 34. Con gavine, 25. Monca, 26. Nasuta, 37. Butterata, 38. Sterile, 39. Gravida, 40. Magra, 41. Grassa, 42. Lentigginosa, 43. Canuta, 44. Scura, 45. Antica, 46. Brutta in generale, 47. Vecchia, 48. Febbricitante, 49. Morta, 50. Sepolta. The fifty sonnets are summarized by a *capitolo* in fifty stanzas, where each stanza outlines the theme of one sonnet. My thanks to Richard Langdon and Luba Frastacky of the Fisher Rare Books Library collection of the University of Toronto Library for allowing me to consult Adimari's book. All quotations from this edition appear here for the first time since their initial publication.
8 One should note that this preoccupation with specific parts of the female body began precisely with Petrarch, who first composed poems on Laura's beautiful hand and was fascinated with her hair. This attraction to single body parts of the beloved continues in the late fifteenth century with Giusto de' Conti's famous poetry for the lady's beautiful hand ('bella mano') and

with Olimpo da Sassoferrato, who in his *Gloria d'amore* (1520) composed in popular style a series of *strambotti* praising every minute detail of a beautiful young girl's body. In France Olimpo had perhaps a larger impact than in Italy itself. As noted in chapter 3, in France in the second quarter of the sixteenth century the anatomical blazon becomes an independent genre, thanks to poets like Antoine Héroet, Maurice Scève, and Clèment Marot. The motif of the birthmark/mole or 'neo' on the white skin of the beloved was inaugurated by Tasso and later appears in Tommaso Stigliani, Paolo Zazzaroni, and Antonio Bruni and, of course, in Marino's *Lira*, just to mention the most famous examples.

9 Despite a revived interest in the last decade in the 'poesia del seicento,' baroque Italian poetry still deserves more research. The first obstacle to a comprehensive study on praise of unconventional beauty is the lack of new editions of baroque poets; we still rely on the classic anthologies of Croce, Getto, Ferrero, and Muscetta, and much remains to be explored in seventeenth-century lyric poetry collections. Luisella Giachino has provided valuable bibliographical information on modern editions of baroque *canzonieri*. Rather than anthological selections, we can now read in their entirety works by poets such as Ciro di Pers, Gianfrancesco Maia Materdona, Giuseppe Battista, Claudio Achillini, Girolamo Preti, Scipione Errico, Girolamo Fontanella, Pietro Casaburi Urries, and Giuseppe Salomoni. Since this book aims at creating a sense of cohesion and closure to the subject matter presented in the previous chapters, in the vast repertoire of seventeenth-century lyric some areas of investigation have been singled out for their direct connection to the general theme of this study.

10 The adjectives 'bruna,' 'brunetta,' or 'mora' are often used ambiguously in pre-baroque and baroque poetry, without indicating whether the woman simply has a darker complexion or whether she is black.

11 The first to praise a brunette was the *Stilnovista* Cino da Pistoia, who compared the lady's dark hair to a blackbird in 'Per una merla, che d'intorno al volto.' Olimpo da Sassoferrato in the early years of the sixteenth century composed in popular style the *canzonetta* 'La brunettina mia,' where a young peasant is praised for her light hair but dark complexion. Giovanni della Casa, too, challenged the cliché in a sonnet praising the beloved's red hair.

12 The non-mimetic nature of blonde hair in literary heroines is demonstrated by a type like Angelica in Ariosto's *Orlando furioso*, who, despite being Chinese, has blonde hair. Angelica is blonde because she is beautiful and because the literary tradition demands that beautiful women be blonde, even defying realism. For more on the topic, see Verina Jones's 'Manzoni's Dark Ladies.'

13 This process of stereotyping is paralleled by an accentuation of the use of metaphors rather than literal designations and by a reduction of the motivations underlying the metaphors to those of splendour and colour. The allowed colours were yellow, red, and white, and only a limited number of tropes were acceptable to designate such colours: gold and amber for yellow, roses for red, a wider range for white including snow, ivory, marble, and pearls. See Pozzi, 'Codici,' 'Il ritratto,' and 'Temi.'

14 The beauty of hair resides in its blondness, and as a consequence its opposite, dark hair, constitutes ugliness. This is merely a literary procedure that elaborates its symbols to designate what is beautiful, creating a cliché. Pozzi sees in the prevalence of light and brightness to designate the beauty of the woman the reason why lyric poetry describes feminine beauty on the basis of the opposition between white/red. If the dark lady comes to replace the canonic blonde one, as happens in baroque poetry, the opposition will no longer be between white/red but white/black. To have a realistic rendering of human complexion, the poets select the motif of praise of the mole or birthmark (a motif that was introduced by Tasso).

15 The theme, then, is a variation on the familiar one of the 'donna dello schermo,' employed as early as Dante in the *Vita nuova.*

16 Taddeo finds Mannerism in Magno's 'similitudine che trapassa in metafora e nella metafora che assume una irreale concretezza spingendo assai avanti l'artificiosità del sonetto' (166).

17 Of course, the same contrast is the founding element of baroque painting, with its revolutionary use of chiaroscuro in painters such as Caravaggio and Caravaggeschi.

18 Marino is aware of the need to change but is also quite conscious of the importance of tradition. In the *Epistolario* he states that 'la vera regola è saper rompere le regole a tempo e luogo' (quoted in Asor Rosa, *La lirica del seicento,* 6).

19 In this poem the only other elements of the lady's beauty are cheeks (like roses) and lips (like rubies), which conform with the canon.

20 Chiabrera's poetry, as well as Tasso's and Marino's, influenced John Milton, who composed among his early *Italian Poems* (circa 1629–30) a sonnet (IV) in praise of an Italian brunette. For more on Milton's *Italian Poems,* see Volpi. As Peter Brandt informs us, Tasso's lyrics were well known and readily available in anthologies in England in the last decades of the sixteenth century (286). A translation of 'Bruna sei tu ma bella' appeared in Nicholas Yonge's volume *Musica transalpina* (1588).

21 For William Crelly, Giovanetti's sonnet 'Chi mi rende a Le Muse, e d'Ippocrene/m'offre a le labra i fugitivi umori?' is 'an almost ecstatic

expression of gratitude for the inspiration he had received from the aging laureate' (5). In turn, Marino praised Giovanetti in the sonnet 'Fra quanti beber mai là in Ippocrene,' which commends the poetic ardour of the young poet beginning his career. The extensive epistolary section in Giovanetti's *Rime* shows how he was acquainted with many of the notable literary personalities of his day; he exchanged verses with Antonio Bruni and Giuseppe Salomoni and appears to have belonged to the Academy of Insensati and Virtuosi. Giovanetti died in Rome in 1632 and was described in a portrait of the *Glorie dell'Accademia degli Incogniti*. For more on Giovanetti's poetry, see Crelly.

22 Much remains to be discovered about the membership and the immense literary output of this academy, founded by Giovan Francesco Loredano in Venice in 1630. Giorgio Spini seems to understate the value of the writers and work of the prolific academy: 'L'accademia degli incogniti ha lasciato ... un qualche ricordo di sé, se non per la qualità degli scritti di ogni genere, che uscirono a fiumi dalle penne instancabili dei sui accademici, per il fatto almeno di avere accolto nelle prorie file la maggior parte dei noti letterati del tempo, dal Cavalier Marino, all'Achillini' (151). This elite group of Venetian libertine intellectuals promoted various artistic activities such as opera, novellas, and poetry. The Incogniti professed themselves followers of Marino and often assumed an attitude of philosophical scepticism intolerant of all preconstituted authority. For a recent informed study of the Accademia degli Incogniti, see Miato.

23 See Rak's introduction to di Pers's *Poesie*, p. xxix.

24 Rak in his edition places [Patto] in brackets to indicate uncertainty about this word. In *Lirici marinisti* (363) Croce, instead, uses the form 'Batto' that I have adopted in my translation.

25 See Bàrberi Squarotti's introduction to *Le sirene*, p. v.

26 In his comment on this sonnet, Evans mentions Elizabethan poet Samuel Daniel; in Daniel's lyric the hair of the beloved Delia is golden in the 1592 edition but has become sable in the 1601 revision (note 3).

27 See Pérez Romero.

28 As early as Giotto (thirteenth century) the Virgin is depicted with golden hair. In the cycle of frescos at the Scrovegni Chapel in Padua, Mary is blonde in the *Nativity* and in *Presentation of Mary at the Temple*. Examples of the Madonna with blonde hair are almost ubiquitously in Renaissance painting. Post-Reformation treaties on religious painting stress the need for more realistic representations of biblical figures and particularly of New Testament characters, such as Saint Joseph, Saint John, and the Virgin, but no precise mention of Mary's physical appearance is made. See Giovanni

Andrea Gilio's *Dialogo nel quale si ragiona degli errori e degli abusi de' pittori circa l'istorie* (1563) and Gabriele Paleotti's *Discorso intorno alle imagini sacre e profane* (1582), collected in Barocchi. Madonnas with dark hair appear in the work of some famous baroque painters such as Caravaggio's *Madonna di Loreto* (1604) and *Madonna dei palafrenieri* (1605–6), where the Virgin was depicted realistically as a peasant. Ludovico Carracci's *Madonna*, at the Pinacoteca Bargellini in Bologna, was also a realistic depiction of a woman with dark hair. Black Madonnas were venerated in popular belief and depicted all over Italy (particularly famous is the Madonna of Loreto) and abroad from very early times, precisely for their dark skin and hair. However, there seems to have been no significant increase in interest in Black Madonnas during the seventeenth century. For more on the Black Madonna, see Chiavola Birnbaum.

29 See Galli Stampino's 'Bodily Boundaries Represented' and Cropper's 'The Beauty of Woman.'
30 The gypsy and the Moor along with the midget could well fit into what Mary Russo calls 'freaks,' types that in the nineteenth century were used as spectacles and provided entertainment in sideshows at the fair or at the circus, and that in seventeenth-century literature exhaust the poets' search for marvel.
31 Thanks to postcolonial studies, blacks, Africans, and other ethnic minorities have become the subject of intense study in Western literature and culture. The United States Pavilion of the 2003 Venice Biennale, for example, presented African American Fred Wilson's exhibit 'Speak of Me as I Am,' an intriguing panorama of the presence of blacks and Africans in Western and Venetian art. As Paul Kaplan observed, Venice, with its particular sensitivity to ethnic identities and cultural boundaries, generated a remarkable variety of visual images of blacks ranging from the 'Mori' of San Marco's clock tower, to the black gondoliers portrayed in Vittore Carpaccio, to the dozens of black servants in Paolo Veronese's canvases (8).
32 Iris Origo ('The Domestic Enemy') in her socio-historic study on slavery in fourteenth- and fifteenth-century Italy notes the decline of slaves in middle-class Italian households after the fifteenth century due to the closure of slave markets to Italian trade.
33 Dark slaves were favourites of noble Renaissance ladies as well as of courtesans. When Isabella of Aragon married Giangaleazzo Sforza in 1488, among her servants were some dark slaves. Isabella d'Este acquired a dark slave girl in 1491 and later tried to find a partner for her. At Isabella's court the 'moretti' were not employed in domestic chores, but were simply viewed as ornament and entertainment. Like buffoons, dark slaves were considered a

source of amusement. Particular interest in dark slaves is shown in the desire to portray them in official paintings. In Titian's portrait of Lucrezia Borgia the lady sits beside a black slave boy. (For more on the connection between slaves and buffoons at the Court of Isabella d'Este, see Luzio and Renier.) Despite their scarcity in sixteenth-century Italy, they appear in many comedies, for example in Delicado's comedy *La Lozana andalusa*. Slaves also appear in Ariosto's *Cassaria* and in Aretino's *Talanta*, and Giovanni Maria Cecchi wrote a comedy called *La stiava*. After the discovery of America, slave routes in Europe quickly shifted to the West Indies. For female Indians and slaves in sixteenth-century Europe, see De Maio's chapter on 'La donna india' (249–62).

34 The contrast between the fair beauty of the lady and the darkness of her maid/servant was already evident in Tasso and would become popular in baroque poetry. See, for example, a sonnet of uncertain attribution quoted in Ferrero (685), 'Per donna mora veduta alla finestra con bella donna'; and Paolo Zazzaroni's sonnet 'La signora e l'ancella,' about a lady and her dark servant. The motif also appears in baroque painting. After Titian's portrait of Lucrezia Borgia with a black slave boy, the theme is found in Van Dyck's *Portrait of Marchesa Elena Grimaldi*, where the lady is accompanied by a young black servant.

35 For the popularity of *Wunderkammern* and *studioli* from the sixteenth century to modern times, see Lugli, who observes that the great impulse to *Wunderkammern* in the sixteenth century derived from the discovery of America, which brought new animals, plants, and new and strange persons (28).

36 In 'Stanze in lode della donna brutta' the same terms, 'inchiostro' and 'ebeno,' were used to describe negatively the face and teeth of the ugly woman. The 'bella negra' appears also in Alessandro Adimari's *Tersicore* (1637), where the sonnet's opening line reveals its indebtedness to Marino: 'Negra, sì ma se' bella, e chi nol crede/di tenebre ammantato il ciel rimiri' (65). In Ludovico Tingoli's 'A brutta donna adorna di gran gioie' (Getto, *I marinisti*, 187), the dark lady is at the centre of a witty redeployment of the metaphors used to describe the beautiful woman. The poet does not intend to praise the dark lady, but rather to reveal her infernal nature. The darkness of her physical aspect stands in contrast with the splendour of the jewels she wears. The poet shifts the objects used by *Petrarchisti* to describe the lady's beauty. Pearls, rubies, and gold, generally referring to teeth, lips, and hair, have materialized as objects decorating the unattractive female body. The jewels produce a brightness and beauty that contrast with the dark and ugly aspect of the lady. This sonnet reveals the return of the misogynist polemic against women's excessive use of ornament.

37 Ciro di Pers defined the beautiful dark hair of the beloved as an 'Ethiopian mane' ('chiome etiope'). Di Pers also describes a Moorish woman in the poem 'Ad un cavaliere innamorato d'una mora che andava a prender fuoco nella sua casa,' where the dark woman is a black and sensuous servant who lures an old man. For other examples of the exotic Other in baroque poetry, see below.

38 In his edition of Marino's *Adone* Giovanni Pozzi notes that the 'ma' signals the superior worth that high-style poetry places on blonde beauty, since dark-haired beauty was allowed only in popular poetry. In *Adone* Marino keeps the distinction of high and low genre, as Venus is blonde when she is portrayed as a goddess, while here, disguised as a gypsy, she is dark haired. Pozzi identifies in *Adone* the two expressions of Marino's poetry: the Petrarchan (blonde Venus) and the ornate modern 'poesia secentesca' (dark Venus; Venus as a gypsy is described in her rich and ornate attire) (576).

39 For more on the motif of the dark lady in English and Spanish seventeenth-century literature, see Pérez Moreno. For issues of race and gender in English anti-Petrarchan poetry, see Dubrow (180–7).

40 Despite Benedetto Croce's general criticism of 'poesia marinista,' he sees some positive energy in Fontanella's poetry (*Saggi*, 402). Capucci and Iannaco also praised Fontanella for expressing with elegance and balance the 'concettismo meridionale' (*Il seicento*, 294). A decade ago Rosario Contarino edited Fontanella's *Ode* and particularly praised the poet's idyllic vein and his predilection for the bucolic pastoral tradition (xii). Despite the limited use in Fontanella of typical baroque witticism and conceit, he shows an interest in the unconventional depiction of female beauty in praising the dark woman.

41 The poem, dedicated to Sig. Cinzio di Tomaso, is in the second book of Fontanella's *Ode* and apppeared for the first time in 1633. The gypsy inspired baroque poets such as Tommaso Stigliani ('A una zingara'), Bartolomeo Tortoletti ('Mascherata delle zingare'), and Paolo Zazzaroni ('A una zingara'). In these poems, however, the gypsy is neither an object of desire nor the recipient of verbal homage; she is the seer, or fortuneteller, invoked by the poet as mediator between him and his distant beloved.

42 In Ciro di Pers's witty canzone addressed 'Ad un cavaliere innamorato d'una mora che andava a prender fuoco nella sua casa,' the dark woman's face is 'etiopica facella' and the poem is structured on the contrast between the bright fire she is carrying and her charcoal face and body. Since this woman is fetching fire in the house of a 'cavaliere' she must be a servant, a female figure that became popular in baroque poetry.

43 See Carmine Chiodo's essay on Salvetti in *Burleschi del seicento*. The choice of burlesque *capitolo* instead of the sonnet or madrigal, normally used by baroque poets, confirms Salvetti's indebtedness to the sixteenth-century Tuscan tradition of burlesque and bernesque poetry.
44 Di Pers does not limit his treatment of woman's aging to the sequence for Nicea, a series that was composed in the earlier period of his life (between 1620 and 1627). After 1636 di Pers expresses his disapproval of the aging Lidia's rejection (sonnets 36–42 and 156–8). With moralistic tones the old woman is scorned for uselessly resorting to cosmetics to repair the damage time has inflicted on her body. Addressing Lidia, di Pers does not use the sympathetic tone found in the sonnets for Nicea. The rejected lover takes his revenge on the old beloved and reproaches her in misogynistic tones for being so distant in the past and for abusing the art of make-up to hide her bodily decay.
45 In the vast repertoire of poetry on the aging woman, Bartolomeo Tortoletti's sonnet 'Bellezza che resiste agli anni' reveals the age of the lady Barbara, who is fifty-five but still retains her charm. Federico Mennini, in his 'Consolatoria' addressed to an aging woman, half seriously and half jokingly states that 'Se con l'oro del crin sembrasti il Sole, / con l'argento del crin sembri la Luna' (Croce, *Lirici marinisti*, 487). Giuseppe Artale in 'Elena invecchiata' lets Helen, symbol of beauty par excellence, mourn the loss of her beauty.
46 The variation on the 'bruna sei tu, ma bella' scheme, inaugurated by Tasso, is evident in the same syntactic structure marked by the adversative 'vecchia sei *ma* leggiadra.'
47 Tommaso Stigliani (1573–1661), the shrewdest critic of Marino and Marinisti, in the section 'Amori giocosi' of his *Canzoniere* (1605 and 1623) critically portrays the 'Musa del secol nostro' (Muse of our century), that is, the inspirer of 'poesia marinista,' as a deformed, ugly, and old woman. The old woman is used as metaphor for a poetic style ('stile poetastrico') that Stigliani despises. For more on this poem, see Besomi's *Esplorazioni secentesche* (55–151).
48 Capucci and Iannaco (279) and Jori (chapter 6, p. 687, section on 'Il grottesco') define the most extreme examples of *Secentismo* as 'baroque grotesque' because of the penchant for the ugly and disgusting displayed by some baroque poets, particularly in the depiction of tainted female beauty. Praz excludes the possibility that the baroque poets had any feeling for the Romantic appeal to ugliness and human deformity: 'Molti di questi temi della bellezza intorbidata riappaiono presso i romantici, ma quello che nei secentisti era spesso soltanto posa dell'intelletto, diventa nei romantici posa

della sensibilità. Al concetto dei secentisti subentra la sensazione dei romantici' (40).
49 Other seventeenth-century authors have dealt with the theme of the flea in comic terms. Antonio Abati wrote a sonnet for 'bella donna che si spulcia' (1676), Cesare Giudici wrote a twenty-five stanza poem 'La caccia alle pulci' (1625) describing how a woman hunts the fleas that prevent her from sleeping at night, and Cesare Orsini devoted some stanzas of his *Selve poetiche* (Padua: Gasparo Ganassa, 1635) to the flea. All these examples are quoted in Belloni (chapter 1, note 55), who says that a whole variety of dirty insects became a common subject in burlesque seventeenth-century poems.
50 Vigarello demonstrates that contemporary concepts of cleanliness did not apply to medieval and early modern people. Furthermore, he states, before the eighteenth century fleas or other vermin were not necessarily believed to be the result of poor bodily hygiene and were equally present on the bodies of peasants and kings (42–3). Yet chapter 3 has shown how Renaissance authors like pseudo-Legacci and Mauro use the uncleanliness, dirt, and infestation of lower-social-class women as a means of distinguishing the elite from the vulgar and the impure.
51 The medieval *Carmen de Pulice* was composed by Ofilius Sergianus, whose name may have been mistaken for Ovidius, given the similarities between the two names. Marcel Françon retraces the motif of animals as privileged company of the loved woman in the Latin poetry of Catullus, in Serafino Aquilano, and in Ariosto. The theme of transformation into and eulogies to animals dates back to Greek anacreontic poetry, Latin classics like Virgil's 'Culex,' Ovid's *Metamorphosis*, Statius, and Lucian, and continues in humanistic examples such as Leon Battista Alberti's 'Laus muscae' and Philip Melanchton's 'Laus formicae.'
52 For a study of this *topos* in Renaissance poetry in Italy, France, Spain, and England, and its earlier tradition, see R.O. Jones, 'Renaissance Butterfly,' and Tomarken. Jones quotes some important pieces on the flea by Spanish poets such as Diego Hurtado de Mendoza and Lope de Vega, and believes that Lope's sonnet ('Picò atrevido un atomo viviente') must have been an imita-tion of an Italian original that the critic failed to identify. John Donne's famous poem 'The Flea' (1633) must have been influenced by the Italian, French, and Spanish examples.
53 The louse is also praised in Ortensio Lando's *Sermoni funebri* (1548). This collection consists of eleven prose sermons attributed to different individuals eulogizing their favourite animals. In fact, the various authors are just the different incarnations of the author's voice. The animals commended here include a horse, a dog, a monkey, an owl, a magpie, a cat, a rooster, and a

cricket. The sermon of 'Frate Puccio nella morte di un suo Pidocchio' is not addressed to an insect housed on the female body. This sermon for the dead louse deals with the most disgusting animal on the list. I am grateful to the University of Toronto's Fisher Rare Book Library for allowing me to consult Lando's sixteenth-century edition of this work.

54 Both of Narducci's sonnets were published in Giacomo Guaccimanni's *Raccolta di sonetti d'autori diversi ed eccellenti dell'età nostra* (Ravenna, 1623) and appear in both Croce's and Ferrero's anthologies. Getto (*Barocco in prosa e in poesia*, 72) seems somehow to skirt the issue; even though he quotes from Narducci's sonnet and mentiones one by Giovanni Giacomo Lavagna (which I was unable to locate), he remains quite elusive about the theme of lice on the beloved's hair, dismissing these poems as 'documenti di interesse essenzialmente stilistico' devoid of any comical or disgusting elements (*Barocco* 73).

55 Among the many examples of baroque lyric's bad taste, in his Second Satire ('La Poesia') Salvator Rosa quotes verses that recall Narducci: 'e dell'amata sua, con qual decoro,/i pidocchi colui cantando, disse/"Sembran fère d'argento in selva d'oro"' (Muscetta and Ferrante, vol. 2, 1827).

56 Since this poem was not found in any anthology, it is quoted here from Belloni's study on the seicento.

57 I quote here the entire sonnet: 'Se del vasto Eritreo conca gemmata / spargesse fra le perle ostri divini, / e tra i cinabri suoi rosa odorata / portasse i gigli aspersi, e i gelsomini; // chi potria rimirar cosa più grata / ne'campi di cristallo alabastrini? / In tal guisa se' tu, beltà macchiata / di coralli sanguigni, e di rubini. // Che se tigre d'Amor sembri alla pelle / (manto condegno al crudo tuo rigore) / sembri anco un vago ciel cinto di stelle: // ma se laceri tè nel tuo candore, / ah pensa, ingrata, a quant'anime ancelle, / con prurito maggior laceri il core' (39).

Bibliography

Adimari, Alessandro. *La Tersicore o vero scherzi e paradossi poetici sopra la Beltà delle Donne fra' difetti ancora ammirabili, e vaghe.* Florence: Nuova Stamperia d'Amadore Massi e Lorenzo Landi, 1637.
Agamben, Giorgio. *Stanze: La parola e il fantasma nella letteratura occidentale.* Turin: Einaudi, 1993.
Alberti, Leon Battista. *Rime e versioni poetiche.* Milan/Naples: Ricciardi, 1975.
Alfie, Fabian. *Comedy and Culture: Cecco Angiolieri's Poetry and Late Medieval Society.* Leeds: Northern University Press, 2001.
Almansi, Guido, and Guido Fink. *Quasi come.* Milan: Bompiani, 1976.
Andreas, Cappellanus. *De amore et amoris remedio.* Rome: Perrella, 1947.
Angiolieri, Cecco. *Le rime.* Ed. Antonio Lanza. Rome: Archivio Guido Izzo, 1990.
Anonymous. *Stanze in lode della donna brutta.* Florence: Doni, 1547.
Aretino, Pietro. *Sei giornate.* Turin: Einaudi, 1975.
Ariosto, Ludovico. *Opere minori.* Milan/Naples: Ricciardi, 1954.
– *Orlando furioso.* Milan: Garzanti, 1990.
Asor Rosa, Alberto. *La lirica del seicento.* Rome/Bari: Laterza, 1975.
– *Il seicento: La nuova scienza e la crisi del Barocco.* Vol. 5, tome 1 of *Letteratura italiana: Storia e testi.* Bari: Laterza, 1974.
Bähr, Rudolf. 'L'influsso della retorica latina sulla *descriptio personarum extrinseca* nella letteratura francese antica.' In *Retorica e poetica: Atti del III convegno italo-tedesco,* ed. D. Goldin, 131–46. Padua: Liviana, 1979.
Bailbè, Jacques. 'Le thème de la vielle femme dans la poésie satirique du XVe siècle.' *Bibliotheque d'Humanisme et Renaissance* 25 (1964): 98–119.
Bakhtin, Mikhail. *Rabelais and His World.* Bloomington, IN: Indiana University Press, 1984.
Baldissone, Giusi. 'Il canto della distanza.' In *Lo specchio che deforma: Le immagini della parodia,* edited by Giorgio Bàrberi Squarotti, 9–34. Turin: Tirrenia Stampatori, 1988.

Banner, Lois W. *In Full Flower. Aging Women, Power, and Sexuality: A History.* New York: Knopf, 1992.
Baransky, Zygmunt, and Patrick Boyde, eds. *The Fiore in Context: Dante, France, Tuscany.* Notre Dame: University of Notre Dame Press, 1997.
Bàrberi Squarotti, Giorgio. 'Introduzione.' In *Rime burlesche,* by Francesco Berni, 5–33. Milan: Rizzoli, 1991.
– 'Introduzione.' In *Rime,* by Giuseppe Salomoni, v–xxiv. Turin: Res, 1996.
– *Lo specchio che deforma: Le immagini della parodia.* Turin: Tirrenia Stampatori, 1988.
Barberino, Francesco. *Documenti d'amore.* Rome: Vitale Mascardi, 1640.
– *Reggimento e costumi di donna.* Ed. Giuseppe Sansone. Rome: Zauli, 1995.
Barocchi, Paola, ed. *Trattati d'arte del cinquecento fra manierismo e riforma.* Bari: Laterza, 1960.
Bartra, Roger. *The Artificial Savage: Modern Myths of the Wild Man.* Ann Arbor: Michigan University Press, 1997.
Battisti, Eugenio. *L'antirinascimento.* Milan: Feltrinelli, 1962.
Baudelaire, Charles. *Les fleurs du mal.* Paris: Garnier, 1961.
Beauvoir, Simone de. *Old Age.* Trans. Patrick O'Brien. New York: Penguin, 1977.
Belloni, Antonio. *Il seicento.* Milano: Vallardi, 1955.
Bembo, Pietro. *Prose e rime.* Turin: Unione tipografico-editrice torinese, 1966.
Berger, John. *Ways of Seeing.* London: BBC / Penguin, 1972.
Bernheimer, Richard. *Wild Men in the Middle Ages: A Study in Art, Sentiment, and Demonology.* Cambridge, MA: Harvard University Press, 1952.
Berni, Francesco. *Rime burlesche.* Ed. Giorgio Bàrberi Squarotti. Milan: Rizzoli, 1991.
– *Rime: Poesie latine lettere edite e inedite.* Ed. Antonio Virgili. Florence: Le Monnier, 1885.
Besomi, Ottavio. *Esplorazioni secentesche.* Padua: Antenore, 1975.
– *Ricerche intorno alla* Lira *di G.B. Marino.* Padua: Antenore, 1969.
Bessi, Rossella. 'Introduzione.' In *Nencia da Barberino,* ed. Rossella Bessi, 13–119. Rome: Salerno, 1982.
Bettella, Patrizia. 'Corpo di parti: Ambiguità e frammentarietà nella rappresentazione della bellezza femminile nei trattati di Trissino e Firenzuola.' *Forum Italicum* 33, no. 2 (1999): 319–36.
– 'Discourse of Resistance: The Parody of Feminine Beauty in Berni, Doni and Firenzuola.' *MLN* 113 (1998): 192–203.
Bettinzoli, Attilio. '"Dolus et error": Di alcuni carmi latini del giovane Poliziano.' *Lettere Italiane* 38, no. 2 (1986): 166–92.
Blamires, Alcuin. *The Case for Women in Medieval Culture.* Oxford: Clarendon Press, 1997.

– ed. *Woman Defamed and Woman Defended: An Anthology of Medieval Texts.* Oxford: Clarendon Press, 1992.
Bloch, Howard R. 'Medieval Misogyny.' *Representations* 20 (1987): 1–24.
– *Medieval Misogyny and the Invention of Western Romantic Love.* Chicago: University of Chicago Press, 1991.
Boccaccio, Giovanni. *Corbaccio.* Milan: Mursia, 1992.
– *The Corbaccio.* Ed. and trans. Anthony Cassell. Urbana: University of Illinois Press, 1975.
– *Tutte le opere.* Vol. 2. Milan: Rizzoli, 1964.
Bologna, Corrado, 'Poesia del centro e del nord.' Chapter 4 in *Storia della letteratura italiana: Dalle origini a Dante,* ed. Enrico Malato, Vol. 1, 409–525. Rome: Salerno, 1995.
Bonadiman, Beatrice. '"Ogni vecchia è una strega": Origine storica della magia in area slava.' In *Geografia storia e poetiche del fantastico,* ed. Monica Farnetti, 61–75. Florence: Olschki, 1995.
Bonfante, G. 'Femmina e donna.' In *Studia philologica et litteraria in Honorem L. Spitzer,* ed. A.G. Hatcher and K.L. Selig. Bern: Francke, 1958.
Bragantini, Renzo, and Pier Massimo Forni, eds. *Lessico critico decameroniano.* Turin: Bollati Boringhieri, 1995.
Braidotti, Rosi. *Nomadic Subjects: Embodiment and Sexual Difference in Contemporary Feminist Theory.* New York: Columbia University Press, 1994.
Brandt, Peter. *Torquato Tasso: A Study of the Poet and His Contribution to English Literature.* Cambridge: Cambridge University Press, 1965.
Brandt, Wolfgang. 'Die Beschreibung hässlicher Menschen in höfischen Romanen: Zur narrativen Integrierung eines *Topos.*' *Germanisch-Romanische Monatsschrift* 35, no. 3 (1985): 257–78.
Brauner, Sigrid. *Fearless Wives and Frightened Shrews: The Construction of the Witch in Early Modern Germany.* Amherst: University of Massachusetts Press, 1995.
Bronzini, Giovanni Battista. 'La predicazione di San Bernardino da Siena fra scrittura e oralità.' In *San Bernardino da Siena predicatore e pellegrino: Atti del convegno nazionale di studi bernardiniani,* ed. Francesco D'Episcopo, 129–50. Galatina: Congedo, 1985.
Bruni, Francesco. 'Dal *De vetula* al *Corbaccio*: L'idea d'amore e i due tempi dell'intellettuale.' *Medioevo Romanzo* 1, no. 2 (1974): 161–216.
Bruni Bettarini, Anna. 'Le rime di Meo dei Tolomei e di Muscia da Siena.' *Studi di filologia italiana* 32 (1974): 31–98.
Burchiello [Domenico di Giovanni]. *I sonetti del Burchiello.* Ed. Michelangelo Zaccarello. Bologna: Commissione per i Testi di Lingua, 2000.
– *Sonetti editi e inediti.* Ed. Michele Messina. Florence: Olschki, 1952.

Burns, Jane E. 'Knowing Women: Female Orifices in Old French Farce and Fabliau.' *Exemplaria* 4, no. 1 (1992): 80–104.

Buzzetti Gallarati, Silvia. 'Sull'organizzazione del discorso comico nella produzione giocosa di Rustico Filippi.' *Medioevo Romanzo* 9, no. 2 (1984): 189–214.

Cadden, Joan. *Meanings of Sexual Difference in the Middle Ages.* Cambridge: Cambridge University Press, 1993.

Callaghan, Karen A. 'Introduction.' In *Ideals of Feminine Beauty. Philosophical, Social, and Cultural Dimensions,* vii–xv. Westport CT: Greenwood Press, 1994.

The Cambridge History of Italian Literature. Ed. Peter Brandt and Lino Pertile. Cambridge: Cambridge University Press, 1999.

Cammelli, Antonio [Il Pistoia]. *I sonetti del Pistoia giusta l'apografo trivulziano.* Turin: Loescher, 1888.

Campani, Niccolò. *Rime.* Siena: Gati, 1878.

Camporesi, Piero. *Rustici e buffoni: Cultura popolare e cultura d'élite fra Medioevo ed età moderna.* Turin: Einaudi, 1991.

Candela, Giuseppe. *Manierismo e condizioni della scrittura in Anton Francesco Doni.* New York: Peter Lang, 1993.

Capucci, Martino, and Carmine Iannaco. *Il seicento.* Milan: Vallardi, 1986.

Carducci, Giosuè. *Cantilene e ballate, strambotti e madrigali nei secoli XIII e XVI.* Bologna: Forni, 1970.

Carter, Angela. *Nights at the Circus.* London: Picador, 1985.

Casaburi Urries, Pietro. *Le sirene.* Ed. Giorgio Bàrberi Squarotti. Turin: Res, 1996.

Casagrande, Carla. 'The Protected Woman' In *Silences of the Middle Ages,* ed. Christiane Klapisch-Zuber, 70–104; Vol. 2 of *A History of Women in the West,* ed. Michelle Perrot and Charles Duby. Cambridge MA.: Belknap, 1992.

Casini, Tommaso. *Studi di poesia antica.* Città di Castello: Lapi, 1913.

Cassata, Letterio, ed. *Guido Cavalcanti: Rime.* Anzio: De Rubeis, 1993.

Cassell, Anthony K. '*Il Corbaccio* and the Secundus Tradition.' *Comparative Literature* 25 (1973): 352–60.

– 'Introduction.' In *The Corbaccio,* by Giovanni Boccaccio, xi–xxvii. Urbana: University of Illinois Press, 1975.

Cavalcanti, Guido. *Rime: Edizione critica, commento, concordanze.* Ed. Letterio Cassata. Anzio: Rubeis, 1993.

Cazalé Bérard, Claude. 'Filoginia/misoginia.' In *Lessico critico decameroniano,* 116–41. Turin: Bollati Boringhieri, 1995.

Cecchi, Emilio, and Sapegno Natalino, eds., *Storia della letteratura italiana.* 9 Vols. Milan: Garzanti, 1965.

Cervigni, Dino. *Dante's Poetry of Dreams.* Florence: Olschki, 1986.

Charlet, Jean-Louis. 'La laideur féminine dans l'Ode 9 *In anum* d'Ange

Politien.' In *Disarmonia bruttezza e bizzarria nel Rinascimento: Atti del VII convegno internazionale*, edited by Luisa Secchi Tarugi, 91–102. Florence: Cesati, 1998. 91–102.
Cherchi, Paolo. 'L'encomio paradossale nel manierismo.' *Forum Italicum* 9 (1975): 368–84.
– 'Per la "femmina balba."' *Quaderni d'Italianistica* 6, no. 2 (1985): 228–32.
Chiabrera, Gabriello. *Canzonette, rime varie, dialoghi.* Turin: Unione tipografico-editrice torinese, 1952.
Chiavola Birnbaum, Lucia. *Black Madonnas: Feminism, Religion and Politics in Italy.* Boston: Northeastern University Press, 1993.
Chierichini, Laura. 'Review of *La battaglia della belle donne di Firenze*, by Franco Sacchetti.' *Italianistica* 27, no. 2 (1998): 29–31.
Chiodo, Carmine. *Burleschi del seicento.* Milan: Treves, 1925.
Chubb, Thomas Caldecott. *The Sonnets of a Handsome and Well-Mannered Rogue.* Hamden, CT: Archon, 1970.
Cian, Vittorio. 'Un codice ignoto di rime volgari appartenuto a B. Castiglione.' *GSLI* 34 (1899): 297–353, 35 (1900): 80–2.
Ciavolella, Massimo. *La 'malattia d'amore' dall'antichità al Medioevo.* Rome: Bulzoni, 1976.
Ciccuto, Marcello. 'Registri parodici e collocazione della *Beca da Dicomano*.' *Italianistica* 6, no. 2 (1977): 264–80.
– 'Una figura del disamore in Guido Cavalcanti.' In *L'immagine del testo: Episodi di cultura figurativa nella letteratura italiana*, 15–31. Rome: Bonacci, 1990.
Cirese, Alberto, Maria. 'Note per una nuova indagine sugli strambotti delle origini romanze, della società quattro-cinquecentesca e della tradizione orale moderna.' *GSLI* 144, no. 1 (1967): 1–54; 144, no. 4 (1967): 491–566.
Contarino, Rosario. 'Introduzione.' In *Ode*, by Girolamo Fontanella, v–xvii. Turin: Res, 1994.
Contini, Gianfranco, ed. *Poeti del duecento.* 2 vols. Milan/Naples: Ricciardi, 1960.
Coppetta, Francesco [Coppetta]. *Rime.* Bari: Laterza, 1912.
Corsi, Giuseppe, ed. *Rimatori del trecento.* Turin: Unione Tipografico-editrice torinese, 1969.
Covito, Carmen. *La bruttina stagionata.* Milan: Bompiani, 1992.
Cowell, Andrew. *At Play in the Tavern: Signs, Coins and Bodies in the Middle Ages.* Ann Arbor: University of Michigan Press, 1999.
Crelly, William. *Marcello Giovanetti: A Poet of the Early Roman Baroque.* Lewiston, NY: Edwin Mellen, 1990.
Croce, Benedetto. *Letteratura della nuova Italia.* Vol. 1. Bari: Laterza, 1914.
– ed. *Lirici marinisti.* Bari: Laterza, 1910.
– *Saggi sulla letteratura italiana del seicento.* Bari: Laterza, 1962.

Croce, Franco. 'Giuseppe Artale.' In *Dizionario Biografico degli italiani*, ed. Alberto Ghisalberti, Vol. 4, 345–8. Rome: Istituto dell'Enciclopedia Italiana, 1962.

Cropper, Elizabeth. 'The Beauty of Woman: Problems in the Rhetoric of Renaissance Portraiture.' In *Rewriting the Renaissance: The Discourses of Sexual Difference in Early Modern Europe*, ed. Margaret W. Ferguson, Maureen Quilligan, and Nancy J. Vickers, 175–90. Chicago: University of Chicago Press, 1986.

– 'Introduction.' In *Concepts of Beauty in Renaissance Art*, ed. Francis Ames-Lewis and Mary Rogers, 1–11. Aldershot: Ashgate, 1998.

Cudini, Piero, ed. *Poesia italiana del duecento*. Milan: Garzanti, 1991.

D'Addario, A. 'Alessandro Adimari.' In *Dizionario Biografico degli italiani*, ed. Alberto Ghisalberti, Vol. 1, 277–78. 1960.

Dante Alighieri. *La divina commedia*. Ed. Natalino Sapegno. Florence: La Nuova Italia, 1978.

– *The Divine Comedy*. Trans. Charles Singleton. Princeton: Princeton University Press, 1973.

– *Vita nuova*. Edited and Trans. Dino Cervigni and Edward Vasta. Bilingual edition. Notre Dame: University of Notre Dame Press, 1995.

Delcorno Branca, Daniela. 'Il laboratorio del Poliziano: Per una lettura delle Rime.' *Lettere Italiane* 39, no. 2 (1987): 190–201.

De Maio, Romeo. *Donne e rinascimento*. Milan: Mondadori, 1987.

Dempsey, Charles. *The Portrayal of Love: Botticelli's Primavera and Humanist Culture at the Time of Lorenzo the Magnificent*. Princeton, NJ: Princeton University Press, 1992.

De Robertis, Domenico. 'Due altri testi della tradizione nenciale.' *Studi di filologia italiana* 25 (1967): 109–90.

Dizionario etimologico della lingua italiana. Ed. Manlio Cortelazzo and Paolo Zolli. 5 vols. Bologna: Zanichelli, 1984.

Doane, Mary Ann. 'Film and the Masquerade: Theorizing the Female Spectator.' *Screen* 23 (1982): 74–87.

Donaldson-Evans, Lance K. *Love's Fatal Glance: A Study of Eye Imagery in the Poets of the École Lyonnaise*. University, MS: Romance Monographs, 1980.

Doni, Anton Francesco. *I marmi*. 2 vols. Bari: Laterza, 1928.

– *La mula la chiave e madrigali satirici*. Bologna: Forni, 1967.

Dubrow, Heather. *Echoes of Desire: English Petrarchism and Its Counterdiscourses*. Ithaca, NY: Cornell University Press, 1995.

Ebreo, Leone. *Dialoghi d'amore*. Bari: Laterza, 1959.

Eco, Umberto. *Art and Beauty in the Middle Ages*. Trans. Hugh Bredin. New Haven, CT: Yale University Press, 1986.

Elwert, Theodor W. *La poesia lirica italiana del seicento: Studio sullo stile barocco.* Florence: Olschki, 1967.
Esposito, Sara. 'Premessa.' In *La battaglia delle belle donne di Firenze*, by Franco Sacchetti, 7–16. Rome: Zauli, 1996.
Faral, Edmond. *Les arts poétiques du XIIe et du XIIIe siècle: Recherches et documents sur la technique littéraire du moyen âge.* Paris: Champion, 1982.
Feminist Encyclopedia of Italian Literature. Ed. Rinaldina Russell. Westport, CT: Greenwood Press, 1997.
Ferrari, Giovanfrancesco. *Rime burlesche.* Venice: Sessa, 1570.
Ferrario, Giulio, ed. *Poesie pastorali e rusticali.* Milan: Società Tipografica de' Classici Italiani: 1808.
Ferrero, Giuseppe Guido, ed. *Marino e i marinisti.* Milan/Naples: Ricciardi, 1954.
Fido, Franco. 'Ameto e Africo precursori del Vallera: Elementi "nenciali" nella poesia di Boccaccio.' *Studi sul Boccaccio* 20 (1991/92): 221–32.
Filippi, Rustico. *Sonetti.* Ed. Pier Vincenzo Mengaldo. Turin: Einaudi, 1971.
Finucci, Valeria, and Regina Schwarz. *Desire in the Renaissance: Psychoanalysis and Literature.* Princeton: Princeton University Press, 1994.
Firenzuola, Agnolo. *On the Beauty of Women.* Translated by Konrad Eisenbichler and Jacqueline Murray. Philadelphia: University of Pennsylvania Press, 1992.
– *Opere.* Ed. Delmo Maestri. Turin: Unione tipografico-editrice torinese, 1977.
Françon, Marcel. 'Un motif de la poésie amoureuse au XVIe siècle.' *PMLA* 57, no. 2 (1941): 307–36.
Freud, Sigmund. *Standard Edition of the Complete Psychological Works.* Ed. James Strachey. London: Hogarth, 1953.
Frugoni, Chiara. 'The Imagined Woman.' In *A History of Women in the West*, Vol. 2: *Silences of the Middle Ages*, ed. Christiane Klapisch-Zuber, 336–422. Cambridge, MA: Belknap, 1992.
Galli Stampino, Maria. 'Bodily Boundaries Represented: The Petrarchan, the Burlesque and Arcimboldo's Example.' *Quaderni d'Italianistica* 16, no. 1 (1995): 61–79.
Genette, Gerard. *Palimpsests: Literature in the Second Degree.* Lincoln: University of Nebraska Press, 1997.
Getto, Giovanni. *Barocco in prosa e in poesia.* Milan: Rizzoli, 1969.
– *Interpretazione del Tasso.* Naples: Edizioni Scientifiche Italiane, 1967.
– 'Introduzione.' In *I marinisti*, 9–73. Turin: Unione tipografico-editrice torinese, 1962.
– ed. *I marinisti.* Turin: Unione tipografico-editrice torinese, 1962.
Giachino Luisella. '"Atomi fecondi": Rassegna di edizioni e studi sulla poesia barocca (1989–1996).' *Lettere italiane* 50, no. 2 (1998): 264–306.

Giallongo, Angela. *L'avventura dello sguardo: Educazione e comunicazione visiva nel Medioevo.* Bari: Dedalo, 1995.
– *Il galateo e le donne nel Medioevo.* Rimini: Maggioli, 1987.
Giambullari, Bernardo. *Rime inedite o rare.* Ed. Italiano Marchetti. Florence: Sansoni, 1955.
Giannetto, Nella. 'Il motivo dell'"amata incanutita" nelle rime di Petrarca e Boccaccio.' In *Boccaccio e dintorni: Miscellanea in onore di Vittore Branca.* 2 vols, 23–49. Florence: Olschki, 1983.
– 'Rassegna sulla parodia in letteratura.' *Lettere italiane* 29, no. 4 (1977): 461–79.
Gilbert, Sandra M., and Susan Gubar. *The Madwoman in the Attic: The Woman Writer and the Nineteenth-Century Literary Imagination.* New Haven: Yale University Press, 1979.
Ginzburg, Carlo. *Il Formaggio e i vermi.* Torino: Einaudi 1976.
Giovanetti, Marcello. 'Chiome, qualor disciolte.' In *I marinisti*, ed. Giovanni Getto, 201–2. Turin: Unione tipografico-editrice torinese, 1962.
Giunta, Claudio. 'La tradizione comico-realistica.' Chapter 3 in *Versi a un destinatario: Saggio sulla poesia italiana del Medioevo*, 267–354. Bologna: Il Mulino, 2002.
Gorni, Guglielmo. 'Manetto tra Guido e Dante. In *Seminario dantesco internazionale: International Dante Seminar*, ed. Zygmunt G. Baranski, 25–39. Florence: Le Lettere, 1997.
Gorni, Guglielmo, Massimo Danzi, and Silva Longhi, eds. *Poeti del cinquecento, Tomo I: Poeti lirici, burleschi satirici e didascalici.* Milano/Naples: Ricciardi, 2001.
Gorni, Guglielmo, and Silvia Longhi. 'La parodia.' In Vol. 5 of *Letteratura Italiana: Le questioni*, ed. Alberto Asor Rosa, 459–87. Turin: Einaudi, 1986.
Gouiran, Gérard. 'La *vielha* au pays de *joven*.' In *Vieillesse et vieillissement au Moyen-Âge*, 91–109. Aix-en-Provence: Centre universitaire d'études et de recherches médiévales d'Aix, 1987.
Graf, Arturo. 'Una cortigiana fra mille: Veronica Franco.' In *Attraverso il cinquecento*, 177–284. Turin: Chiantore, 1926.
– 'Petrarchismo e antipetrarchismo.' In *Attraverso il cinquecento*, 3–71. Turin: Chiantore, 1926.
Guinizzelli, Guido. *Poesie.* Ed. Edoardo Sanguineti. Milan: Mondadori, 1986.
Hendrix, Harald. 'The Construction of an Author: Pietro Aretino and the Elizabethans.' In *Betraying Our Selves: Forms of Self-Representation in Early Modern English Texts*, ed. Henk Dragstra, Sheila Ottway, and Helen Wilcox, 31–44. New York: St. Martin's Press, 2000.
Hillman, David, and Carla Mazzio, eds. *The Body in Parts: Fantasies of Corporeality in Early Modern Europe.* New York: Routledge, 1997.
Hösle, Johanne. *Texte zum Antipetrarchismus.* Tubingen: Max Niemeyer, 1970.
Horace (Orazio). *Odi e epodi.* Italian and Latin edition. Milan: Rizzoli, 1994.

Hurwitz, Siegmund. *Lilith, the First Eve: Historical and Psychological Aspects of the Dark Feminine.* Einsiedeln: Daimon, 1992.
Jacobson Schutte, Anne. 'Introduction.' In *Autobiography of an Aspiring Saint*, 3–18. Chicago: University of Chicago Press, 1996.
Jannaco, Carmine, and Martino Capucci. *Il seicento.* Milan: Vallardi, 1986.
Jones, R.O. 'Renaissance Butterfly, Mannerist Flea: Tradition and Change in Renaissance Poetry.' *MLN* 80, no. 2 (1965): 166–84.
Jones, Verina. 'Manzoni's Dark Ladies.' *Romance Studies* 19 (1991): 37–52.
Jordan, Mark D. *The Invention of Sodomy in Christian Theology.* Chicago: University of Chicago Press: 1997.
Jori, Giacomo. 'Poesia lirica marinista e "antimarinista" tra classicismo e barocco.' In *Storia della letteratura italiana*, ed. Enrico Malato, Vol. 5. Rome: Salerno Editrice, 1997.
Kaplan, Ann E. 'Is the Gaze Male?' In *Powers of Desire: The Politics of Sexuality*, ed. Ann Snitow, Christine Stonsell, and Sharon Thompson, 309–27. New York: Monthly Review Press, 1983.
Kaplan, Paul H.D. 'Local Color: The Black African Presence in Venetian Art and History.' In *Speak of Me as I Am: The United States Pavilion 50th International Exhibition of Art, The Venice Biennale 2003*, by Fred Wilson, 8–10. Cambridge, MA: List Visual Arts Center, MIT, 2003.
Klein, Melanie, and Joan Riviere. *Developments in Psychoanalysis.* London: Hogarth Press, 1952.
Köhler, Erich. 'Senso e funzione del termine *joven*.' In *Sociologia della fin amore*, 233–56. Padua: Liviana, 1976.
Kramer, Heinrich, and James Sprenger. *The Malleus Maleficarum of Heinrich Kramer and James Springer.* Trans. Montague Summers. New York: Dover, 1971.
Kristeva, Julia. *Powers of Horror: An Essay on Abjection.* New York: Columbia University Press, 1982.
Kuehn, Thomas, and Anne Jacobson Schutte. 'Introduction.' In *Time, Space, and Women's Lives in Early Modern Europe*, vii–xvii. ed. by Anne Jacobson Schutte, Thomas Kuehn, and Silvana Seidel Menchi. Kirksville, MO: Truman State University Press, 2001.
Lando, Ortensio. *Sermoni funebri de vari authori nella morte de diversi animali.* Genoa, 1558.
Lanza, Antonio. 'Aspetti e figure della poesia comico-realistica toscana del secolo XV.' *La rassegna della letteratura italiana* 89, no. 8 (1985): 403–43.
– 'Caratteri e forme della poesia per musica del secolo XIV.' In *Studi sulla lirica del Trecento*, 129–90. Rome: Bulzoni, 1975.
– *Freschi e minii del due, tre e quattrocento.* Florence: Cadmo, 2002.
– 'Introduzione.' In *Rime*, by Cecco Angiolieri, vii–lvi. Rome: Archivio Guido Izzo, 1990.

- ed. *Lirici toscani del quattrocento*. 2 vols. Rome: Bulzoni, 1975.
- *Polemiche e berte letterarie nella Firenze del primo rinascimento (1375–1449)*. Rome: Bulzoni, 1989.

Laqueur, Thomas. *Making Sex: Body and Gender from the Greeks to Freud*. Cambridge, MA: Harvard University Press, 1990.

Larivaille, Paul. *Pietro Aretino fra rinascimento e manierismo*. Rome: Bulzoni, 1980.

Letteratura italiana Zanichelli. CD-ROM. Bologna: Zanichelli, 1993.

Liborio, Mariantonia. 'L'"effictio ad vituperium": Le funzioni del *brutto*.' *Annali-Istituto-Universitario-orientale-Napoli-sezione-Romanza* 27, no. 1 (1985): 39–48.

Lobanov-Rostovsky, Sergei. 'Taming the Basilisk.' In *The Body in Parts: Fantasies of Corporeality in Early Modern Europe*, ed. David Hillman and Carla Mazzio, 195–217. New York: Routledge, 1997.

Lomperis, Linda, and Sarah Stanbury, eds. *Feminist Approaches to the Body in Medieval Literature*. Philadelphia: University of Pennsylvania Press, 1993.

Longhi, Silvia. *Lusus: Il capitolo burlesco nel cinquecento*. Padua: Antenore, 1983.

- 'Le rime di Francesco Berni: Cronologia e strutture del linguaggio burlesco.' *Studi di filologia italiana* 34 (1970): 249–99.
- ed. (Gugliemo Gorni and Massimo Danzi). *Poeti del cinquecento, Tomo I: Poeti lirici, burleschi satirici e didascalici*. Milan/Naples: Ricciardi, 2001.

Lorenzo il Magnifico. *Poesie*. Milan: Rizzoli, 1992.

Lugli, Adalgisa. *Wunderkammer*. Turin: Umberto Allemadi, 1997.

Luzio, Alessandro, and Rodolfo Renier. 'Buffoni, nani e schiavi dei Gonzaga al tempo d'Isabella d'Este.' *Nuova antologia* 34, no. 2 (1891): 113–46.

Maestri, Delmo. 'Le rime di Agnolo Firenzuola: Proposta di ordinamento del testo e valutazione critica.' *Italianistica* 3, no. 1 (1974): 78–96.

Malato, Enrico, ed. *Storia della letteratura italiana*. 12 Vols. Rome: Salerno, 1995.

Marchetti, Italiano. 'Note sulla poesia rusticale.' *Studi Secenteschi* 1 (1960): 61–81.

Marino, Giovan Battista. *Adone*. Ed. Giovanni Pozzi. Milan: Mondadori, 1976.

- *Amori*. Ed. Alessandro Martini. Milan: Rizzoli, 1982.

Marrani, Giuseppe. 'I sonetti di Rustico Filippi.' *Studi di filologia italiana* 57 (1999): 33–195.

Marsh Heywood, Melinda. 'The Withered Rose: Seduction and Poetics of Old Age in *Roman de la Rose* of Guillaume de Lorris.' *French Forum* 25, no. 1 (2000): 5–22.

Martelli, Mario. 'La semantica del Poliziano e la "Centuria secunda" dei *Miscellanea*.' *Rinascimento* 13 (1973): 21–84.

Marti, Mario. *Cultura e stile nei poeti giocosi del tempo di Dante*. Pisa: Nistri-Lischi, 1953.

- *Letteratura italiana: I minori*. Milan: Marzorati, 1961.

- ed. *Poeti giocosi del tempo di Dante.* Milan: Rizzoli, 1956.
Martial. *Epigrams.* Vol. 1. New York: Putnam, 1925.
Martìn, Adrienne. *Cervantes and the Burlesque Sonnet.* Berkeley: California University Press, 1991.
Massera, Aldo Francesco, ed. *Sonetti burleschi e realistici dei primi due secoli.* Bari: Laterza, 1920.
Matthew of Vendôme. *Ars versificatoria: The Art of the Versemaker.* Trans. Roger P. Parr. Milwaukee: Marquette University Press, 1981.
Mauro, Giovanni. 'Capitolo delle donne di montagna.' In *Poeti del cinquecento, Tomo I: Poeti lirici, burleschi, satirici e didascalici,* ed. Guglielmo Gorni, Massimo Danzi, and Silvia Longhi, 904–10. Milan/Naples: Ricciardi, 2001.
Maylender, Michele. *Storia delle accademie d'Italia.* 5 vols. Bologna: Forni, 1970.
Mazzi, Curzio. 'Prefazione.' In *Rime,* by Niccolò Campani, vii–xxvii. Siena: Gati, 1878.
Meglio, Giovan Matteo. *Rime.* Ed. Giuseppe Brincat. Florence: Olschki. 1977.
Mengaldo, Pier Vincenzo. 'Introduzione.' In *Sonetti,* by Rustico Filippi, 5–16. Turin: Einaudi, 1971.
Merlini, Domenico. *Saggio di ricerche sulla satira contro il villano.* Turin: Loescher, 1894.
Miato, Monica. *L'accademia degli incogniti di Giovan Francesco Loredan: Venezia 1630–1661.* Florence: Olschki, 1998.
Montanile, Milena. 'Le chiome antipetrarchiste di Berni.' *Esperienze letterarie* 21, no. 2 (1996): 59–65.
Mormando, Franco. 'Bernardino of Siena: "Great Defender" or "Merciless Betrayer" of Women?' *Italica* 75, no. 1 (1998): 22–40.
Mulvey, Laura. 'Visual Pleasure and Narrative Cinema.' *Screen* 16 (1975): 6–18.
Musacchio, Enrico. 'Passione d'amore e scienza ottica in un sonetto di Giacomo da Lentini.' *Letteratura italiana antica* 4 (2003): 337–69.
Muscetta, Carlo, and Pier Paolo Ferrante, eds. *Poesia del seicento.* 2 vols. Turin: Einaudi, 1964.
Muscetta, Carlo, and Daniele Ponchiroli, eds. *Poesia del quattrocento e del cinquecento.* Turin: Einaudi, 1959.
Muscia, Niccola. 'Deh, guata Ciampol.' In *Le rime* by Cecco Angiolieri, ed. Antonio Lanza, 398. Rome: Archivio Guido Izzo. 1990.
Mutini, Claudio. 'Idee per il Berni.' In *L'autore e l'opera: Saggi sulla letteratura del cinquecento,* 27–56. Rome: Bulzoni, 1973.
Nelson, Lowry, Jr. *The Poetry of Guido Cavalcanti.* New York: Garland, 1986.
La Nencia da Barberino. Ed. Rossella Bessi. Rome: Salerno, 1982.
Newman, Cathy. 'The Enigma of Beauty.' *National Geographic,* January 2000.

Oldcorn, Anthony. 'Berni e berneschi' In *The Cambridge History of Italian Literature*, ed. Peter Brandt and Lino Pertile, 270–1. Cambridge: Cambridge University Press, 1999.

Onians, John. 'The Biological Basis of Renaissance Aesthetics.' In *Concepts of Beauty in Renaissance Art*, ed. Francis Ames Lewis and Mary Rogers, 12–22. Aldershot: Ashgate, 1998.

Opere burlesche di Francesco Berni, del Molza, di M. Bino, di M. Lodovico Martelli, di Mattio Franzesi, dell'Aretino et di diversi Autori. Florence: Giunti, 1555.

Origo, Iris. 'The Domestic Enemy: The Eastern Slaves in Tuscany in the Fourteenth and Fifteenth Century.' *Speculum* 30 (1955): 321–66.

– *The World of San Bernardino*. New York: Harcourt Brace, 1962.

Orvieto, Paolo. *Pulci medievale*. Rome: Salerno, 1978.

Orvieto, Paolo, and Lucia Brestolini. *La poesia comico-realistica: Dalle origini al cinquecento*. Rome: Carocci, 2000.

Pacteau, Francette. *The Symptom of Beauty*. Cambridge: Harvard University Press, 1994.

Pagani, Walter. *Repertorio tematico della scuola poetica siciliana*, Bari: Adriatica, 1968.

Panizza, Letizia, and Sharon Wood. *A History of Women's Writing in Italy*. Cambridge: Cambridge University Press, 2000.

Parker, Patricia. *Literary Fat Ladies: Rhetoric, Gender, Property*. London: Methuen, 1987.

– 'On the Tongue: Cross Gendering, Effeminacy, and the Art of Words.' *Style* 23, no. 3 (1989): 445–65.

Parr, Roger P., ed. and trans. *Ars Versificatoria: The Art of the Versemaker*. Milwaukee: Marquette University Press, 1981.

Partner, Nancy. *Studying Medieval Women*. Cambridge, MA: Medieval Academy of America, 1993.

Pascal, C. 'Misoginia medievale: Due carmi contro le donne.' *Studi Medievali* 2 (1906–7): 242–8.

Pasquini, Emilio. 'La poesia popolare e giullaresca.' Chapter 7 of *Letteratura italiana storia e testi. Il duecento dalle origini a Dante*, edited by Carlo Muscetta, Vol. 1, tome 2, 115–81. Bari: Laterza, 1970.

Passera, Elsa. 'The Semantic Evolution of the Latin Terms *domina, femina* and *mulier* in the Italian Language.' *Quaderni d'Italianistica* 22, no. 1 (2000): 105–25.

Pérez Romero, Carmen. 'El motivo de la mujer morena come antihéroina petrarquista: Retrato y etopeya.' In *Actas del IX Simposio de la Sociedad Española de Literatura General y Comparada*, 301–11. Zaragoza: Universidad de Zaragoza, 1994.

Pers, Ciro di. *Poesie.* Ed. Michele Rak. Turin: Einaudi, 1978.
Petrarch, Francesco. *Canzoniere.* Ed. Piero Cudini. Milan: Garzanti, 1991.
Poggi Salani, Teresa. 'Motivi e lingua della poesia rusticale: Appunti.' *Acme* 20 (1967): 233–86.
Poliziano, Angelo. *Opera Omnia.* Turin: Bottega d'Erasmo, 1970.
– *Rime.* Ed. Daniela Delcorno Branca. Venice: Marsilio, 1990.
Pozzi, Giovanni. 'Codici, stereotipi, topoi e fonti letterarie.' *Intorno al codice: Atti del III convegno della Associazione Italiana di Studi Semiotici (AISS),* 37–76. Florence: La Nuova Italia, 1976.
– 'Il ritratto della donna nella poesia d'inizio cinquecento.' *Lettere Italiane* 31, no. 1 (1979): 3–30.
– 'Temi, topoi, stereotipi.' In *Letteratura italiana: Le forme del testo I; Teoria e poesia,* ed. Alberto Asor Rosa, 391–436. Turin: Einaudi, 1984.
Praz, Mario. *La carne, la morte e il diavolo nella letteratura romantica.* Florence: Sansoni, 1966.
Previtera, Carmelo. *La poesia giocosa e l'umorismo: Dalle origini al Rinascimento.* Milan: Vallardi, 1939.
Psaki, Regina, F. '"Women Make All Things Lose Their Power": Women's Knowledge, Men's Fear in the *Decameron* and the *Corbaccio.*' *Helitropia* 1, no. 1 (2003), http://www.helitropia.org.
Pulci, Luigi. *Morgante.* Ed. Franca Ageno. Milan/Naples: Ricciardi, 1955.
– *Opere minori.* Milan: Mursia, 1986.
Quondam, Amedeo. *Il naso di Laura.* Modena: Panini, 1991.
Rak, Michele. 'Introduzione.' In *Poesie,* by Ciro di Pers, vii–xlv. Turin: Einaudi, 1978.
Randisbacher, Hans J. *The Smell of Books: A Cultural-Historical Study of Olfactory Perception in Literature.* Ann Arbor: University of Michigan Press, 1992.
Rebay, Luciano. *Italian Poetry: A Selection from St. Francis of Assisi to Salvatore Quasimodo in Italian with English Translation.* New York: Dover, 1969.
Renier, Rodolfo. *Il tipo estetico della donna nel Medioevo.* Bologna: Forni, 1972.
Ricci, Pier Giorgio. 'La tradizione dell'invettiva tra il Medioevo e l'Umanesimo.' *Lettere Italiane* 26, no. 4 (1974): 405–14.
Rivkin, Julie, and Michael Ryan, eds. *Literary Theory: An Anthology.* Malden, MA: Blackwell, 1998.
Robathan, Dorothy M. *The Pseudo Ovidian De Vetula.* Amsterdam: Hakkert, 1968.
Robbins, R.H. 'Metamorphosis.' In *Encyclopedia of Witchcraft and Demonology,* 343–6. New York: Crown, 1958.
Rodnite Lemay, Helen. *Women's Secrets: A Translation of the Pseudo-Albertus Magnus's* De Secretis mulierum *with Commentaries.* Albany: State University of New York Press, 1992.

Rogers, Katharine M. *The Troublesome Helpmate: A History of Misogyny in Literature.* Seattle: University of Washington Press, 1966.

Rogers, Mary. 'The Decorum of Women's Beauty: Trissino, Fiorenzuola, Luigini and the Representation of Women in Sixteenth-Century Painting.' *Renaissance Studies* 2, no. 1 (1988): 41–88.

Roper, Lyndal. 'Madri di depravazione: Le mezzane nel cinquecento.' *Memoria* 17 (1986): 7–23.

Rosenthal, Margaret. *The Honest Courtesan: Veronica Franco, Citizen and Writer in Sixteenth-Century Venice.* Chicago: University of Chicago Press, 1992.

Rossi, Nicolò de'. *Canzoniere.* Ed. Furio Brugnolo. Padua: Antenore, 1974.

Russo, Mary. *The Female Grotesque.* New York: Routledge, 1995.

Sacchetti, Franco. *La battaglia delle belle donne di Firenze.* Ed. Sara Esposito. Rome: Zauli, 1996.

– *Il libro delle rime.* Ed. Franca Brambilla Ageno. Florence: Olschki, 1990.

Saffioti, Tito. *I Giullari in Italia: Lo spettacolo, il pubblico, i testi.* Milan: Xenia, 1990.

Salmon, Paul. 'The Wild Man in *Iwein* and Medieval Descriptive Technique.' *Modern Language Review* 56 (1961): 520–8.

Salomoni, Giuseppe. *Rime.* Ed. Catia Giovannini. Turin: Res, 1996.

Savona, Eugenio. *Repertorio tematico del Dolce Stil Nuovo.* Bari: Adriatica, 1973.

Schiesari, Juliana. 'Libidinal Economies: Machiavelli and Fortune's Rape.' In *Desire in the Renaissance: Psychoanalysis and Literature,* ed. Valeria Finucci and Regina Schwarz, 169–83. Princeton: Princeton University Press, 1994.

Sgruttendio de Scafato, Felippo [Giulio Cesare Cortese]. *Opere poetiche.* Rome: Edizioni dell'Ateneo, 1967.

Shahar, Shulamith. 'The Old Body in Medieval Culture.' In *Framing Medieval Bodies,* ed. Sara Kay and Miri Rubin, 160–86. Manchester: Manchester University Press, 1999.

Shakespeare, William. *The Sonnets.* Ed. G. Blakemore Evans. Cambridge: Cambridge University Press, 1996.

Sherman, Cindy. *Cindy Sherman: Retrospective.* New York: Thames and Hudson, 1997.

Sissa, Giulia. *Greek Virginity.* Cambridge, MA: Harvard University Press, 1990.

Spackman, Barbara. '*Inter musam et ursam moritur:* Folengo and the Gaping "Other" Mouth.' In *Refiguring Woman: Perspectives on Gender and the Italian Renaissance,* ed. Marilyn Migiel and Juliana Schiesari, 19–34. Ithaca: Cornell University Press, 1991.

Specht, Henrik. 'The Beautiful, the Handsome, and the Ugly: Some Aspects of the Art of Character Portrayal in Medieval Literature.' *Studia Neophilologica* 56, no. 2 (1984): 129–46.

Spini, Giorgio. *Ricerca dei libertini*. Florence: La Nuova Italia, 1983.
Stallybrass, Peter. 'Patriarchal Territories: The Body Enclosed.' In *Rewriting the Renaissance: The Discourse of Sexual Difference in Early Modern Europe*, ed. Margaret W. Ferguson, Maureen Quilligan, and Nancy J. Vickers, 123–42. Chicago: University of Chicago Press, 1986.
Stallybrass, Peter, and Allon White. *Politics and Poetics of Transgression*. Ithaca: Cornell University Press, 1986.
Stanbury, Sarah. 'Feminist Masterplots: The Gaze on the Body of *Pearl*'s Dead Girl.' In *Feminist Approaches to the Body in Medieval Literature*, edited by Linda Lomperis and Sarah Stanbury, 96–115. Philadelphia: University of Pennsylvania Press, 1993.
– 'The Virgin's Gaze: Spectacle and Transgression in Middle English Lyrics of the Passion.' *PMLA* 106 (1991): 1083–93.
Stapleton, M.L. '"My False Eyes": The Dark Lady and Self-Knowledge.' *Studies in Philology* 90, no. 2 (1993): 213–30.
Stephens, Walter. *Demon Lovers: Witchcraft, Sex and the Crisis of Belief*. Chicago: University of Chicago Press, 2002.
– 'Il ruolo dello sgradevole nella caccia alle streghe.' In *Disarmonia bruttezza e bizzarria nel Rinascimento: Atti del VII convegno internazionale*, ed. Luisa Secchi Tarugi, 383–403. Florence: Cesati, 1998.
Storia della letteratura italiana. Ed. Enrico Malato. 12 vols. Rome: Salerno, 1995.
Suitner, Franco. *La poesia satirica e giocosa nell'età dei comuni*. Padua: Antenore, 1983.
Taddeo, Edoardo. *Manierismo letterario e i lirici veneziani del tardo cinquecento*. Rome: Bulzoni, 1974.
Tarchetti, Iginio Ugo. *Fosca*. Milan: Mondadori, 1988.
Tasinato, Maria. 'Presentazione.' In *Gli ornamenti delle donne* by Tertullian, 5–11. Parma: Nuova Pratiche, 1995.
Tasso, Torquato. *Opere*. Ed. Bruno Maier. Vol. 1. Milan: Rizzoli, 1963.
Tateo, Francesco. 'Angelo Poliziano.' In *Letteratura italiana storia e testi: Il Quattrocento. L'età dell'umanesimo*, ed. Achille Tartaro et al., Vol. 2, tome 2, 155–245. Bari: Laterza, 1972.
Tertullian. *The Apparel of Women*. In *Disciplinary, Moral and Ascentical Works*, trans. Rudolph Abersmann, Sister Emily Joseph Daly and Edwin Quain, Vol. 40, 111–49. New York: Fathers of the Church, 1959.
– *Gli ornamenti delle donne [De cultu feminarum]*. Ed. Maria Tasinato. Parma: Nuova Pratiche Editrice, 1995.
Tomarken, Annette. 'Flea Encomia and Other Mock Eulogies of Animals.' *Fifteenth Century Studies* 11 (1985): 137–48.
Trubiano, Marisa S. 'Lyric Poetry: Seventeenth Century.' In *Feminist Encyclopedia*

of Italian Literature, ed. Rinaldina Russell, 177–80. Westport, CT: Greenwood Press, 1997.

Ulysse, Georges. *Théâtre et société au cinquecento: Le rapports sociaux dans la comedie italienne de la fin du XVe siècle au premier tiers du XVIe.* Aix en Provence: Publications Université de Provence, 1984.

Usher, Jonathan. 'Guido Cavalcanti.' In *The Cambridge History of Italian Literature*, ed. Peter Brandt and Lino Pertile, 22–5. Cambridge: Cambridge University Press, 1999.

Valenti, Cristina. *Comici artigiani: Mestiere e forme dello spettacolo a Siena nella prima metà del cinquecento.* Modena: Panini, 1992.

Vickers, Brian. 'Epideictic and Epic in the Renaissance.' *New Literary History* 14 (1983): 497–537.

Vickers, Nancy. '"The Blazon of Sweet Beauty's Best": Shakespeare's *Lucrece*.' In *Shakespeare and the Question of Theory*, ed. Patricia Parker and Geoffrey Hartman, 95–115. New York: Methuen, 1985.

– 'Diana Described: Scattered Woman in Scattered Rhyme.' In *Writing and Sexual Difference*, ed. Elizabeth Abel, 95–109. Chicago: Chicago University Press, 1982.

– 'Members Only: Marot's Anatomical Blazons.' In *The Body in Parts: Fantasies of Corporeality in Early Modern Europe*, ed. David Hillman and Carla Mazzio, 3–21. New York: Routledge, 1997.

Vigarello, Georges. *Concepts of Cleanliness.* Cambridge: Cambridge University Press, 1988.

Volpi, Angiola. '"Pellegrina bellezza": Recherche su "Peregrino" et nostalgie épique dans la poésie italienne du jeune Milton.' In *Prelude au matine d'un poete: 'Such sights as youthful poets dream,' Traditions humanistes chez le jeune Milton*, 17–32. Paris: Université de Paris IV Sorbonne, 1983.

Williams, Linda. 'When the Woman Looks.' In *Re-Vision: Essays in Feminist Film Criticism*, ed. Mary Ann Doane, Patricia Mellencamp, and Linda Williams, 83–99. Los Angeles: American Film Institute, 1984.

Woodward, Kathleen. 'Youthfulness as Masquerade.' *Discourse* 11, no. 1 (1989): 119–42.

Wright, Charlotte M. *Plain and Ugly Janes: The Rise of the Ugly Woman in Contemporary American Fiction.* New York: Garland, 2000.

Wulff, August. *Die Frauenfeindliche Dichtungen in den Romanische Literaturen des Mittelalters bis zum Ende des XIII Jahrhunderts.* Halle: Max Niemeyer, 1914.

Yandell, Cathy. 'Of Lice and Women: Rhetoric and Gender in *La Puce de Madame Des Roches*.' *Journal of Medieval and Renaissance Studies* 20 (1990): 123–35.

Young, Robert. *Postcolonialism: An Historical Introduction.* Oxford: Blackwell, 2001.
Zancan, Marina. *Il doppio itinerario della scrittura: La donna nella tradizione letteraria italiana.* Turin: Einaudi, 1998.
Zemon Davis, Natalie. 'Women on Top.' In *Society and Culture in Early Modern France*, 124–51. Stanford: Stanford University Press, 1975.
Zetzel Lambert, Ellen. *The Face of Love: Feminism and the Beauty Question.* Boston: Beacon Press, 1995.
Ziino, Agostino. 'Rime per musica e danza.' In *Storia della letteratura italiana: Il trecento*, edited by Enrico Malato, Vol. 2, 455–529. Rome: Salerno Editrice, 1995.
Ziolkowski, Jan. 'Avatars of Ugliness in Medieval Literature.' *Modern Language Review* 79, no. 1 (1984): 1–20.

Index

Abriani, Paolo 129
Achillini, Claudio 140, 222n2, 224n9, 226n22
Adimari, Alessandro 8, 129–32, 161, 163, 222nn3–4, 223nn4–5, 223n7, 228n36
Agamben, Giorgio 34, 197n60, 199n75
aging, 3, 7, 9, 14, 15, 18, 74, 81, 132–3, 152–8, 166, 188n7
Albert the Great 14, 192n20, 192n22
Alberti, Leon Battista 208n69, 231n51
Alesso di Guido Donati 53, 201n 20
Alfie, Fabian 19, 30, 194n29
Almansi, Guido 83
Andreas, Cappellanus 39, 42, 43, 52, 197n62, 201n23
Angiolieri, Cecco 6, 14, 19, 21, 27, 28, 29, 30, 31, 38, 46, 68, 71, 191n15, 194n29, 196nn48–9, 198nn70–1, 200n14
antifeminist discourse. *See* misogyny
Anti-Petrarchism 8, 82, 101, 114–15, 117–18, 120–3, 129, 133, 156, 163, 218n55, 219n65, 220nn70–1, 221n73, 228n36
Anti-Stilnovism 27, 34

Aretino, Pietro 83, 89, 114, 120–2, 205n46, 220n71, 221n 74, 228n33
Ariosto, Ludovico 81, 165, 168, 198n69, 205n46, 207n58, 208n67, 208n71, 210n5, 213n24, 224n12, 228n33, 231n51
Artale, Giuseppe 159, 230n45
Asor Rosa, Alberto 128, 155, 157, 222n1, 225n18
Authority, male/female 3, 42, 45, 46, 48, 51, 52, 54, 55, 56, 57, 61, 62, 65, 67, 79, 107, 165–6

Bähr, Rudolf 192n25
Bakhtin, Mikhail 5, 7, 55, 56, 58, 76, 92, 94, 114, 126, 202n30, 207n62, 213n23, 214n26
Baldissone, Giusi 197n55, 197n57
Banner, Lois 15, 29, 78, 188n7, 192n21, 207n58
Bàrberi Squarotti, Giorgio 157–8, 197n55, 218n55, 226n25
Barberino, Francesco da 21, 29, 42, 56, 196n50
Battista, Giuseppe 155, 224n9
Battisti, Eugenio 53, 205n48
Baudelaire, Charles 169

Beauvoir, de, Simone 15
Beca da Dicomano 75, 87, 89, 96, 215n31
Beccuti, Francesco (Coppetta) 168, 207n58, 209n72
Belloni, Antonio 130, 231n 49, 232n56
Bembo, Pietro 7, 87, 99, 114–16, 210n7, 212n18, 215n38, 218–19n56
Beolco, Angelo 215n36
Berger, John 44
Bernard de Gordon 39, 40, 199n75
Bernardino da Siena 67, 206n49
Bernheimer, Richard 63, 64, 204nn42–3, 205n48
Berni, Francesco 7, 68, 83, 89–92, 97, 99, 100–2, 104–8, 110–12, 114–20, 123, 125, 130, 133, 152–3, 156, 168, 212nn14–15, 212n17, 214n27, 215nn32–4, 215nn36–7, 216n38, 217n49, 218nn55–6, 219n58
Beroe 17, 18, 21, 22, 32, 69, 79–80, 126, 193n27
Besomi, Ottavio 137, 160, 162, 230n47
Bettella, Patrizia 216n39, 219n56
Blamires, Alcuin 189n1, 189n4, 190n6, 190n14
blazon 7, 120, 143, 220n70, 224n8
Bloch, Howard 11, 12, 21, 70, 189nn1–2, 202n29
Boccaccio, Giovanni 13, 30, 31, 48, 83–4, 87, 90, 130, 134, 152–4, 165, 168, 191n14, 192n20, 196n51, 198n74, 199n3, 204n42, 204n44, 210n5, 210n7, 211n8, 214n29, 215n38
Bologna, Corrado 13
Bonadiman, Beatrice 67

Bonichi, Bindo 14, 191n19
Braidotti, Rosi 42, 165
Brandt, Wolfgang 17
Brauner, Sigrid 67
Brestolini, Lucia 13, 26, 50, 53, 191n15, 201n19, 201n23, 211n11, 214n27
Bruni, Antonio 219
Burchiello (Domenico di Giovanni) 7, 24, 66, 68–73, 99, 119, 168, 201n20, 206n52, 215n33
Burns, Jane 59
Buzzetti Gallarati, Silvia 25

Cadden, Joan 10, 61, 192n20, 192n22, 222n80, 230n39
Callaghan, Karen, 3
Cammelli, Antonio (Pistoia) 60, 73, 75, 79, 99, 207n60, 215n33
Campani, Nicolò (Strascino) 7, 89–92, 96, 98–100, 102, 104–13, 212n15, 212n17, 212n19, 213n20, 213n22, 214n26, 214n31
Canale, Giovanni 155
canon of beauty, 4–8, 81–4, 86, 88–90, 94–6, 100, 105, 114, 117, 119, 125, 133–4, 167, 187n1, 210n7, 225n19
Caravaggio 144, 225n17, 227n28
Carnivalesque 5, 64, 76, 91, 94, 96, 110, 207n62, 214n62, 222n82
carpe diem 152–3
Carter, Angela 169–70
Casa, Giovanni della 83, 11, 113, 215n35, 224n11
Casaburi Urries, Pietro 8, 133, 141–2, 224n9
Casagrande, Carla 12, 202n33
Casini, Tommaso 46, 55, 56, 62, 63, 171, 202n28, 203n34

Casoni, Guido 137
Cassata, Letterio 34, 197n57, 197n64, 198n69
Castiglione, Baldassar 87, 91, 176, 210n7, 212n19, 213n21
Cavalcanti, Guido 7, 19–21, 32–40, 71, 78, 114, 129, 168, 194n30, 197n56, 198n65,198nn67–9, 207n61
Cenne da la Chitarra 32
Cervigni, Dino 25, 195n42, 196n47, 198n66
Charlet, Jean Louis 80
Cherchi, Paolo 40, 199n75
Chiabrera, Gabriello 138, 225n20
Cian, Vittorio 26, 176, 192n23, 202n28, 203n40
Ciavolella, Massimo 198n73
Ciccuto, Marcello 34, 197n60
Cicero 14
Cino da Pistoia 144, 224n11
Cirese, Alberto Maria 211n8
Comic-realistic poetry 3, 4–8, 13, 15–16, 18–19, 21, 27, 31, 42, 45, 66, 87, 119, 123, 126, 128, 134, 152, 187n2, 194n28, 194n32, 196n53
Contini, Gianfranco 22, 191n16, 194n28, 198n65, 198n71
Corsi, Giuseppe 54, 203n38
Cortese, Giulio Cesare 163
Covito, Carmen 169–70
Cowell, Andrew 58
Crelly, William 138, 225n21
Croce, Benedetto 137, 155, 160, 224n9, 229n40, 230n45, 232n54
Cropper, Elizabeth 210n7, 227n29

D'Alessandro, Giuseppe 150
Dante Alighieri 21, 25, 28, 34–6, 39–41, 90, 165, 191n15, 192n21, 196n74, 197n59, 197n65, 198n67, 199n1, 210n3, 213n24, 225n15
Dark lady: 8, 122, 127, 133–8, 143, 149–51, 163–4, 225n14, 225n20, 228n34, 228n36, 229n37, 229n39; in Shakespeare 122, 143, 221n74
Delcorno Branca, Daniela 78–9, 205n47, 207n63, 208nn67–8
De Maio, Romeo 205n48, 228n33
Dempsey, Charles 210n5
De Robertis, Domenico 34, 37, 39, 198n69, 211n12
descriptio or descriptive portrait 16–17, 22, 36, 51, 55, 57, 65, 78, 82, 84, 86, 88, 90, 98–100, 102–5, 107, 113, 118, 125, 156, 168, 193n25, 210n3, 210n5, 212n14, 216n39
desire 29, 35, 37, 45, 96, 101, 104–5, 107, 167
De vetula 41, 47, 199n3
Doane, Mary Ann 44
Dolce, Lodovico 160, 220n69
Donato da Cascia 53, 54, 63, 67, 201n20
Doni, Anton Francesco 7, 83, 114, 117–20, 123, 125, 133, 153, 156, 181, 211n9, 219n60, 220n66, 220n68
Donne, John 160, 231n52
Du Bellay, Joachim 220n70
Dubrow, Heather 221n74, 229n39

Eco, Umberto 11, 190n7
Erasmus 82
Errico, Scipione 129, 224n9
Esposito, Sara 200n16

Faitinelli, Pietro de' 27, 28, 32, 49, 191n15, 196n53
Faral, Edmond 16, 17, 193n27

254 Index

female body: as abject 5, 188n6, 217n48, 217n50; as deformed 7, 34–5, 37, 40, 46, 61, 89–90, 100, 110, 113, 125, 130, 156, 158, 163, 169, 223n5, 230nn47–8; as disgusting 7, 10, 17, 22–5, 28, 31, 37, 40, 54–5, 61, 64, 69, 70, 78–80, 95–6, 98, 101, 107–12, 126–7, 158–60, 162, 166, 196n36, 230n48; dismemberment of 7, 25, 27, 46, 48, 52, 91, 102; excess of 54, 65, 71, 80–2, 92, 94, 100–1, 105, 107, 114, 125; as fragmented 5, 7, 91, 102, 104, 106–7, 109, 114, 120, 143, 189n8; as grotesque 7, 45, 55–6, 58, 64, 91–2, 97, 99, 101, 105, 107, 109, 113–14, 126, 159, 169, 188n6, 204n43, 208n69, 213n24, 222n82; as masculine 24–5, 58, 61, 63, 64; objectified 91, 102, 105, 107, 120, 158; old 7, 9, 14, 55, 196n48

female speech/silence 4–5, 55–7, 59–62, 65, 166, 188n3, 188n5, 202n29, 202n33, 203nn35–7

female subjectivity, construction of 4, 188n5

female ugliness: as aesthetic deviancy 81, 92, 94, 166, 167; and bad smell 5, 6, 8, 22–5, 39–40, 49, 58, 69, 78, 114, 166, 195nn41–2, 195n44; and dehumanization 72; and disproportion 6, 7, 94–6, 100–1, 105, 108, 110, 113, 119, 166, 214n31; and evil 6, 15, 17, 21, 27; and gender hybridity 24–5, 55, 58, 61, 64–5; and lust 10, 18, 21–3, 25, 61, 63–4, 67, 69, 72–3, 79–80, 112, 126, 166; and moral deviancy 10, 17–18, 32, 35, 166; and old age 17–18, 21, 74, 80, 109, 116, 195n48, 197n61,
204n45; and sexual deviancy 6, 23–5, 67, 69, 166; and transgression 55, 58, 61, 81, 125

feminist criticism, 5, 7, 42, 44, 165

Ferrario, Giulio 211n9

Ferrero, Giuseppe Guido 138, 146–7, 160, 224n9, 228n34, 232n54

Filippi, Rustico 6, 18, 20–7, 32, 34, 37, 39, 58, 69, 72, 78, 119, 194n32, 195n41, 195n45, 197n64, 220n67

film theory 5, 44

Fink, Guido 83

Firenzuola, Agnolo 7, 8, 83, 90–2, 99, 102–7, 110, 112, 114, 119, 212n17, 214n27, 215n35, 216n39, 216n42, 216n44, 220n69

Folgore da San Gimignano 32

Fontanella, Girolamo 149, 224n9, 229nn40–1

Franco, Niccolò 80–1, 207n58, 208n71, 209n72

Françon, Marcel 159, 231n51

Freud, Sigmund 5, 24, 195n40

Frugoni, Chiara 67

Gandino, Ludovico 220n65

gaze, male/female 42–6, 47, 48, 50, 51–2, 60, 70, 75, 200n10, 201n21

gender 3, 24, 39, 44, 61, 64–5, 99, 163, 209n1

Genette, Gerard 32, 197n55

Geoffrey of Vinsauf 16, 84

Getto, Giovanni 129, 135, 138–9, 150–1, 154, 160, 224n9, 232n54

Gherardo, Quinto 168, 207n58, 209n72

Giallongo, Angela 196n50, 199n4

Giambullari, Bernardo 65, 201n20, 211n9

Giannetto, Nella 152–3

Gilbert, Sandra, 4
Giotto 226n28
Giovanetti, Marcello 8, 130, 133, 138, 141–2, 222n3, 225n21
Giunta, Claudio 34, 197nn60–1, 197n63
Giustinian, Leonardo 205n47
Gorni, Guglielmo 34, 197n55, 197n60, 197n63
Graf, Arturo 209n65, 220n65
Gramsci, Antonio 209n1
Guazzo, Stefano 219n65
Gubar, Susan, 4
Guinizzelli, Guido 6, 18–19, 60, 21, 25–6, 29, 32, 34, 37, 39, 43, 52, 54, 65, 69, 196n45, 197n64, 202n28

hegemony 3, 5, 81, 86, 88, 92, 98–9, 101, 106, 114, 163, 166, 209n1, 212n19, 220n65
Horace 10, 22, 66, 73, 79, 192n23
Hugo, Victor 169
Hurtado de Mendoza, Diego 220n70, 231n52
Hurwitz, Siegmund 204n41

invective 7, 17, 21, 26, 54, 60, 68, 71, 73, 83, 113, 120, 126–8, 132, 203n38, 211n12
Isabella d'Este 73, 145, 227n33

Jacobson Schutte, Anne 190n13, 203n37
Jones, Verina 187n1, 224n12
Juvenal 10, 189n3

Kaplan, Ann 200n10
Kaplan, Paul 227n31
Klein, Melanie 216n44
Köhler, Erich 15, 192n23

Kristeva, Julia 5, 192n23
Kuehn, Thomas 190n13

Lando, Ortensio 159, 231n53
Lanza, Antonio 28, 68, 71, 196n49, 197n64, 198n70, 200n14, 201n20, 202n26, 206n57
Laqueuer, Thomas 195n40
Larivaille, Paul 220n71
lauda, or *laus*, or praise 16, 19, 21, 26
Legacci Stricca, Pier Antonio 8, 107, 109–10, 112, 114, 123, 125–6, 178, 213n20, 216n45, 231n50
Lentini, Giacomo 43, 199n55
Leonida, Fabio 155
Lessing, Gotthold Ephraim 91
Liborio, Maria Antonia 17
Lippi, Filippo 144
Lobanov-Rostovsky, Sergei 43, 200n12, 201n21
Longhi, Silvia 82, 90, 92, 100, 115, 168, 197n55, 211n12, 212nn15–17, 214n28, 217n51, 218n54
Lorenzo il Magnifico (de'Medici) 65, 87, 89, 99, 108, 212n13
Lugli, Adalgisa 228n35
lusus 11, 33, 76, 82, 115, 165–6, 207n63

Machiavelli, Niccolò 168, 209n72
Maestri, Delmo 102
Magno, Celio 134, 136, 141, 225n16
male imagination 3, 5, 23, 31, 65, 80–1, 130, 158, 161
Malleus Maleficarum 67, 192n22
Mamiani, Giambattista 160–1, 163
Marchetti, Italiano 87
Marino, Giambattista 8, 9, 124, 128, 135–8, 140, 145–50, 222n1, 224n8,

256   Index

225n20, 226nn21–2, 229n38, 230n47
Marot, Clement 120, 224n8
Marrani, Giuseppe 23, 194n36, 195n39
Marti, Mario 18, 27, 34, 68, 187n2, 194n32, 218n55
Martial 10, 22, 26, 66, 192n23
Massera, Aldo Francesco 47–8, 220n14
Matthew of Vendôme 16–17, 21, 80, 84, 193n27
Mauro, Giovanni 7–8, 83, 92, 107, 110–14, 125, 162, 212n17, 215n35, 217n51, 218n54, 231n50
Meglio, Giovan Matteo 7, 66, 71–3, 75, 80, 206n57, 207n59
Mengaldo, Pier Vincenzo 23, 195n39
Merlini, Domenico 108, 217n47, 222n79
Messina, Michele 69, 71
Michelangelo, Buonarroti 89, 218n55
Michelangelo, Buonarroti il Giovane 89, 212n14
Michiele, Pietro 139–40, 155
Milton, John 225n20
minstrel poetry 52–3, 55, 67, 203n35
misogyny 4–6, 10–16, 19, 21, 23, 27–8, 30–3, 37, 40, 42, 49, 57, 60, 67, 69, 72, 120, 122–3, 152, 156, 165–8, 187n2, 189nn1–3, 189n5, 190n6, 190nn8–9, 190n14, 191n15, 196n51, 206n57, 221n76
Montanile, Milena 120, 220n69
Morando Bernardo 130, 154
Mulvey, Laura 5, 220n10
Musacchio, Enrico 199n5
Muscia, Niccola 6, 32, 37–40, 60, 65, 78, 198n70, 207n61

Narducci, Anton Maria 160–1, 163, 232n54
Nencia da Barberino 75, 87–9, 96, 98, 100, 108, 125, 211n8, 211n10, 211n12, 214n28, 214n30
Neoplatonism 105, 148, 153, 192n21
Newman, Cathy 187n1

Onians, John 98
Origo, Iris 206n46, 222n81, 227n32
Orvieto, Paolo 13, 18, 26, 50, 53, 89, 168, 187n2, 191n15, 191n23, 201n19, 201n23, 204n45, 210n5, 211n11, 212n13, 214n27
Ovid 10, 39, 41, 66, 72, 79, 191n17, 192n23, 198n74, 231n51

Pacteau, Francette 144
Paoli, Pier Francesco 133
paradoxical praise 5, 7, 81–3, 90–1, 99, 102, 104, 106–7, 110, 113–15, 120–1, 123, 125, 127–30, 132, 156, 162, 166, 221n76
parody 5–6, 26, 28, 32–5, 37, 83, 87–8, 90, 99–100, 102, 104–5, 113, 116, 118, 120, 123, 125, 156, 158, 162–3, 165–6, 169, 197n55
Pasini, Pace 140
Pasquini, Emilio 202n25
Pers, Ciro di 8, 133, 140–2, 153, 224n9, 226n23, 229n37, 229n42, 230n44
Petrarch, Francesco 6–7, 83, 86, 90, 114–15, 119–20, 133–4, 140, 152–3, 165, 210n6, 215n37, 219n58, 223n8
Petrarchism 7–8, 99–100, 102–3, 105, 115–22, 124–5, 129–30, 133, 136–7, 139, 141, 143, 147, 149, 152, 154–5, 161, 163, 167

Poliziano, Angelo 7, 66, 71, 75–8, 80, 99, 165, 207n4, 208n68, 208nn70–1, 210n2, 210n5, 214n29
power male/female. *See* authority
Pozzi, Giovanni 84, 134, 210n4, 225nn13–14, 229n38
Praz, Mario 130, 223n5, 230n48
Propertius 66, 72
Proverbia quae dicuntur super natura feminarum 13–14, 28, 32, 191n17, 221n78
Pseudo-Legacci. *See* Legacci
Pucci, Giambattista 155
Pulci, Luigi 87, 89, 168, 205n45, 215n31

Quevedo, Francisco 220n70
Quirini, Leonardo 140, 150
Quondam, Amedeo 219n65

race 144, 146, 150–1, 165–6
Randisbacher, Hans 24, 195n43
Raphael 144
Renier, Rodolfo 20, 84, 134, 210n6, 228n33
rhetoric 6, 10–11, 15–18, 20–1, 23, 34, 40, 51, 54–5, 57, 60, 62, 83–4, 96, 113, 144, 156, 166
Rinaldi, Cesare 137
Rodnite Lemay, Helen 192n22
Rogers, Katharine 10, 189n2, 189n4
Ronsard, Pierre 160
Roper, Lyndal 79, 208n66
Rosa, Salvator 160, 232n55
Rossi, Nicolo de' 6, 27, 31–2, 191n15, 196n53
Russo, Mary 5, 127, 169–70, 188n6, 222n82, 227n30
rustic poetry 62, 75, 81–3, 87, 89, 90, 98–9, 104–5, 107–8, 110, 112, 211nn8–9, 211nn11–12, 212n14, 215n31, 215n36, 222n79
Sacchetti, Franco 41, 48–52, 60, 65, 191n15, 200n17
Saffioti, Tito 53, 201n24, 203nn34–6
Salomoni, Giuseppe 9, 129, 155–8, 222nn2–3, 224n9, 226n21
Salvetti, Pier 151, 230n43
Schiesari, Juliana 209n72
Sempronio, Giovan Leone 129, 133
Sgruttendio de Scafato. *See* Giulio Cesare Cortese
Shakespeare, William 122, 143, 221nn74–5
Sherman, Cindy 169–70
Sissa, Giulia 195n40
social class 6, 15, 81, 99, 101, 105, 107–8, 110, 163, 167
Song of Songs 17, 133–4
Spackman, Barbara 92, 213n24
Spini, Giorgio 139, 226n22
Stallybrass, Peter 5, 7, 56, 96, 101, 109–10, 113, 166, 214n24, 217n48, 217n53
Stanbury, Sarah 44, 220n9
standards of beauty 3, 7, 39, 75, 81–3, 86, 115, 165, 169
'Stanze in lode della donna brutta' 7, 8, 107, 110, 123–7, 132, 145, 162, 181
Stephens, Walter 67, 70, 72, 206n50, 206n54, 206n56
Stigliani, Tommaso 137, 162, 224n8, 229n41, 230n47
Stilnovism 6, 18, 19–21, 24, 27–8, 32, 34–7, 43, 45, 54, 87, 196n53
Strascino. *See* Campani

Taddeo, Edoardo 136, 225n16
Tarchetti, Iginio Ugo 169, 188n4

258 Index

Tasso, Torquato 134–7, 141–4, 146–7, 150, 153, 155–6, 224n8, 225n20, 228n34, 230n46
Tedaldi, Pieraccio 14, 191n19
Tertullian 12, 14, 28, 29, 37, 189n2
Tingoli, Ludovico 228n36
Titian 228nn33–4
transgression 3, 5, 7, 11, 14, 23–4, 27, 29, 32–3, 41–2, 44–5, 48, 51–2, 55, 58, 63–4, 66, 70, 75, 78–81, 90, 94, 96, 101, 107, 113, 115, 119, 124, 133, 165, 166
Trubiano, Marisa 133

Ulysse, George 93, 108, 213n20, 214n25
unconventional beauty: 8, 101, 127–8, 128, 134, 136, 139–40, 156, 158, 163, 219n59, 224n9; as ambiguous 9, 129, 156; and bodily contamination 133, 159–63, 167; and imperfection 6, 129, 132; and tainted beauty 8, 9, 129, 131, 161, 222n3

Valenti, Cristina 91, 108, 213nn20–1, 216n45
Varchi, Benedetto 83
Vasari, Giorgio 144
Vickers, Brian 16
Vickers, Nancy 143, 189n8, 210n6, 216n39, 220n70
Vigarello, Georges 159, 231n50
visual pleasure 35, 44–6, 101, 105, 114, 166
vituperation, *vituperatio vetulae* 5, 16–17, 21, 23–4, 26, 34, 37–9, 41, 45, 49, 51–2, 62, 70, 73, 75, 79, 107, 123, 125, 132, 194n34, 200n16

Young, Robert 209n1

White, Allon 5, 7, 96, 102, 109–10, 166, 217n48, 217n53
Williams, Linda 46, 200n11
witticism 5–6, 9–11, 28–30, 73, 112, 127, 129, 146–7, 150, 157, 159–60, 229n40
woman: as angel-like 6, 20–1, 24, 26–8, 32, 34, 87; as animal-like 23–4, 58, 62, 64, 72, 112; as anti-Laura 7, 81–2, 114, 117–18, 120, 127, 167; blonde 3, 133–4, 167, 187n1, 224n12, 226n28; dark-haired 6, 8, 122, 133–4, 136, 138–44, 149, 167, 224n11, 225n14, 229n38; dark-skinned 6, 8, 133, 136, 144–9, 167, 229n42; devilish 6, 27–8, 49–50, 220n17; exotic 8, 127, 144–5, 148–51, 163; *facchino* 8, 107–11, 114, 126; filthy 6, 8, 23, 80, 108, 110, 112, 114, 126, 160, 163, 165; as guardian 7, 41–2, 44–8, 50–5, 59–62, 64–5, 166, 201n20, 206n53; gypsy 8, 9, 145, 148, 229n4; hag 6–7, 21, 23, 25–6, 35–9, 49, 52, 55, 60, 65, 70, 72, 78–80, 110, 119–20, 125, 165, 220n16, 205n45; as heretic 53, 69, 70; hunchback 33, 35–7, 63, 129, 131, 163, 198n67; and make-up 12, 13, 156, 190n50; as metaphor 11–12, 157; mountain-dweller 7, 8, 107–8, 110, 112–14, 204n42; as object 44–5, 106–7, 130, 132, 143, 145, 147, 164, 166; old 5, 8, 10, 14–15, 22, 24, 26, 32, 34–5, 37–42, 45–73, 75–81, 110, 113, 115, 119–20, 125, 132, 134, 152–8, 163, 165, 188n7, 192nn20–1, 192n23, 199nn2–3, 204n40, 204n45, 205n47, 209n72, 230nn44–5; and ornamentation

11–13, 60, 66, 112, 189n2; as Other 4–5, 8, 15, 81–2, 89–90, 95–6, 99, 101, 105, 107–8, 110, 112, 114, 126–7, 144–5, 148–51, 158, 162, 166, 209n1, 229n37; peasant 6–7, 52, 68, 81–2, 87, 89–90, 93–7, 99, 101, 105–14, 128; prostitute 7, 22–3, 41, 60, 66, 68, 71–2, 76, 79–81, 166, 195n39, 205n46, 207n58, 208n66, 209nn71–2; slanderer 55–7, 59–60, 65; slave/servant 9, 146–7, 163–4, 167, 227nn31–2; widow 30, 68, 73–5, 198n74, 203n35; wild 58, 61, 63–5, 67–9, 203n39, 204n42; witch 7, 16, 24, 32, 41, 54, 58, 61, 63–73, 75, 79, 166, 192n22, 205nn48–9, 205n51, 205n54, 205n56, 208n68
Wright, Charlotte, 169

Zaccarello, Michelangelo 70–1, 206n52
Zancan, Marina 188n3
Zazzaroni, Paolo 140, 154, 159, 224n8, 228n34, 229n41
Zemon Davis, Natalie 55, 92, 202n31, 204n43, 214n24
Zetzel, Labert, Ellen 91

www.ingramcontent.com/pod-product-compliance
Lightning Source LLC
Chambersburg PA
CBHW030311080526
44584CB00012B/531